12.95

CONFUCIAN THOUGHT:
Selfhood as Creative Transformation

SUNY Series in Philosophy
Robert C. Neville, Editor

CONFUCIAN THOUGHT:

Selfhood As Creative Transformation

Tu Wei-Ming

State University of New York Press

Published by
State University of New York Press, Albany

© 1985 State University of New York

For information, address State University of New York
Press, State University Plaza, Albany, N.Y., 12246

Library of Congress Cataloging in Publication Data

Tu, Wei-ming.
  Confucian thought.

  (SUNY series in philosophy)
  Bibliography: p.
  Includes index.
  1. Philosophy, Confucian. I. Title. II. Series.
B5233.C6T8 1985   181'.09512   84-16263
ISBN 0-88706-005-6
ISBN 0-88706-006-4 (pbk.)

IN MEMORY OF

T'ang Chün-i, an exemplary teacher at New Asia College in Hong Kong

and

Lee Sang-eun, an inspiring scholar at Korea University in Seoul

Contents

Acknowledgements

"The 'Moral Universal' from the Perspectives of East Asian Thought" was originally published in *Morality as a Biological Phenomenon*, edited by Gunther S. Stent, as *Life Sciences Research Report* 9 of the Dahlem Konferenzen (Berlin, 1978). The article was reprinted, with commentary by Clifford Geertz, in *Philosophy East and West*, vol. XXXI, no. 3 (July 1981). I am grateful to Professor Geertz for his thought-provoking comments and to the Dahlem Konferenzen for its permission to have the article included in this volume.

"The Continuity of Being: Chinese Visions of Nature" was first presented as one of the basic motifs in the Chinese mode of thinking at a meeting of the Association of the History of Chinese Philosophy in Beijing in the summer of 1980 during my six-month research tour of China under the sponsorship of the Committee on Scholarly Communication with the People's Republic of China of the National Academy of Sciences. My conversations on the subject with Professors Chang Liwen, Fang Keli, Feng Qi, Pang Pu, and Tang Ijie encouraged me to write an essay in Chinese on the three basic motifs in Chinese philosophy. The essay was published in the *Study of the History of Chinese Philosophy*, a newly established journal of the Institute of Philosophy in the Chinese Academy of Social Sciences. The invitation from Leroy S. Rouner, Director of the Boston University Institute for Philosophy and Religion, to deliver a public lecture on the Chinese visions of nature in the Institute's Wednesday Evening Series of 1983 enabled me to share my thoughts with an English-speaking audience. I benefited greatly from discussions with Professors Peter Berger, John Carman, Ewert Cousins, L. S. Rouner, and Huston Smith. The article is included in *On Nature*, ed., Leroy S. Rouner (Notre Dame: Ind., University of Notre Dame Press, 1984). Copyright © 1984 by University of Notre Dame Press. Reprinted by permission.

"A Confucian Perspective on Learning to be Human" was written as a current perspective in religious studies for a collection of essays in honor of Professor Wilfred Cantwell Smith. It is included in *The World's Religious Traditions*, ed., Frank Whaling (Edinburgh: T. & T. Clark, 1984). Copywright © by T. & T. Clark, 1984. Reprinted by permission.

"The Value of the Human in Classical Confucian Thought" first appeared in *Humanitas*, vol. XV, no. 2 (May 1979). I am grateful to Professor John R. MacCormack, Director of the Institute of Human Values at Saint Mary's University in Halifax, Nova Scotia for his kind invitation which enabled me to share my thoughts with scholars of a variety of disciplines in the humanities.

"*Jen* as a Living Metaphor" was first presented at the Harvard Workshop on Classical Chinese Thought in August 1976. I benefited from inspiring comments by Professors H. G. Creel, Herbert Fingarette, Henry Rosemont, and Benjamin I. Schwartz. The article was published in *Philosophy East and West*, vol. XXXI, no. 1 (January 1981). Copyright © 1981 by the University Press of Hawaii. Reprinted by permission.

"The Idea of the Human in Mencian Thought: An Approach to Chinese Aesthetics," was first presented at a conference on "Theories of the Arts in China," sponsored by the American Council of Learned Societies in June 1979. Useful suggestions from Professors James Cahill, Mary Mothersill, Stephen Owen, and Maureen Robertson enabled me to revise the paper for publication in *Theories of the Arts in China*, eds., Susan Bush and Christian Murck (Princeton: Princeton University Press, 1984). Copyright © 1983 by Princeton University Press. Reprinted by permission.

"Selfhood and Otherness: Father-Son Relationship in Confucian Thought" was written as a response to Robert Bellah's seminal essay on "Father and Son in Christianity and Confucianism." It is included in *Culture and Self*, eds., Anthony Marsella, George De Vos and Francis Hsü (London: Tavistock Press, 1985). Copyright © 1984 by Tavistock Press. Reprinted by permission.

"On Neo-Confucian Religiosity and Human-Relatedness" was first presented at the 5th Annual Taniguchi Symposium for the Promotion of Ethnology, held at the National Museum of Ethnology, Osaka, in September 1981. I learned much from the fellow participants of the Symposium. I am particularly grateful to Professors Bito Masahide, Lee Kwang Kyu, Morioka Kiyomi, and Suenari Michio for their enlightening thoughts on the Confucian family in East Asia. The article, under a slightly different title, is included in

Religion and the Family in East Asia, eds., George A. De Vos and Takao Sofue (Osaka: National Museum of Ethnology, 1984). Copyright © 1984 by the National Museum of Ethnology. Reprinted by permission.

"Neo-Confucian Ontology: A Preliminary Questioning" was first presented at the Berkeley Regional Seminar in Confucian Studies, under the sponsorship of the American Council of Learned Societies, on March 5, 1976. I am indebted to my colleagues and friends there for their searching criticisms and constructive suggestions. The paper was subsequently published in *Journal of Chinese Philosophy* (1980). A German translation is included in *Max Webers Studie über Konfuzianismus und Taoismus*, edited by Wolfgang Schluchter (Frankfurt and Main: Suhrkamp, 1983). Reprinted by permission of *Journal of Chinese Philosophy*.

I am indebted to Song-bae Park for taking the initiative of recommending this book to the SUNY Series in Philosophy, to David Hall for his insightful comments, to Betsy Scheiner and Rosanne V. Hall for editing both the published and unpublished portions of the manuscript, to Thomas Selover for his painstaking effort at proofreading and indexing and to Robert Neville for his encouraging Foreword.

Foreword

Wang Yang-ming (1472–1529) is generally credited with a revolution in Confucian thinking, inaugurating a philosophical project that dominated China for two hundred years and Japan down into this century. Strange as it may seem to Westerners, the vehicle of his revolution was an attack on an editorial change that Chu Hsi (1130–1200) had made in the order of items in a list in the text of the ancient *Great Learning*. Wang restored the text to its supposed original order. By implication, Chu Hsi's original editorial change was a core component of his own revolution which has been even more influential than Wang's and is usually thought now to be truer to the heart of Confucianism than Wang's. One way of looking at these two events is to see a tradition with enormous creativity and diversity punctuating its radical turning points by scholarly moves that appear to be aiming at continuity.

Professor Tu Wei-ming sees himself as transmitting the Confucian tradition and introducing it to the West. This volume like his others is interpretive of Confucian ideas and figures. Unlike many scholars, however, he understands that the true meaning of transmission is not merely translation and the conveying of "knowledge about." It is also the conveying of the felt merit of the ideas and practices, a transmission of the reasons why they are true and worthy of adoption. This is not a simple matter.

The reasons why a great figure such as Wang Yang-ming said what he did are given only in part in his explicit expressions. The rest come from his feeling for his age, from the way his own parents treated him, from the things that made him dream the dreams he had. True transmission of Wang's thought would require a thorough, empathetic social and psycho-history of his own situation. Of course that is impossible. The records are simply inadequate and most of what one would need to get inside Wang's mind probably was never recorded. Nevertheless, with careful scholarship an expert can come close to understanding the context and thereby grasping the affect in Wang's ideas. Professor Tu set the standard in the par-

1

ticular case of Wang with his own *Neo-Confucian Thought in Action: Wang Yang-ming's Youth (1472–1509)* (Berkeley: University of California Press, 1976). One might go so far as to say that a great scholar can understand a previous time even better than most of us can understand our own. The usual effect of coming to understand a prior age and its tastes is that our own minds are put back in that age, perhaps with considerable empathy. In rare cases our own experience is simply expanded so as to include that age as well as ours. The historical interest does not directly answer the question, however, whether Confucian ideas in any form have merit as a contemporary philosophical option. To answer that question one might begin with a thorough engagement with contemporary life, an engagement often avoided (unconsciously?) by the historical orientation.

The opposite transmission strategy is to bracket the historical dimension, assuming that human nature and social context are pretty much the same everywhere and always. Books such as the recently popular *Tao of Physics* by Fritjof Capra allow for great comparative generalizations. Truly sophisticated philosophical studies in this genre can apply analytical methods to unravel and state the meanings of ideas. Again, Professor Tu has offered us a fine example of this genre, his *Centrality and Commonality: An Essay on Chung-yung* (Honolulu: the University Press of Hawaii, 1976). The limitation of this approach is that without strict historical controls it allows the questions that nudge our own minds to guide the hermeneutics of the old texts. These might not be the questions in the minds of the original authors at all. And then since the understanding of the text in turn guides our own self-understanding, this a-historical approach to ideas may lead us recursively to delusions about our own situation.

Students of hermeneutics have argued in this century that we need to unite both approaches in an ever-circling process of interpretation. To this I would like to add one emphasis, that we have a particular responsibility to engage our own time from more angles than those of hermeneutical circles catching up ancient texts. The very habit of interpreting the past puts a bias on our participation in the present. Please do not think I believe we can effectively engage the present without bringing it into relation with the past and our understanding of it. But there are other approaches, theoretical, appreciative, and practical, by which we come to terms with ourselves and our time; each approach has its own strength which corrects and completes the others. These many approaches need to be registered in any metaphysics for our own time to be embodied in an adequate philosophy of life.

Now it is Professor Tu's particular interest to present Confucianism as an adequate philosophy of life. This requires him both to be faithful to the tradition's texts and to present Confucianism as a responsible resource for our own philosophic needs. There are two stages, as I see it, to this interest. The first is to present Confucianism as a world class philosophy, not just the historic expression of Chinese culture. To do this requires developing Confucian ideas to address the major issues and life situation of the major groups of people in the contemporary era. Professor Tu, I believe, is well along in doing this, as Whitehead did it for Platonism and McKeon for Aristotelianism.

The second stage goes beyond showing the relevance of a set of basic ideas to the explicit elaboration of them from an idiosyncratic author's point of view. This means the creation of a new authorial perspective that allows us to grasp our situation in new and improved ways. Whitehead and McKeon also did this, the former by developing process metaphysics and the latter by establishing a school of historical criticism. Professor Tu is now in this stage, a stage of creativity in which he stands in danger of being rejected by the mere repeaters of Confucianism. I know of no one more successful at developing a twentieth-century Confucian philosophy than he.

Like Wang and Chu Hsi, Professor Tu's creative revolution centers around a point of authority within the tradition. As mentioned before, Chu Hsi's philosophy has generally been taken to be the orthodox line of Confucian interpretation, despite two hundred years of competition from Wang Yang-ming. Chu Hsi's interpretation, for instance, formed the examination system in China up to our own century. Professor Tu, however, in his *Humanity and Self-Cultivation: Essays in Confucian Thought* (Berkeley: Asian Humanities Press, 1979), argues that Wang's is the more faithful interpretation of the line beginning with Confucius and Mencius. What this means for Professor Tu's philosophy is the importance he thus can put on the will and its cultivation. Wang said that the decision to become a sage is itself the root of sagehood, not just the beginning but the stuff, as it were, of which sagehood is made. This leads Professor Tu in the current volume to focus on the transformation of the self. As much as any scholar, he has told us that Confucianism is a social philosophy, a philosophy of practice and engagement with the moral affairs of the world. With striking parallels to Dewey's pragmatism, Confucianism as it comes to us through Mencius, Wang, and Tu emphasizes the transformation of the moral quality of action through careful learning. But whereas Dewey moved from there to considerations of public policy, Tu turns instead to the cultivation of the self. This volume, even more than his earlier ones, displays this orientation.

Questions of authentic Confucianism aside, what does Professor Tu's emphasis mean for Confucianism as a contemporary philosophy? For one, it means a corrective emphasis to pragmatism, one that can capture and discipline the often silly and narcissistic personal "seeker" phenomenon which arose in reaction against crude pragmatism. Confucian self-cultivation is a rigorously disciplined path. Another meaning of Professor Tu's emphasis is that the religious dimensions of self-cultivation can be given new expression in an avowedly atheistic cosmology. To be sure, there are categories in Neo-Confucianism's ontology (the topic of one of the chapters here) that function like the "ultimate" categories of Western thought. But there is not the belief in a God with a definite, historically particular will such as characterized most non-mystical Western religion and philosophy. Insofar as we live after the "death of God," Professor Tu's reconstruction of a viable religio-philosophy is appropriate.

I mentioned earlier the need for an authentic metaphysics to be embodied in any philosophy which is viable for our time. By that I mean that we need to discern the most general thought forms expressed in the assumptions that make life vital today — assumptions in science, economics, efforts at distributive justice, and the like — because these thought-forms must also be embodied in the philosophies by which we can reflect on and guide that vital life. The most devastating criticism of a philosophy is that its root patterns are not those which engage the vital activities of life. This is not to assume that there is a single consistent set of assumptions, or only one metaphysics, or only one philosophy of life. Yet a philosophy which is metaphysically connected to nothing vital is of no serious interest. The Confucian tradition would be the first to acknowledge this. (It may be of great playful interest. The Taoists insist on this point.)

The formation of a metaphysics is no easy matter, coming as it does both from a dialectic with past metaphysical ideas and from an articulation and extrapolation of vigorous areas of inquiry and activity. In this volume Professor Tu makes significant strides toward a metaphysics that would make Confucianism a way of wisdom for our common life. Ethical considerations constitute a good starting point for a metaphysical construction where the sources come from such diverse traditions as those of China and the West. Professor Tu makes ingenious uses of psychology as well in this volume. The Neo-Confucian tradition presents many notions concerning principle and nature that will move him on to basic issues of aesthetics and cosmology.

The essays in this volume present themselves as attempts at transmission and interpretation, Confucius' own self-understanding. But embodied in that task is one of the most exciting and creative philosophical projects of our time: the evocation of a world philosophy for the twentieth century from Confucian roots.

Robert C. Neville
Professor of Philosophy and Religious Studies
SUNY Stony Brook

Introduction

In the opening discussion of the final meeting of the five-year Berkeley-Harvard program in the comparative study of social values,[1] Robert Bellah, my teacher and friend for over two decades, in commenting on my paper, "The 'Moral Universal' From the Perspectives of East Asian Thought" (Chapter 1), raised the challenging question, "What is the Confucian self?" The nine essays included in this book attempt to answer this question. They do not, however, offer a simple answer. Rather, they explore dimensions of Confucian thought which illuminate the meaning of Confucian selfhood as creative transformation.

If we Confucians have a coherent conception of the self, why was it difficult for me to give Bellah a straightforward answer? Part of the problem is contextual. Unless we fully understand a question, we cannot hope to offer the right answer. Often the way a question is posed is deceptively simple, but the background that gives meaning to it is immensely complex. Because the question emanates from the *Problematik* of the questioner, we need to know not only the propositional content of the question but also the thinking person behind it. For me, then, Bellah's question occasioned a living encounter rather than a mere exchange of information. The essays in this book are, in this sense, all living encounters. To be sure, they offer basic information on the Confucian tradition; but, primarily, they are self-consciously "Confucian" responses to perennial human concerns.

Had I been asked the same question by someone else, by a language student for example, I could have answered the question by simply listing the cluster of terms which, for all practical purposes, can be accepted as functional equivalents of the classical or modern Chinese terms for the English word "self." (This may have been what the student was really after, although he might have continued to wonder whether a one-to-one translation would work in some cases.) But, the weight of Bellah's question lies elsewhere, for in reflecting on my attempt to discern the shared orientations of East Asian thought, he was troubled by the centrality of "self-cultiva-

tion" in my characterization of the Mencian line of Confucian
thought, Chuang Tzu's version of Taoism, and Ch'an (Zen) Buddhism. What about the other salient features of East Asian culture:
the sense of community, the importance of the sacred texts, the
power of tradition, convention and sharable values, the significance
of the exemplary teacher, and the primacy of the political order?
Moreover, self-cultivation smacks of preoccupation with one's individuality, one's inner spirituality, indeed one's own private self.
Bellah, a most eloquent critic of individualism in our society, is particularly concerned about the radical individualistic tendencies that
have been undermining the social fabric of American civil religion.[2]

In light of this *Problematik*, one of the most intriguing areas for me
to explore is the authentic possibility of a new vision of the self which
is rooted in the reality of a shared life together with other human beings and inseparable from the truth of transcendence. Chapter 1,
which was prepared as a background paper for an interdisciplinary
examination of the truth claims of sociobiologists, sketches the ra-
tionale for a twofold approach to self-realization in East Asian
thought. (1) Each human being has sufficient internal resources for
ultimate self-transformation; we can become a sage, a buddha, or a
true person through our self-effort because sageliness, buddhahood, or
the *Tao* is inherent in our human nature. (2) The path to the highest
good, to *nirvāna*, or to oneness with the *Tao* is long and strenuous.
Self-cultivation is ceaseless. We can never say at any juncture of our
life that we have already made it. This interplay between faith in the
strength of humanity in ordinary daily existence and the wisdom of
infinite human potential for personal growth enables the three East
Asian traditions to perceive the self as a dynamic, holistic, open
system, just the opposite notion of the privatized ego. However,
whether such a self can be grounded in society without losing sight of
the transcendent reality remains problematical. In order to address
this issue, we need to examine the metaphysical assumption
underlying this conception of the self.

Chapter 2 propounds the thesis that the "continuity of being," a
characteristic of Chinese cosmological thinking, frames the whole
question of self-cultivation in a specific context. Particularly
noteworthy is the implicit conceptual apparatus which allows a vision of the self significantly different from what Bellah, following
Alasdair MacIntyre, calls "bureaucratic individualism."[3] The
familiar dichotomies such as self/society, body/mind, sacred/
profane, culture/nature, and creator/creature, in light of the

"continuity of being," are relegated to the background. A different mode of thinking, which emphasizes part/whole, inner/outer, surface/depth, root/branches, substance/function, and Heaven/man, becomes prominent. The central question does not involve static, mechanistic, analytical distinctions but subtle relationships, internal resonance, dialogical interplay, and mutual influence. As a result, the cosmos envisioned by Chinese thinkers is a "spontaneously self-generating life process." Inherent in such a life process "is not only inner connectedness and interdependence but also infinite potential for development."[4] Thus, the Chinese conceive of the cosmos, like the self, as an open system. "As there is no temporal beginning to specify, no closure is ever contemplated. The cosmos is forever expanding; the great transformation is unceasing."[5] The message for us humans is as follows:

> The precondition for us to participate in the internal resonance of the vital forces in nature is our own inner transformation. Unless we can first harmonize our own feelings and thoughts, we are not prepared for nature, let alone for an "interflow with the spirit of Heaven and Earth." It is true that we are consanguineous with nature. But as humans, we must make ourselves worthy of such a relationship.[6]

The Confucian emphasis on humanism may seem to be in conflict with Taoist naturalism. However, in light of their shared concern for self-cultivation, we cannot say that the Confucian insistence on social participation and cultural transmission is incompatible with the Taoist quest for personal freedom. Both the Taoist critique of Confucian ritualism and the Confucian critique of Taoist escapism are dialogical interplays reflecting a much deeper point of convergence. This is not to deny the nuanced differences between the two spiritual traditions; but, despite their divergence, they belong to the same symbolic universe in which they not only co-exist but help each other to grow through mutual influence.

"A Confucian Perspective on Learning to be Human" (Chapter 3) was written for a collection of essays intended to offer some current perspectives in religious studies in honor of the work of Wilfred Cantwell Smith.[7] Bellah's question, against the background of Smith's concerted effort to address the dual problem of cumulative tradition and faith in human religiosity,[8] takes on new significance. The Confucian project of learning to be human, defined by Confucius as "learning for the sake of the self," takes the concrete person living here and now as its point of departure. This seemingly particularistic, temporal, secular, and individualistic focus is predicated on a holistic vision of humanity which transcends not only self-centeredness, nepotism, ethnocentrism, nationalism, and culturalism but also anthropocentrism. Indeed, the Confucian vision of "forming one body with Heaven and Earth and the myriad things"[9] is anthropocosmic in the sense that the complete realization of the self, which is tantamount to the full actualization of humanity, entails the unity of humankind with Heaven. Therefore, the Confucian insistence that the journey of self-realization begins with the concrete experience of the self should not be construed as an assertion of the finite, historical, and culturally specific to the exclusion of the infinite, trans-historical, and universal. The significance of the Confucian project of learning to be human, in a comparative religious perspective, lies in its insight into the creative tension between our earthly embeddedness and our great potential for self-transcendence.

As Bellah notes, "bureaucratic individualism" is "the logical consequence of that process of instrumental rationalization that Max Weber analyzed so profoundly."[10] The economic and psychological mobilization of resources for the purpose of mastering the world, as portrayed in Weber's *The Protestant Ethic and The Spirit of Capitalism*, may have so much distorted the spirit of Calvinism that, to use Weber's vivid expression, the cloak lightly placed on the shoulder of the modern West has now become an "iron cage" for the industrial world.[11] This is certainly not the place to assess the historical accuracy of Weber's interpretation. Nor can we take much comfort in noting that the Confucian ethic did not contribute to that process of instrumental rationalization that fundamentally transformed the West and, by extension, the world at large. However, Weber's depiction of the Confucian spiritual orientation as "adjustment to the world"[12] in his *The Religion of China* is relevant here. The Confucian recommendation for harmonizing society appears to be a reasonable corrective to the rampant individualism seen in the West. What Weber detected as a deficiency in the rationalizing potential of Confucian ethics is now recognized as a strength for forging social solidarity.

Notwithstanding the possible relevance of the Confucian message to us, "The Value of the Human in Classical Confucian Thought" (Chapter 4) addresses much broader concerns. Such a discussion, in the context of the symbolic resources of the Confucian tradition itself, may provide a fresh perspective on the idea of the self without evoking sentiments about individualism. As I observe in the conclusion of this Chapter,

> Historically, the emergence of individualism as a motivating force in Western society may have been intertwined with highly particularized political, economic, ethical, and religious traditions. It seems reasonable that one can endorse an insight into the self as a basis for equality and liberty without accepting Locke's idea of private property, Adam Smith's and Hobbes' idea of private interest, John Stuart Mill's idea of privacy, Kierkegaard's idea of loneliness, or the early Sartre's idea of freedom.[13]

Recent scholarship, notably Thomas Metzger's *Escape from Predicament*, suggests that Weber was probably wrong in making such a sharp distinction between the inner asceticism of the Calvinist Puritan and the this-worldliness of the Confucian literatus.[14] The Confucian, like the Puritan, was greatly energized by an internal measure of self-worth. His rationalizing potential was as high as the Puritan's, even though it did not engender a comparable spirit of capitalism. In fact, the Confucians may have fashioned the East Asian world into a particular kind of socio-political order through their transformative ethics, even though they did not shape their society in the direction of bourgeois capitalism.

If the Confucian project, either in its spiritual self-definition or in its historical function, is not "adjustment to the world," what is the ontological status of the human community in its ultimate concern? Herbert Fingarette's seminal study on *Confucius — The Secular as Sacred* persuasively argues that the Confucian perception of society as the "holy rite" makes the presumption of an inner psyche superfluous.[15] By implication, there is no need to posit the idea of the psychological self in our understanding of the "personal locus" in Confucius' *Analects*. While I have enormously benefited from Fingarette's insightful observations, I do not totally share his interpretation of the core value in Confucian thought, *jen* (humanity). My attempt to study "*Jen* as a Living Metaphor in the Confucian *Analects*" (Chapter 5) is thus both an appreciation and a critique of Fingarette's treatment of the initial formulation of the Confucian project.

A major contribution of Fingarette's study is his emphasis on the universality of the Confucian idea of "ritual" (*li*). This underscores the significance of Hsün Tzu as a contributor to the Confucian Way.[16] However, traditional as well as modern Chinese interpretive literature repeatedly notes that without self-cultivation as the root of a participatory moral community, the imposition of the rules of decorum by the elite on the unsuspecting masses easily degenerates into authoritarianism. Mencius, the transmitter of the Confucian Way, was also intensely interested in the continuation of the moral community, the preservation of the classics, the vitality of the sagely tradition, of well-established rituals and of the good common sense of the people, the respect for the teacher, and the stability of the political order. Nevertheless, he took the ultimate self-transformation of the person as the key to the realization of social and political values. His theory of human nature, far from being a romantic advocacy of human perfectibility, calls our attention to our internal resources for spiritual growth. Learning to be human, in the Mencian perspective, is to refine ourselves so that we can become good, true, beautiful, great, sagely, and spiritual. Chapter 6, intended to suggest an approach to Chinese aesthetics for a research conference in theories of the arts in China, depicts the Mencian self as body, heart, and spirit.

The first six chapters in this book should demonstrate why, in answering Bellah's challenging question, I felt reluctant to shift my emphasis from self-cultivation in order to avoid a possible misunderstanding. The difference between the Confucian perception of the self as a center of relationships and Western individualism is so obvious that by stressing the sociality of Confucian selfhood we may have further deepened the mistaken impression that personal dignity, independence, and autonomy are not deep-rooted Confucian values. A more serious reason for my insistence on the centrality of self-cultivation is the rightness that I sense in articulating the Confucian project as I best understand it. I must hasten to add that this sense of rightness is not momentary. It is neither a heuristic device nor an expedient corrective, but a personal realization. In other words, my deliberate choice to proceed in such a manner is not only dictated by a desire to adopt the best interpretive strategy but also prompted by my own understanding of what the Confucian spiritual orientation is all about.

I do not believe that we can discuss Confucian ideas in English in the twentieth-century United States as if the terms used by Confucius, Mencius, and Wang Yang-ming in classical Chinese were transparently clear through translation. Whenever my compatriots teaching in American universities assure me that a distinctive advantage of discussing Confucian ethics with an English-speaking audience is that we are unencumbered with layer after layer of commentary and sub-commentary sedimentation, I feel extremely uneasy. For one thing, I do not believe that it is possible to present an undifferentiated Confucian position on vital issues, such as the idea of the self, as if there were a trans-temporal wisdom which, once revealed, would remain essentially the same. There is no monolithic Confucian self to speak of.

My attempt to explore those dimensions of Confucian thought that are particularly relevant to Confucian selfhood has been painstakingly difficult. I am critically aware that to understand Confucius in the light of the Mencian rather than the Hsün Tzuan interpretation or to understand Mencius in the Wang Yang-ming rather than the Chu Hsi line impels me to reason from a particular vantage point. Thus, my intellectual claim to universality or, if you will, ecumenicalism, even within the Confucian tradition, is limited. Nevertheless, the parochialism in which I am inevitably circumscribed provides a concrete basis for encountering perennial human concerns in a comparative perspective. Of course, I did not hold these views as self-evidently true when I was first attracted to them. Nor do I intend to defend them, if I am persuaded that they are untenable. I have come to realize that they are sharable, indeed universalizable, mainly because I have been inspired to speak on their behalf by those who challenge me to relate my particularistic study to broad interpretive issues.

How could Confucius, informed by Mencius' *Problematik* which had been, in turn, informed by Wang Yang-ming's *Problematik* have responded to the question of the self that is framed by Bellah's *Problematik*? Chapters 7 and 8 intend to show that the possibility to imagine such a response is itself profoundly meaningful. Chapter 7 addresses the common assumption that the Confucian self, in the context of a hierarchical structure of social roles, is inevitably submerged in the group. The father-son relationship seems to provide an excellent case in which the Confucian son submits himself to the parental authority for the maintenance of social order. Bellah suggests that "the Confucian phrasing of the father-son relationship blocks any outcome of Oedipal ambivalence except submission — submission not in the last analysis to a person but to a pattern of personal relationships that is held to have ultimate validity."[17] This emphasis on the primacy of political and familial authority leads Bellah to the view that in Confucian culture "creative social innovation as in the Protestant case was precluded by the absence of a point of transcendent loyalty that could provide legitimation for it."[18]

However, if we take seriously the centrality of self-cultivation in the Confucian tradition, the governing principle of the father-son relationship is reciprocity rather than subjugation. It is the realization of the father's ego-ideal, not merely the respect for the father in the flesh, that defines the son's filial piety. Furthermore, a social dyad, in the Confucian sense, "is not a fixed entity, but a dynamic interaction involving a rich and ever-changing texture of human-relatedness woven by the constant participation of other significant dyadic relationships."[19] Viewed in this broader context, the father-son relationship in Confucian thought specifies a given and yet transformable human condition for self-realization. Nevertheless, to say that Confucian selfhood entails the participation of the other is not to imply that it is pre-eminently sociological and thus devoid of any profound religious import.

> The answer lies in the Confucian conception of the self not only as a center of relationships but also as a dynamic process of spiritual development. Ontologically, selfhood, our original nature, is endowed by Heaven. It is therefore divine in its all-embracing fullness. Selfhood, in this sense, is both immanent and transcendent. It is intrinsic to us; at the same time, it belongs to Heaven.[20]

Chapter 8, "Neo-Confucian Religiosity and Human-Relatedness" presents further reflectoins on the same theme. Learning, to reiterate an earlier point, is for the sake of the self. Since the self as a center of relationships is an open system, self-realization involves the establishment of an ever-expanding circle of human-relatedness. Such a circle must develop through the structures of the self, the family, the country, and the world; it must also transcend selfishness, nepotism, ethnocentrism, and anthropocentrism to maintain its dynamism and authenticity.[21] This broadening and deepening of the self can be characterized, in Mencian terminology, as the manifestation of the "great self" and the concomitant dissolution of the "small self."[22]

Mencius maintained that the unlimited sensitivity of the human heart-and-mind provides the basis for ceaseless self-growth.

Through the full realization of our human sensitivity, we can truly understand our nature and, by understanding our nature, we can know Heaven. By taking the self-cultivation of a single person as the root of not only human self-understanding but also divine knowledge, Mencius suggested that ultimate self-transformation, instead of being a lonely quest for one's inner spirituality, is a communal act. Human-relatedness is thus an integral part of one's quest for spiritual fulfillment. To take one's situatedness in a particular network of dyadic relationships as the given is not total submission to the prescribed social roles but a recognition of the most immediate and fruitful way of initiating and completing one's task of learning to be human. After all, in the Confucian view, the ultimate meaning of life is never found in a radical otherness, for it is inseparable from our ordinary daily existence.

The final essay, "Neo-Confucian Ontology: A Preliminary Questioning," explores the metaphysical foundation of humanity as perceived by the principal Neo-Confucian thinkers. Intent on transmitting the Mencian faith in the perfectibility of human nature through self-effort, the central question for them is, How do I learn to become a sage? Since sagehood means the most genuine and authentic manifestation of humanity, the question is virtually identical with, How do I learn to be fully human? Furthermore, since, as we have already discussed, learning to be human, in the Confucian sense, entails learning for the sake of the self, the question is tantamount to, How do I really know myself? or, in more elaborate Neo-Confucian terminology, How do I cultivate my "body and mind" so that I can truly understand my human nature and, by implication, know Heaven?

In a comparative perspective, it seems that Neo-Confucian ontology, grounded in the ultimate certitude of human sensitivity, our ability to feel, sense, and experience an ever-enlarging reality as an integral part of our selfhood, is diametrically opposed to Kantian metaphysics in which the objectivity of the moral will, devoid of any emotional content, features prominently. Yet, since I wrote my "preliminary questioning" almost ten years ago, I have been continuously encouraged by the points of convergence lurking behind the two apparently conflicting metaphysical visions. If we probe Kant's awe-inspiring attempt to lay the metaphysical foundation for autonomous morality in "the realm of ends,"[23] Kant's deep concern for the form and principle from which "the categorical imperative" results may find a sympathetic echo in the Neo-Confucian insistence that the "Heavenly Principle" inherent in human nature is the real source of moral creativity. The alleged Kantian formalism, which provoked a strong negative response from Bellah in the aforementioned Berkeley-Harvard meeting, may turn out to be a surface manifestation of Kant's, and I believe also Neo-Confucian thinkers', fully justified anxiety about selfish desires, private interests, and self-deception.

I have learned, through numerous conversations with my mentor, Benjamin I. Schwartz, that, in broad comparative study, the clear boundaries that define East and West, or for that matter North and South, usually do not provide the necessary intellectual impetus for deep thinking. Rather, the subtle, nuanced differences in between offer greater opportunity for critical scholarship. The "fruitful ambiguity"[24] of Confucian selfhood may prevent us from giving a straightforward answer to Bellah's challenging question, but it can prompt us to consider the question itself in fresh perspectives. The nine essays, written over a fairly long period of time for a variety of purposes are, in the kind words of Robert C. Neville, "attempts at transmission and interpretation, Confucius' own self-understanding."[25] However, these attempts, far from transmitting and interpreting the Confucian conception of selfhood, suggest ways of exploring the rich resources within the Confucian tradition so that they can be brought to bear upon the difficult task of understanding Confucian selfhood as creative transformation.

Notes

1. The Berkeley-Harvard program in the comparative study of social values (also referred to as the comparative ethics project) has been co-directed by Mark Juergensmeyer, Associate Professor of Religious Studies at the Graduate Theological Union and the University of California, Berkeley, and John Carman, Professor of Comparative Religion and Director of the Center for the Study of World Religions at Harvard University.

2. For Bellah's recent reflection on "civil religion," see R. N. Bellah and P. E. Hammond, *Varieties of Civil Religion* (San Francisco: Harper & Row, 1980). For his criticism of individualism, see his "Religion and the University: The Crisis of Unbelief" (The W. B. Noble Lectures; Harvard University, 1982).

3. Bellah, "Discerning Old and New Imperatives in Theological Education" (Address to the Association of Theological Schools, Pittsburgh, June 21, 1982), p. 8. See A. MacIntyre, *After Virtue* (Notre Dame, Ind.: University of Notre Dame Press, 1981), p. 33.

4. Chapter 2, "The Continuity of Being: Chinese Visions of Nature," p. 39.

5. Ibid.

6. Ibid., p. 47.

7. *The World's Religious Traditions; Current Perspectives in Religious Studies; Essays in Honor of Wilfred Cantwell Smith*, ed. Frank Whaling (Edinburgh: T.&T. Clark, 1984).

8. W.C. Smith's scholarly proposal is succinctly set forth in *The Meaning and End of Religion: A New Approach to the Religious Traditions of Mankind* (New York: Macmillan, 1963). Since its publication, the book has been reissued: New York, New American Library (Mentor Books), 1964; San Francisco, Harper & Row, 1978.

9. Wang Yang-ming, "Inquiry on the Great Learning," in *Instructions for Practical Living and Other Neo-Confucian Writings*, trans. Wing-tsit Chan (New York: Columbia University Press, 1963), p. 272.

10. Bellah, "Discerning Old and New Imperatives in Theological Education," p. 8.

11. Weber's original statement reads:

> The Puritan wanted to work in a calling; we are forced to do so. For when asceticism was carried out of monastic cells into everyday life, and began to dominate worldly morality, it did its part in building the tremendous cosmos of the modern economic order. This order is now bound to the technical and economic conditions of machine production which today determine the lives of all the individuals who are born into this mechanism, not only those directly concerned with economic acquisition, with irresistible force. Perhaps it will so determine them until the last ton of fossilized coal is burnt. In Baxter's view the care for external goods should only lie on the shoulders of the saint "like a light cloak, which can be thrown aside at any moment." But fate decreed that the cloak should become an iron cage.

See Max Weber, *The Protestant Ethic and the Spirit of Capitalism*, trans. T. Parsons (New York: Scribners, 1958), p. 181.

12. Max Weber, *The Religion of China: Confucianism and Taoism*, trans. Hans H. Gerth (Glencoe, Ill.: Free Press, 1951), p. 235.

13. Chapter 4, p. 78.

14. Thomas A. Metzger, *Escape from Predicament; Neo-Confucianism and China's Evolving Political Culture* (New York: Columbia University Press, 1977), pp. 3-4, 18-19, 198-204.

15. Herbert Fingarette, *Confucius — The Secular as Sacred* (New York: Harper & Row, 1972), pp. 1-17.

16. Fingarette's interpretation of Confucius is based on his hermeneutic reading of the *Analects*. He does not himself associate his interpretive position with the Hsün Tzu tradition. However, his emphasis on ritual as communal performance helps us to appreciate an important dimension of Hsün Tzu's moral education.

17. Robert Bellah, "Father and Son in Christianity and Confucianism," in his *Beyond Belief: Essays on Religion in a Post-Traditional World* (New York: Harper & Row, 1976), p. 95.

18. Ibid.

19. Chapter 7, p. 118.

20. Ibid, p. 125.

21. Chapter 8, p. 137.

22. *Mencius*, 6A:15.

23. *Immanuel Kant, Foundations of the Metaphysics of Morals*, trans. Lewis White Beck (New York: Bobbs-Merrill, 1959), pp. 58–61.

24. I am indebted to B. I. Schwartz for this thought-provoking idea. His refusal to tie up loose ends prematurely both as a style of scholarship and as an intellectual commitment to a sympathetic and sophisticated method of comparative intellectual history has been a major inspiration for my own work. His forthcoming *The World of Thought in Ancient China* (Harvard University Press) will give us further insight into his brilliant critique of reductionism.

25. R. C. Neville, Foreword, p. 5.

I. The "Moral Universal" from the Perspectives of East Asian Thought

A defining characteristic of East Asian thought is the widely accepted proposition that human beings are perfectible through self-effort in ordinary daily existence. This proposition is based on two interrelated ideas: (1) The uniqueness of being human is an ethicoreligious question which cannot be properly answered if it is reduced to biological, psychological, or sociological considerations; and (2) the actual process of self-development, far from being a quest for pure morality or spirituality, necessarily involves the biological, psychological, and sociological realities of human life. For the sake of convenience, the first idea will be referred to as an ontological postulate and the second as an experiential assertion. I begin this chapter with a few general observations on the proposition. After I have noted some of the salient features of the East Asian mode of thinking relevant to the present deliberation, I will proceed to a more focused investigation of the two basic ideas. For brevity, the discussion of East Asian thought will be confined to the Mencian line of Confucianism, the Chuang Tzu tradition of Taoism, and the Ch'an (Zen) interpretation of Buddhism.

It should be mentioned from the outset that the primary focus of the "Three Teachings" under study is self-knowledge. Since the conception of a Creator as the ultimate source of morality or spirituality is not even a rejected possibility, there is no appeal to the "wholly other" as the real basis of human perfectibility. Rather, the emphasis is on learning to be human, a learning that is characterized by a ceaseless process of inner illumination and self-transformation. The Confucian ideal of sagehood, the Taoist quest for becoming a "true person," and the Buddhist concern for returning to one's "original mind" are all indications that to follow the path of knowledge backward, as it were, to the starting point of the true self is the aim of East Asian thought.

Knowledge so conceived is not a cognitive grasp of a given structure of objective truths; nor is it an acquisition of internalized skills. It is basically an understanding of one's mental state and an appreciation of one's inner feelings. Since presumably a genuine knowledge of the self entails a transforming act upon the self, to know in this sense is not only to reflect and comprehend, but also to shape and create. To know oneself is simultaneously to perfect oneself. This, I think, is the main reason that East Asian thought lays as much stress on how to cultivate oneself as on who and what the true self is. To the Confucians, Taoists, and Buddhists, self-knowledge is predominantly an ethicoreligious question, although it is inevitably laden with epistemological implications.

In a deeper sense, self-knowledge is neither "knowing that" nor "knowing how"; it is, in essence, an objectless awareness, a realization of the human possibility of "intellectual intuition." Self-knowledge is nothing other than the manifestation of one's real nature (inner sageliness in Confucianism and buddhahood in Ch'an), and that real nature is not only a being to be known but also a self-creating and self-directing activity. However, although self-knowledge does not depend upon empirical knowledge, it is not incompatible with sense experience, or the "knowledge of hearing and seeing." Thus the relation between self-knowledge and empirical knowledge can be either mutually contradictory or mutually complementary. In an extreme formulation, the Taoist maintains that in the pursuit of the Way one must first lose all that one has already acquired in order to embody the Tao. But it is one thing to lose the fragmented and confusing opinions of the world and quite another to lose a sense of reality by enclosing oneself in a totally narcissistic state. Generally speaking, East Asian thought takes empirical knowledge seriously, while focusing its attention on the supreme value of self-knowledge.

The idea of "intellectual intuition" needs some elaboration. For one thing, it is significantly different from either irrationalism or esoterics. It does claim a direct knowledge of reality without logical reasoning or inference. But, unlike what is commonly associated with mysticism, it has very little to do with revelation. Actually, the whole tradition of contemplation as a way of coming to an immediate cognizance of the true essence of God without rational thought is alien to the East Asian mode of thinking. Rather, the possibility for each human being to have "intellectual intuition" is predicated on the presumption that since humanity forms an inseparable unity with heaven, earth, and the myriad things, its sensibility is in principle all-embracing. The theological distinction between Creator and creature, signifying an unbridgeable gap between divine wisdom and human rationality, is here transformed into what Joseph Needham characterizes as an organismic vision.[1] Human beings are therefore thought to have as their birthright the potential power and insight to penetrate the things-in-themselves, or, in Ch'an terminology, the suchness and thusness of *samsāra*. This resembles the Christian notion of divinity inherent in human nature: in the prelapsarian state man is created in the image of God; and in medieval Christian thought man is sometimes defined as divinity circumscribed.

It would be unfortunate if this organismic vision were understood as no more than a form of primitive animism, a doctrine which apparently conflicts with the scientific explanations of natural phenomena. Far from being an unexamined belief in the continued existence and mutual interaction of individual disembodied spirits, organismic vision here seems to have been the result of a philosophical anthropology which neither denies nor slights the uniqueness of being human. As a matter of fact, it subscribes to the non-evolutionary observation that human phylogeny has its own specific structure which cannot be fully explained in terms of the general laws governing the animal kingdom as a whole. Needless to say, it also rejects the attribution of a discrete indwelling spirit to any material form of reality. It is perhaps not far-fetched to consider the organismic vision as an ecological insight, locating humanity in a highly complex web of interdependency.

It would be equally unfortunate if, instead of animism, the organismic vision were taken as a form of anthropocentrism. The human possibility of "intellectual intuition" must not be viewed as a license for manipulative imposition of the human will upon nature. Promethean defiance and Faustian restlessness are not at all compatible with the cherished value of harmony, as both societal goal and cosmic ideal, in East Asian thought. On the contrary, the authentic manifestation of the human will is thought to be ultimate self-transformation, a liberation rather than a conquest. To Confucians, Taoists, and Buddhists, knowledge is enlightenment, a power of self-illumination. And only in its corrupt form does knowledge become a power of conquest. According to this line of thinking, to be fully human requires the courage and wisdom of constantly harmonizing oneself with an ever-enlarging network of relationships, which necessitates a perspective going beyond the restrictions of anthropocentrism.

Yet the transcending perspective never allows a departure from the lived world here and now. This is part of the reason why all major spiritual traditions in East Asia emphasize inner experience as a basis for ethicoreligious deliberation, not only the abstract "inner experience" as a category of thought for systematic analysis but also the concrete inner experience of the thinker engaged in philosophizing.

The line between religion and philosophy is inevitably blurred. What is normally associated with the discipline of psychoanalysis becomes religiously and philosophically relevant and significant. The conscious refusal or, if you will, the inability of East Asian thought to submit itself to the academic compartmentalization characteristic of modern universities is not simply a sign of its lack of differentiation but also an indication of its wholeness with all of its fruitful ambiguities. Indeed, common experiences, such as eating and walking, are respected as having great symbolic significance for moral and spiritual self-development.

For example, to the Confucian every human act is perceived as the reenactment of a time-honored ritual. Each gesture, such as eating, requires numerous practices before it takes the proper form. Only through socially recognized forms can one establish the communication necessary for self-cultivation. Human growth can thus be described as a process of ritualization. However, it is misleading to characterize Confucianism as a kind of ritualism. A coercive imposition of well-established social norms upon the individual who cannot choose but adjust to the all-powerful society is at best the result of a highly politicized Confucian ideology of control. Confucian ethics, on the contrary, is built upon commonly shared human feelings, such as empathy. Ritual in this connection is not a fixed norm but a flexible and dynamic procedure by which self-realization as a concrete means for communal participation rather than as an isolated quest for inner truth becomes possible. The Ch'an teaching of *satori* may on the surface seem diametrically opposed to the ritualized world, but, as the Ch'an masters have never failed to note, the enlightening experience is a confirmation rather than a rejection of common sense because simple acts such as carrying water and chopping wood are the Way of Buddha. Taoism, too, for that matter, affirms the intrinsic value of ordinary human existence. They are all, in a sense, involved in the art of practical living.

It is vitally important to mention at this juncture that the East Asian concept of the human as a self-perfectible being in common ordinary existence without the intervention of a transcendent God is atheistic only in a profoundly religious sense. The ultimate concern of self-realization actually necessitates a ceaseless process of inner moral and spiritual transformation. The purposefulness of life, however, is not a form of teleology in the sense of a preconceived cosmic design. In fact, human beings often remain tragically aimless and helpless, like "rudderless ships on restless waves." It is misleading to define sageliness or buddhahood in the language of entelechy. Human beings can become sages and buddhas because they are endowed with the "germinations" of morality or "seeds" of enlightenment, but it is highly problematical to perceive these germinations and seeds as the functional equivalents of what some vitalists claim to be the suppositiously immanent but immaterial agency responsible for the achievement of maturity in the human organism. For one thing, in both Confucianism and Buddhism, the duality of spirituality and materiality is meaningless. The Confucian *hsin*, which must be awkwardly rendered as "heart-mind," is a case in point. Intent on integrating the emotive aspects of human life with other dimensions of self-development, Mencius considers the fulfillment of the "bodily design" the highest manifestation of self-cultivation. In Ch'an, the assertion that *nirvāna* is *samsāra*, with all its ramifications, clearly rejects the artificial dichotomy between the body and the enlightened mind. Suggestively, the root metaphor shared by all Three Teachings in East Asian thought is the Way.

In light of the above discussion, the rhetorical situation in which the East Asian Way is articulated has, at least, the following features: (1) the inquirer is as much an inside participant as an outside observer. It is inconceivable that the general question of self-knowledge can be completely independent of the questioner's own self-knowledge. Indeed, as the questioning process unfolds, the inquirer deepens and broadens his understanding of the general issue only to the extent that his personal transformation confirms it. However, (2) it would be mistaken to infer that the East Asian Way is subjectivistic because it lays much emphasis on inner experience. Actually, the idea of "intellectual intuition" does not give any particular individual privileged access to truth. Indeed, the concept of individuality is not at all compatible with it. Rather, it is predicated on a strong sense of sharability and commonality. In other words, the experience that is considered truly personal is not at all private to the individual; self-knowledge is a form of inner experience precisely because it resonates with the inner experiences of the others. Accordingly, internality is not a solipsistic state but a concrete basis of communication, or, in the Taoist expression, of "spiritual communion."

It is in this sense that (3) the aforementioned organismic vision is the result of neither animism nor anthropocentrism but of a transcending perspective which seeks the ultimate meaning of life in ordinary human existence. Of course, it is often taken for granted that the ultimate meaning of life is never found in ordinary human existence. The commonly observed distinctions between soul and body or between sacredness and profanity are clear indications that this is so. Paradoxically, all Three Teachings of the East Asian Way endorse the view that everydayness is not only the point of departure but also the eventual return of any significant moral and spiritual journey. They believe that the true test of lasting values in any ethicoreligious tradition is common sense and good reasons. But they by no means glorify the trite and plain languages of everyday speech. It is actually in what Herbert Fingarette calls the "secular as sacred"[2] that the spirit of their concern for ordinariness really lies.

Against this background, the ontological postulate can be introduced with one more observation. The uniqueness of being human must first transcend many familiar forms of reductionism. It is fallacious to define human nature merely in terms of biological, psychological, or sociological structures and functions because, viewed holistically, a more comprehensive grasp of its many-sidedness is required. However, an empirical enumeration of as many "human" traits as is practically feasible is not satisfactory either. Such a procedure cannot address one question without in principle changing it in a fundamental way. To put it differently, the question about the uniqueness of being human will always be scientifically unanswerable, as advances in biology, psychology, and sociology never intend to provide it with an answer.

The postulate about the perfectibility of human nature is thus empirically unprovable. Yet it is certainly not an unexamined faith in something beyond rational comprehension. Its status is ontological because it specifies a mode of understanding the being of the human. To be sure, perfectibility presupposes malleability and changeability. Ordinarily it is quite conceivable that malleation or change may not lead to the desired perfection. As a result, it seems that human nature can be seen as corruptible no less than as perfectible. However, common to all Three Teachings is the further claim that inherent in human nature is the moral and spiritual propensity for self-development. Only when this original propensity is frustrated by a complexity of internal and external causes is human nature destroyed or led astray. It is in this connection that Mencius insists upon the goodness of human nature as the real basis for self-realization. The Mencian thesis deserves a brief exposition.

Each human being, Mencius asserts, is endowed with a "moral sense," also known as the sensibility of the *hsin*. Inherent in the *hsin* are the four germinations of the four basic human feelings: commiseration, shame and dislike, deference and compliance, and right and wrong. Although environment, both social and psychological, features prominently in human growth, the germination power of these feelings is the structural reason for moral and spiritual self-development. In a strict sense, morality or spirituality is not internalized by but expressed through learning. Learning to be human in the Mencian tradition is therefore conceived of as the "mutual nourishment" of inner morality and social norms rather than the imposition of external values upon an uncultured mind. Indeed, *hsin* is both a cognitive and an affective faculty, symbolizing the functions of conscience as well as consciousness. For it not only reflects upon realities but, in comprehending them, shapes and creates their meaningfulness for oneself.

Similarly, in the view of Taoism, the inner illumination of the mind is the real basis for self-liberation. Confucian values, such as humanity and righteousness, are rejected by Chuang Tzu as unnecessary and are considered harmful social and cultural constraints detrimental to the spontaneity of nature. However, the pursuit of the Way requires a process of ultimate self-transformation which appeals neither to the immortality of the soul nor to the existence of God but to the "intellectual intuition" inherent in the true self. The *prajñā* in Ch'an, commonly rendered as "intuitive wisdom" or "nondual knowledge," also refers to an inalienable quality of the mind which manifests itself as the true buddha nature in each person.

Accordingly, despite divergent approaches to the actual process of moral and spiritual self-development, Confucianism, Taoism, and Buddhism all share this fundamental belief. Although existentially human beings are not what they ought to be, they can be perfected through self-cultivation; and the reason that they can become fully realized is inherent in what they are. Therefore, the human condition here and now, rather than either the original position in the past or a utopian projection into the future, is the central concern. It is in this sense that the ontological postulate of human perfectibility must be supplemented by an experiential assertion about the concrete path by which one's own "germinations" and "seeds" can eventually be brought to fruition. This may account for some of the deceptively simple paradoxes in East Asian thought, such as:

(a) There is sageliness in every human being/Virtually no one, not even Confucius, can claim to be a sage.

(b) Every sentient being is endowed with buddhahood/*Nirvāna* can never be attained except through Great Death.

(c) *Tao* is everywhere/Only the most sensitive and subtle mind can hear the Way.

It should be mentioned that germinations and seeds constitute only one of the many forms of the metaphorical language used in this connection. A frequently used analogy is the digging and drilling of a well, suggesting many degrees and layers of personal knowledge. Only after one has penetrated the deepest ground of one's existence can one truly experience the "taste" of one's enlightening self, which significantly also provides the authentic possibility for communicating with others and understanding things as they really are. The self so conceived, far from being an isolated and enclosed individual, signifies a sharable commonality accessible to every member of the human community. However, it is vitally important to note that commonality here by no means implies sameness, for it inevitably assumes different shades of meaning as it is perceived and manifested in different persons. The idealists' claim that all rational beings will finally agree is too restrictive a notion to account for the complex structure of common selfhood in East Asian thought. It is also in this sense that all Three Teachings assume that moral and spiritual self-development involves not only a convergence of stages to be perfected but also a multiplicity of ways to be pursued. Exclusivism in ethicoreligious thought is rejected mainly because by insisting upon a single path it would be incapable of accommodating the divergent interests and concerns of human beings as a whole. The recognition that the best way for me is not necessarily the best for my neighbor is a psychology essential for the peaceful coexistence of different and even conflicting beliefs in East Asian society and culture. The Confucian Golden Rule, for instance, is deliberately stated in a negative form: "Do not do to others what you would not want others to do to you."

The reluctance to impose one's own way on others is a consideration for the integrity of the other, and also a recognition that one can never fully comprehend another to the same extent and in the same degree as one can comprehend oneself. The veil of ignorance, however, must not prevent one from constantly trying to empathize with other human beings as an integral part of one's own quest for self-knowledge. Indeed, a sense of community, which is a manifestation of the organismic vision, is absolutely essential for moral and spiritual self-development. Only Confucianism among the Three Teachings unequivocally asserts that society is both necessary and intrinsically valuable for self-realization. Taoism and Ch'an do not seem to have attached much importance to human relations. But neither Taoism nor Ch'an belittles the lived world as a meaningful context in which ethicoreligious developments are assessed, as problems of afterlife, heaven and hell are deliberately relegated to the background. It is this sense of togetherness in the secular world, I suppose, that accounts for much of the concerted efforts of the Three Teachings to eradicate the alleged fallacy of "individualism." The Confucian instructions on the falsehood of self-centeredness, the Ch'an warning against egoist attachments, and the Taoist advocacy of self-forgetfulness all seem to point to the necessity of going beyond the private in order to participate in a shared vision.

The underlying thesis, then, is equality without uniformity. Moral and spiritual self-development can be understood as a process toward an ever-deepening subjectivity, but this must not be taken as a quest for pure morality or spirituality. The idea that inner truth is mysteriously connected with a transcendent reality not accessible to the human community at large does not feature prominently in East Asian thought at all. The perfected self is never conceived of as a depersonalized entity assuming a superhuman quality. This partly explains the absence of priesthood, presumably a spiritual elite mediating between the secular and the sacred, in any of the Three Teachings. Confucian, Taoist, and Ch'an masters are supposed to be exemplary teachers. They may try to instruct, discipline, and enlighten the student. But the purpose is always to inspire the self-effort of the student because the ultimate reason for self-realization is one's own inner strength.

The "Moral Universal," viewed from these perspectives, assumes a twofold significance: (1) Human beings are moral because, as self-perfectible beings, they cannot be circumscribed merely by the instinctual demands for survival or, for that matter, by the necessities and needs for the solidarity of the group or the perpetuation of the species. The meaning of being human is so uniquely personal that functional explanations, no matter how broad the scope they attempt to encompass, rarely escape the danger of reductionism. Indeed, simple human acts such as eating and walking have profound symbolic significance, making them qualitatively different from similar "acts" in other animals. Human hunger, for example, may from a naturalistic point of view be no more than a common physiological condition in the animal kingdom, but symbolically it is a phenomenon *sui generis*. Human development, therefore, involves much more than the combination of biological growth, psychological maturation, and the continuous internalization of social norms. (2) However, human beings are also inescapably biological, psychological, and social; and in order to realize themselves they must transform these circumscriptions into necessary "instrumentalities" for self-development. To learn to become what one ought to be, far from being a total rejection of what one is, must begin with a critical self-examination, "a reflection on things at hand." Commonly experienced feelings are therefore the points of departure for cultivating personal knowledge. It is not asceticism but perhaps a balanced diet, and certainly not occultism but a disciplined mind, that can really broaden one's vision and sharpen one's awareness. Methods of "quiet-sitting," "regulated breathing," or *zazen*, notwithstanding their varying degrees of seriousness in different traditions, all seem to suggest that the given "body and mind" is after all the concrete place where great ethicoreligious insight occurs. Pure morality and spirituality, admitting no biological, psychological, or sociological factors, is a kind of formalism as unacceptable to the East Asian mode of thinking as an extreme kind of behavioral reductionism would be. Mencius may have a point when he claims that if we can fully extend the common experience of feeling unable to bear the sufferings of others, our humanity will become inexhaustibly abundant.

FURTHER THOUGHTS

Having prepared a general statement on East Asian thought as a background paper for the Workshop and having participated in the discussions of its relevance to a critical examination of the "biological foundations of morality," I propose to offer in retrospect, especially in the light of Clifford Geertz's thought-provoking comments on my presentation, some observations that may have a direct bearing on the psychological and philosophical issues raised in our joint endeavor. For expediency, I would call our attention to the thought of Wang Yang-ming, who is said to have combined the wisdom of Ch'an Buddhism and the aesthetic sensitivity of Taoism with the humanist concerns of Confucianism. This may help us to focus more sharply on the salient features of the so-called Three Teachings. To begin, it should be remarked that Yang-ming, hailed as a most original and influential thinker in premodern China, was a distinguished scholar-official who consciously and conscientiously put into practice his metaphysical vision and demonstrated through his own personal spiritual development the beliefs he held. Indeed, his life history was an exemplification of the "unity of knowledge and action" idea which he advocated as a defining characteristic of his mode of thinking.

I. *The Great Man Regards Heaven, Earth, and the Myriad Things as One Body*. Thus begins the first line of Wang Yang-ming's "Inquiry on the *Great Learning*," a synoptic view of the central theme he had been formulating throughout his life. What he intends to convey here is neither an intellectual ideal nor an ethical injunction but, as Geertz noted, primarily "a common experience of feeling that undergirds morality." This shared feeling is explicitly described as the "emotional inability to bear the sufferings of others." Underlying these deceptively simple experiential assertions is an ontological claim about the "humanity of the heart." The reason that the great man can manifest his empathic and sympathetic feelings toward another (human being, animal, plant, or stone) in a genuine and spontaneous manner is thought to be in the structure of the heart (*hsin*) itself. Indeed, following Mencius, Yang-ming maintained that the "emotional inability to bear the sufferings of others" is an inborn capacity, not acquired (although it must be enhanced and refined) through imitative learning. Of course this does not mean, to paraphrase P. H. Wolff, that human sensitivity "matures in isolation from specific socioenvironmental influences." On the contrary, from a developmental point of view, it is like a delicate bud which can be easily frustrated without proper nourishment.

The opposite of this kind of unpremeditated human sensitivity is often depicted as selfishness (or self-centeredness), a deliberate refusal to share with, care for, and show affection toward others. Selfish acts are obviously in conflict with what H. L. Rheingold and D. F. Hay call the "prosocial behavior of the very young." Viewed from this perspective, the humane qualities of the infant as empirically identified by Rheingold and Hay are ontologically as well as ontogenetically inherent in the original capacity of the heart. Understandably, the growth of a human being depends as much upon the active participation of the learner (the infant, for example) as a "partner," indeed a "socializer" (a sharing, caring, and feeling "great man" in process) as on what we commonly call "socialization" from outside. This middle path must also reject both "normative biologism" and "normative sociologism."

Yang-ming's interpretive position is actually predicated on a metaphysical vision. If properly understood, such a vision is in accord with the Aristotelian, and for that matter Kantian, assertion

that what makes "reason" most valuable and essential to human beings is precisely the fact that it is beyond genetic constraints and thus
"biologically irrelevant." For one thing, the innateness of universalizable feelings shared by the human community is conceived as a
manifestation of the same "principle" (*li*) which underlies Heaven,
Earth, and the myriad things. Indeed, there is only one "principle" in
all beings and that "principle" is inherently in and intrinsically
knowable to the "humanity of the heart." Unlike the Platonic idea,
the "principle" that is embodied in each concrete thing is the "principle" in its all-embracing fullness. There is no distinction here between man and animal, plant or stone. The uniqueness of man,
however, lies in his ability to know and manifest through self-effort
the "principle" in him.

Man has this ability because ontologically he is endowed with the
"humanity of the heart" for self-realization which, in the tradition of
Chung-yung (Doctrine of the Mean), necessitates a concomitant realization of the other. But, in practice, unless a consistent and strenuous
effort at self-development is applied, man can in actuality become as
insensitive as stone. This metaphor, widely used in Chinese
literature, seems to imply that although man is the most sentient being that embodies the "principle" in the cosmos, what he is existentially may turn out to be a parody of what he can and ought to
become. It is therefore not only man's right but also his duty to be
moral. This reminds us of Kant. However, unlike Kant, Yang-ming
believed that the "principle," which has also been rendered as
"reason," is what human nature in the ultimate sense really means.
As a result, the formalist approach in Kantianism is here replaced by
an appeal to the universality of moral feelings which are biologically
based but not genetically determined. For the "principle" and the
"humanity of the heart" are one and the same reality.

II. *The Preservation of the Heavenly Principle and the Elimination of
Human Desires.* Implicit in the claim that the "humanity of the heart"
is universal and that the greatness of being human lies in the max-
imum development of this commonly shared feeling are two conflicting images of man. He can "embody" (*t'i*) the cosmos in his heart as
a concretely lived experience rather than a mere intellectual projection. Man so conceived symbolizes, in the words of Chou Tun-i
(1017–73), "the highest excellence" of the creative process of the
universe. Unfortunately, it is also probable that man is so cir-

cumscribed and corrupted by his "human desires" (jen-yü), biologically rooted and socioenvironmentally conditioned as well, that he can in fact inflict inhumanity upon himself and his closest kin. Even without the myth of the Fall, the range of human possibility for morality and immorality is frightfully extensive. Man can go beyond anthropocentrism (let alone egoism and ethnocentrism) and serve as a guardian of nature; or he can exhibit an aggression toward himself as well as all other beings as the most destructive force in the universe.

The contrast between the "Heavenly Principle" and "human desires" is of great significance in light of the above. Yang-ming took it for granted that what is truly human necessarily manifests the "principle" in its most generalized sense. Paradoxically "human desires," as limited and distorted expressions of the self, are detrimental to the original rhythm of the heart. This is why "human desires" are also described as "selfish desires" (ssu-yü). Just as selfishness endangers the authentic development of the self, "human desires" frustrate the true manifestation of humanity. Thus Yang-ming stated that learning to become a great man "consists entirely in getting rid of the obscuration of selfish desires in order by his own efforts to make manifest his clear character, so as to restore the condition of forming one body with Heaven, Earth, and the myriad things, a condition that is originally so, that is all."

Actually, the preservation of the Heavenly Principle and the elimination of human desires must be taken as a unitary effort of self-cultivation, signifying a holistic process of ultimate personal transformation. A key concept in this connection is i (intention), especially an act of the will to manifest one's "clear character" informed by the Heavenly Principle. For without a continuous quest for self-knowledge by an ever deepening psychology of purification, selfish desires cannot be eliminated and the quality of one's life, so far as the "principle" is concerned, remains obscure. This, I suppose, is the main reason why Yang-ming attached so much importance to "establishing the will" (li-chih) as the first essential step in the ceaseless process of learning to be truly human. This view seems remarkably similar to F. A. Jenner's observation in which he suggests that "we cannot live in everyday life without acting as though the moral depends on intention, indeed intentionality". For Yang-ming, we can surmise, morality entails intending, both as a state of conscious knowing (directionality of the mind) and as a process of conscientious acting (transforming effect of the heart). Perhaps in this sense we can follow E. Turiel's distinction between morality and convention without necessarily committing ourselves to the claim that they are "different aspects of social regulation."

III. *The Full Realization of Primordial Awareness.* I mentioned earlier that the Confucian *hsin* must be glossed as "heart-mind" because it involves both cognitive and affective dimentions of human awareness. This "fruitful ambiguity" is perhaps the result of a deliberate refusal rather than an unintended failure to make a sharp distinction between conscience and consciousness. To Yang-ming, consciousness as cognition and conscience as affection are not two separable functions of the mind. Rather, they are integral aspects of a dynamic process whereby man becomes aware of himself as a moral being. Indeed, the source of morality depends on their inseparability in a pre-reflective faculty. Borrowing a classical term from Mencius, Yang-ming defines this pre-reflective faculty as *liang-chih* (commonly translated as "innate knowledge" but here rendered as "primordial awareness"), signifying an innermost state of human perception wherein knowledge and action form a unity. This primordial awareness, which can also be understood as a more subtle way of characterizing the "humanity of the heart," creates values of human understanding as it encounters the world. Learning to be human, in this sense, involves a continuous development of one's "primordial awareness." The expression *chih liang-chih*, often translated as "the extension of innate knowledge," may be more appropriately interpreted here as the full realization of one's primordial awareness. I do not see any obvious conflict between this line of thinking and T. Nagel's analysis that "a capacity to subject their prereflective or innate responses to criticism and revision, and to create new forms of understanding" is that unique quality that human beings have discovered in themselves. Yet I must admit that Yang-ming's "primordial awareness" is not merely a rational capacity; nor is it simply a perceptual and motivational starting point. Needless to say, it also has little to do with biological nativism. Rather, it is a mode of perceiving which I earlier noted as the function of "intellectual intuition." A feature of it is that, as a critical self-awareness, it can understand our true nature and apprehend the thing-in-itself, a capacity which Kant thought is humanly impossible. The justification for this seemingly outrageous claim is relatively simple: "Knowing thyself" means to realize the "principle" inherent in one's nature. Since the same "principle" also underlies humans and things in general, the procedure by which other forms of understanding are created is, in the ultimate sense, identical to that of self-knowledge. But the assumption that the level of self-knowledge attained entails a comparable depth of knowledge about humans and things in general is not an expression of subjective idealism. The true self so conceived is never an isolated entity. The solipsistic predicament (an extreme case of self-centeredness perhaps), so far as it may have a bearing on this, is rejected by a direct appeal to the common experience of feeling. The sense of cosmic togetherness, or in Chang Tsai's (1020–77) poetic expression that "Heaven is my father and Earth is my mother . . . . All people are my brothers and sisters, and all things are my companions," is a primary background understanding in this tradition. As a result, the whole philosophical activity centered around the skeptic's questions about the outside world and about other minds is never developed. Whether or not this mode of thinking will eventually lead to a form of panpsychism is beyond the scope of our present discussion. It is clear, however, that the position introduced here is basically at odds with the view that biological or any physical structures can in themselves explain human morality.

The apparent divergence between this line of inquiry, focusing on the commonality and sharability of human experience, indeed on the unity and continuity of being, and Charles Fried's plea for a greater tolerance of diversity is perhaps a matter of emphasis. I wonder, however, whether the centrality of recognizing the identity of persons as a background assumption for the morality of free, rational choosing beings does not itself presuppose a primordial awareness that despite the distinctness of persons, equality of respect is possible. After all, Kant "who sees in freedom the heart of moral value" feels it is fitting to define moral *choice* as a duty, a categorical imperative. A fiduciary commitment (in Michael Polanyi's sense) to the value of the human, I believe, is a basis for the "principle of the autonomy of morals."

NOTES

1. Needham, J. and Wang, L., *Science and Civilization in China*, 6 vols. (Cambridge: Cambridge University Press, 1954-), 2-287.

2. Fingarette, H., *Confucius: The Secular as Sacred* (New York: Harper & Row, 1972).

II. The Continuity of Being: Chinese Visions of Nature

The Chinese belief in the continuity of being, a basic motif in Chinese ontology, has far-reaching implications in Chinese philosophy, religion, epistemology, aesthetics, and ethics. F. W. Mote comments:

> The basic point which outsiders have found so hard to detect is that the Chinese, among all peoples ancient and recent, primitive and modern, are apparently unique in having no creation myth; that is, they have regarded the world and man as uncreated, as constituting the central features of a spontaneously self-generating cosmos having no creator, god, ultimate cause, or will external to itself.[1]

This strong assertion has understandably generated controversy among Sinologists. Mote has identified a distinctive feature of the Chinese mode of thought. In his words, "[t]he genuine Chinese cosmogony is that of organismic process, meaning that all of the parts of the entire cosmos belong to one organic whole and that they all interact as participants in one spontaneously self-generating life process."[2]

However, despite Mote's insightfulness in singling out this particular dimension of Chinese cosmogony for focused investigation, his characterization of its uniqueness is problematic. For one thing, the apparent lack of a creation myth in Chinese cultural history is predicated on a more fundamental assumption about reality; namely, that all modalties of being are organically connected. Ancient Chinese thinkers were intensely interested in the creation of the world. Some of them, notably the Taoists, even speculated on the creator (*tsao-wu chu*) and the process by which the universe came into being.[3] Presumably indigenous creation myths existed although the written records transmitted by even the most culturally sophisticated historians do not contain enough information to reconstruct them.[4] The real issue is not the presence or absence of creation myths, but the underlying assumption of the cosmos: whether it is continuous or discontinuous with its creator. Suppose the cosmos as we know it was created by a Big Bang; the ancient Chinese thinkers would have no problem with this theory. What they would not have accepted was a further claim that there was an external intelligence, beyond human comprehension, who willed that it be so. Of course the Chinese are not unique in this regard. Many peoples, ancient and recent, primitive and modern, would feel uncomfortable with the idea of a willful God who created the world out of nothing. It is not a creation myth as such but the Judeo-Christian version of it that is absent in Chinese mythology. But the Chinese, like numerous peoples throughout human history, subscribe to the continuity of being as self-evidently true.[5]

An obvious consequence of this basic belief is the all-embracing nature of the so-called spontaneously self-generating life process. Strictly speaking, it is not because the Chinese have no idea of God external to the created cosmos that they have no choice but to accept the cosmogony as an organismic process. Rather, it is precisely because they perceive the cosmos as the unfolding of continuous creativity that it cannot entertain "conceptions of creation *ex nihilo* by the hand of God, or through the will of God, and all other such mechanistic, teleological, and theistic cosmologies."[6] The Chinese commitment to the continuity of being, rather than the absence of a creation myth, prompts them to see nature as "the all-enfolding harmony of impersonal cosmic functions."[7]

The Chinese model of the world, "a decidedly psychophysical structure" in the Jungian sense,[8] is characterized by Joseph Needham as "an ordered harmony of wills without an ordainer."[9] What Needham describes as the organismic Chinese cosmos consists of dynamic energy fields rather than static matter-like entities. Indeed, the dichotomy of spirit and matter is not at all applicable to this psychophysical structure. The most basic stuff that makes the cosmos is neither solely spiritual nor material but both. It is a vital force. This vital force must not be conceived of either as disembodied spirit or as pure matter.[10] Wing-tsit Chan, in his influential *Source Book of Chinese Philosophy*, notes that the distinction between energy and matter is not made in Chinese philosophy. He further notes that H. H. Dubs's rendering of the indigenous term for this basic stuff, *ch'i*, as "matter-energy" is "essentially sound but awkward and lacks an adjective form."[11] Although Chan translates *ch'i* as "material force," he cautions that since *ch'i*, before the advent of Neo-Confucianism in the eleventh century, originally "denotes the psychophysiological power associated with blood and breath," it should be rendered as "vital force" or "vital power."[12]

The unusual difficulty in making *ch'i* intelligible in modern Western philosophy suggests that the underlying Chinese metaphysical assumption is significantly different from the Cartesian dichotomy between spirit and matter. However, it would be misleading to categorize the Chinese mode of thinking as a sort of pre-Cartesian naïveté lacking differentiation between mind and body and, by implication, between subject and object. Analytically Chinese thinkers have clearly distinguished spirit from matter. They fully recognize that spirit is not reducible to matter, that spirit has an independent ontological status, and that axiomatically spirit is of more enduring value than matter. There are of course notable exceptions. But these so-called materialist thinkers are not only rare but also too few and far between to constitute a noticeable tradition in Chinese philosophy. Recent attempts to reconstruct the genealogy of materialist thinkers in China have been painful and, in some cases, far-fetched.[13] Indeed, to characterize the two great Confucian thinkers, Chang Tsai (1020–1077) and Wang Fu-chih (1619–1692), as paradigmatic examples of Chinese materialism is predicated on the false assumption that *ch'i* is materialistic. Both of them did subscribe to what may be called philosophy of *ch'i* as a critique of speculative thought but, to them, *ch'i* was not simply matter but vital force endowed with all-pervasive spirituality.[14]

The continuous presence in Chinese philosophy of the idea of *ch'i* as a way of conceptualizing the basic structure and function of the cosmos, despite the availability of symbolic resources to make an analytical distinction between spirit and matter, signifies a conscious refusal to abandon a mode of thought that synthesizes spirit and matter as an undifferentiated whole. The loss of analytical clarity is compensated by the reward of imaginative richness. The fruitful ambiguity of *ch'i* allows philosophers to explore realms of being which are inconceivable to people constricted by a Cartesian dichotomy. To be sure, the theory of the different modalities of *ch'i* cannot engender ideas such as the naked object, raw data, or the value-free fact, and thus cannot create a world out there, naked, raw, and value-free, for the disinterested scientist to study, analyze, manipulate, and control. *Ch'i*, in short, seems inadequate to provide a philosophical background for the development of empirical science as understood in the positivistic sense. What it does provide,

however, is a metaphorical mode of knowing, an epistemological attempt to address the multidimensional nature of reality by com-
parison, allusion, and suggestion.

Whether it is the metaphorical mode of knowing that directs the
Chinese to perceive the cosmos as an organismic process or it is the
ontological vision of the continuity of being that informs Chinese
epistemology is a highly intriguing question. Our main concern
here, however, is to understand how the idea of the undifferentiated
ch'i serves as a basis for a unified cosmological theory. We want to
know in what sense the least intelligent being, such as a rock, and
the highest manifestation of spirituality, such as heaven, both consist
of *ch'i*. The way the Chinese perceive reality and the sense of reality
which defines the Chinese way of seeing the world are equally important in our inquiry, even though we do not intend to specify any
causal relationship between them.

The organismic process as a spontaneously self-generating life
process exhibits three basic motifs: continuity, wholeness, and
dynamism.[15] All modalities of being, from a rock to heaven, are integral parts of a continuum which is often referred to as the "great
transformation" (*ta-hua*).[16] Since nothing is outside of this continuum, the chain of being is never broken. A linkage will always be
found between any given pair of things in the universe. We may
have to probe deeply to find some of the linkages, but they are there
to be discovered. These are not figments of our imagination but solid
foundations upon which the cosmos and our lived world therein are
constructed. *Ch'i*, the psychophysiological stuff, is everywhere. It
suffuses even the "great void" (*t'ai-hsü*) which is the source of all beings in Chang Tsai's philosophy.[17] The continuous presence of *ch'i* in
all modalities of being makes everything flow together as the unfolding of a single process. Nothing, not even an almighty creator, is
external to this process.

This motif of wholeness is directly derived from the idea of continuity as all-encompassing. If the world were created by an intelligence higher than and external to the great transformation, it
would, by definition, fall short of a manifestation of holism. Similarly, if the world were merely a partial or distorted manifestation of
the Platonic Idea, it would never achieve the perfection of the
original reality. On the contrary, if genuine creativity is not the creation of something out of nothing, but a continuous transformation of
that which is already there, the world as it now exists is the authentic
manifestation of the cosmic process in its all-embracing fullness. Indeed, if the Idea for its own completion entails that it realize itself

through the organismic process, the world is in every sense the concrete embodiment of the Idea. Traditional Chinese thinkers, of course, did not philosophize in those terms. They used different conceptual apparatuses to convey their thought. To them, the appropriate metaphor for understanding the universe was biology rather than physics. At issue was not the eternal, static structure but the dynamic process of growth and transformation. To say that the cosmos is a continuum and that all of its components are internally connected is also to say that it is an organismic unity, holistically integrated at each level of complexity.

It is important to note that continuity and wholeness in Chinese cosmological thinking must be accompanied by the third motif, dynamism, lest the idea of organismic unity imply a closed system. While Chinese thinkers are critically aware of the inertia in human culture which may eventually lead to stagnation, they perceive the "course of heaven" (*t'ien-hsing*) as "vigorous" (*chien*) and instruct people to model themselves on the ceaseless vitality of the cosmic process.[18] What they envision in the spontaneously self-generating life process is not only inner connectedness and inter-dependence but also infinite potential for development. Many historians have remarked that the traditional Chinese notion of cyclic change, like the recurrence of the seasonal pattern, is incompatible with the modern Western idea of progress. To be sure, the traditional Chinese conception of history lacks the idea of unilinear development, such as Marxian modes of production depicting a form of historical inevitability. It is misleading, however, to describe Chinese history as chronicling a number of related events happening in a regularly repeated order.[19] Chinese historiography is not a reflection of a cyclic world view. The Chinese world view is neither cyclic nor spiral. It is transformational. The specific curve around which it transforms at a given period of time is indeterminate, however, for numerous human and nonhuman factors are involved in shaping its form and direction.

The organismic life process, which Mote contends is the genuine Chinese cosmogony, is an open system. As there is no temporal beginning to specify, no closure is ever contemplated. The cosmos is forever expanding; the great transformation is unceasing. The idea of unilinear development, in this perspective, is one-sided because it fails to account for the whole range of possibility in which progress constitutes but one of several dominant configurations. By analogy, neither cyclic nor spiral movements can fully depict the varieties of cosmic transformation. Since it is open rather than closed and dynamic rather than static, no geometric design can do justice to its complex morphology.

Earlier, I followed Mote in characterizing the Chinese vision of nature as the "all-enfolding harmony of impersonal cosmic function" and remarked that this particular vision was prompted by the Chinese commitment to the continuity of being. Having discussed the three basic motifs of Chinese cosmology — wholeness, dynamism, and continuity — I can elaborate on Mote's characterization by discussing some of its implications. The idea of all-enfolding harmony involves two interrelated meanings. It means that nature is all-inclusive, the spontaneously self-generating life process which excludes nothing. The Taoist idea of *tzu-jan* ("self-so"),[20] which is used in modern Chinese to translate the English word *nature*, aptly captures this spirit. To say that *self-so* is all-inclusive is to posit a nondiscriminatory and nonjudgmental position, to allow all modalities of being to display themselves as they are. This is possible, however, only if competitiveness, domination, and aggression are thoroughly transformed. Thus, all-enfolding harmony also means that internal resonance underlies the order of things in the universe. Despite conflict and tension, which are like waves of the ocean, the deep structure of nature is always tranquil. The great transformation of which nature is the concrete manifestation is the result of concord rather than discord and convergence rather than divergence.

This vision of nature may suggest an unbridled romantic assertion about peace and love, the opposite of what Charles Darwin realistically portrayed as the rules of nature. Chinese thinkers, however, did not take the all-enfolding harmony to be the original naïveté of the innocent. Nor did they take it to be an idealist utopia attainable in a distant future. They were acutely aware that the world we live in, far from being the "great unity' (*ta-t'ung*) recommended in the *Evolution of the Rites*,[21] is laden with disruptive forces including humanly caused calamities and natural catastrophes. They also knew well that history is littered with internecine warfare, oppression, injustice, and numerous other forms of cruelty. It was not naïve romanticism that prompted them to assert that harmony is a defining characteristic of the organismic process. They believed that it is an accurate description of what the cosmos really is and how it actually works.

One advantage of rendering *ch'i* as "vital force," bearing in mind its original association with blood and breath, is its emphasis on the life process. To Chinese thinkers, nature is vital force in display. It is continuous, holistic, and dynamic. Yet, in an attempt to understand the blood and breath of nature's vitality, Chinese thinkers discovered that its enduring pattern is union rather than disunion, integration rather than disintegration, and synthesis rather than separation. The eternal flow of nature is characterized by the concord and convergence of numerous streams of vital force. It is in this sense that the organismic process is considered harmonious.

Chang Tsai, in his celebrated metaphysical treatise, "Correcting Youthful Ignorance," defines the cosmos as the "Great Harmony":

> The Great Harmony is called the Tao. It embraces the nature which underlies all counter processes of floating and sinking, rising and falling, and motion and rest. It is the origin of the process of fusion and intermingling, of overcoming and being overcome, and of expansion and contraction. At the commencement, these processes are incipient, subtle, obscure, easy and simple, but at the end they are extensive, great, strong and firm. It is *ch'ien* ("heaven") that begins with the knowledge of Change, and *k'un* ("earth") that models after simplicity. That which is dispersed, differentiated, and discernible in form becomes *ch'i*, and that which is pure, penetrating, and not discernible in form becomes spirit. Unless the whole universe is in the process of fusion and intermingling like fleeting forces moving in all directions, it may not be called "Great Harmony."[22]

In his vision, nature is the result of the fusion and intermingling of the vital forces that assume tangible forms. Mountains, rivers, rocks, trees, animals, and human beings are all modalities of energy-matter, symbolizing that the creative transformation of the Tao is forever present. Needham's idea of the Chinese cosmos as an ordered harmony of wills without an ordainer is, however, not entirely appropriate. Wills, no matter how broadly defined, do not feature prominently here. The idea that heaven and earth complete the transformation with no mind of their own clearly indicates that the harmonious state of the organismic process is not achieved by ordering divergent wills.[23] Harmony will be attained through spontaneity. In what sense is this what Mote calls "impersonal cosmic function"? Let us return to Chang Tsai's metaphysical treatise:

> *Ch'i* moves and flows in all directions and in all manners. Its two elements (yin and yang) unite and give rise to the concrete. Thus

the multiplicity of things and human beings is produced. In their ceaseless successions the two elements of yin and yang constitute the great principles of the universe.[24]

This inner logic of *ch'i*, which is singularly responsible for the production of the myriad things, leads to a naturalistic description of the impersonal cosmic function. Wang Fu-chih, who developed Chang Tsai's metaphysics of *ch'i* with great persuasive power, continues with this line of thinking:

> The fact that the things of the world, whether rivers or mountains, plants or animals, those with or without intelligence, and those yielding blossoms or bearing fruits, provide beneficial support for all things is the result of the natural influence of the moving power of *ch'i*. It fills the universe. And as it completely provides for the flourish and transformation of all things, it is all the more spatially unrestricted. As it is not spatially restricted, it operates in time and proceeds with time. From morning to evening, from spring to summer, and from the present tracing back to the past, there is no time at which it does not operate, and there is no time at which it does not produce. Consequently, as one sprout bursts forth it becomes a tree with a thousand big branches, and as an egg evolves, it progressively becomes a fish capable of swallowing a ship. . . .[25]

The underlying message, however, is not the impersonality of the cosmic function, even though the idea of the moving power of *ch'i* indicates that no anthropomorphic god, animal, or object is really behind the great transformation. The naturalness of the cosmic function, despite human wishes and desires, is impersonal but not inhuman. It is impartial to all modalities of being and not merely anthropocentric. We humans, therefore, do not find the impersonal cosmic function cold, alien, or distant, although we know that it is, by and large, indifferent to and disinterested in our private thoughts and whims. Actually, we are an integral part of this function; we are ourselves the result of this moving power of *ch'i*. Like mountains and rivers, we are legitimate beings in this great transformation. The opening lines in Chang Tsai's *Western Inscription* are not only his article of faith but also his ontological view of the human:

> Heaven is my father and earth is my mother, and even such a small being as I finds an intimate place in their midst. Therefore,

> that which fills the universe I regard as my body and that which
> directs the universe I regard as my nature. All people are my
> brothers and sisters, and all things are my companions.[26]

The sense of intimacy with which Chang Tsai, as a single person,
relates himself to the universe as a whole reflects his profound
awareness of moral ecology. Humanity is the respectful son or
daughter of the cosmic process. This humanistic vision is distinctively
Confucian in character. It contrasts sharply with the Taoist idea of
non-interference on the one hand and the Buddhist concept of
detachment on the other. Yet the notion of humanity as forming one
body with the universe has been so widely accepted by the Chinese,
in popular as well as elite culture, that it can very well be
characterized as a general Chinese world view.

Forming one body with the universe can literally mean that since
all modalities of being are made of *ch'i*, human life is part of a continuous flow of the blood and breath that constitutes the cosmic process. Human beings are thus organically connected with rocks,
trees, and animals. Understandably, the interplay and interchange
between discrete species feature prominently in Chinese literature,
notably popular novels. The monkey in the *Journey to the West* came
into being by metamorphosis from agate,[27] the hero in the *Dream of
the Red Chamber* or the *Story of the Stone*, Pao-yü, is said to have been
transformed from a piece of precious jade,[28] and the heroine of the
Romance of the White Snake has not completely succeeded in transfigur-
ing herself into a beautiful woman.[29] These are well-known stories.
They have evoked strong sympathetic responses from Chinese au-
diences young and old for centuries, not merely as fantasies but as
great human drama. It is not at all difficult for the Chinese to imagine that an agate or a piece of jade can have enough potential
spirituality to transform itself into a human being. Part of the pathos
of the White Snake lies in her inability to fight against the spell cast
by a ruthless monk so that she can retain her human form and be
united with her lover. The fascinating element in this romance is
that she manages to acquire the power to transfigure herself into a
woman through several hundred years of self-cultivation.

Presumably, from the cosmic vantage point, nothing is totally fixed.
It need not be forever the identity it now assumes. In the perceptive
eye of the Chinese painter Tao Chi (1641–1717), mountains flow
like rivers. The proper way of looking at mountains, for him, is to
see them as ocean waves frozen in time.[30] By the same token, rocks
are not static objects but dynamic processes with their particular

configuration of the energy-matter. It may not be far-fetched to suggest that, with this vision of nature, we can actually talk about the different degrees of spirituality of rocks. Agate is certainly more spiritual than an ordinary hard stone and perhaps jade is more spiritual than agate. Jade is honored as the "finest essence of mountain and river" (*shan-ch'uan ching-ying*).[31] By analogy, we can also talk about degrees of spirituality in the entire chain of being. Rocks, trees, animals, humans, and gods represent different levels of spirituality based on the varying compositions of *ch'i*. However, despite the principle of differentiation, all modalities of being are organically connected. They are integral parts of a continuous process of cosmic transformation. It is in this metaphysical sense that "all things are my companions."

The uniqueness of being human cannot be explained in terms of a preconceived design by a creator. Human beings, like all other beings, are the results of the integration of the two basic vital forces of yin and yang. Chou Tun-i (1017–1073) says, "the interaction of these two *ch'i* engenders and transforms the myriad things. The myriad things produce and reproduce, resulting in an unending transformation."[32] In a strict sense, then, human beings are not the rulers of creation; if they intend to become guardians of the universe, they must earn this distinction through self-cultivation. There is no preordained reason for them to think otherwise. Nevertheless, the human being, in the Chinese sense of *jen* which is gender neutral, is unique. Chou Tun-i offers the following explanation:

> It is man alone who receives [the Five Agents] in their highest excellence, and therefore he is most intelligent. His physical form appears, and his spirit develops consciousness. The five moral principles of his nature (humanity, rightness, propriety, wisdom, and faithfulness) are aroused by, and react to, the external world and engage in activity; good and evil are distinguished; and human affairs take place.[33]

The theory of the Five Agents or the Five Phases (*wu-hsing*) need not concern us here. Since Chou makes it clear that "by the transformation of yang and its union with yin, the Five Agents of Water, Fire, Wood, Metal, and Earth arise" and that since "the Five Agents constitute a system of yin and yang."[34] they can be conceived as specific forms of *ch'i*.

That humankind receives *ch'i* in its highest excellence is not only manifested in intelligence but also in sensitivity. The idea that humans are the most sentient beings in the universe features prominently in Chinese thought. A vivid description of human sensitivity is found in the "recorded sayings" (*yü-lu*) of Ch'eng Hao (1032–1085):

> A book on medicine describes paralysis of the four limbs as absence of humanity (*pu jen*). This is an excellent description. The man of humanity regards heaven and earth and all things as one body. To him there is nothing that is not himself. Since he has recognized all things as himself, can there be any limit to his humanity? If things are not part of the self, naturally they have nothing to do with it. As in the case of paralysis of the four limbs, the vital force (*ch'i*) no longer penetrates them, and therefore they are no longer parts of the self.[35]

This idea of forming one body with the universe is predicated on the assumption that since all modalities of being are made of *ch'i*, all things cosmologically share the same consanguinity with us and are thus our companions. This vision enabled an original thinker of the Ming Dynasty, Wang Ken (1483–1540), to remark that if we came into being through transformation (*hua-sheng*), then heaven and earth are our father and mother to us; if we came into being through reproduction (*hsing-sheng*), then our father and mother are heaven and earth to us.[36] The image of the human that emerges here, far from being the lord of creation, is the filial son and daughter of the universe. Filial piety connotes a profound feeling, an all-pervasive care for the world around us.

This literal meaning of forming one body with the universe must be augmented by a metaphorical reading of the same text. It is true that the body clearly conveys the sense of *ch'i* as the blood and breath of the vital force that underlies all beings. The uniqueness of being human, however, is not simply that we are made of the same psychophysiological stuff that rocks, trees, and animals are also made of. It is our consciousness of being human that enables and impels us to probe the transcendental anchorage of our nature. Surely, the motif of the continuity of being prevents us from positing a creator totally external to the organismic cosmic process, but what is the relationship between human nature and heaven which serves as the source of all things? Indeed, how are we to understand the ontological assertion in the first chapter of the *Doctrine of the Mean* that our nature is decreed by heaven?[37] Is the Mandate of Heaven a one-time operation or a continuous presence? Wang Fu-chih's general response to these questions is suggestive:

> By nature is meant the principle of growth. As one daily grows, one daily achieves completion. Thus by the Mandate of Heaven is not meant that heaven gives the decree (*ming*, mandate) only at the moment of one's birth. . . . In the production of things by heaven, the process of transformation never ceases.[38]

In the metaphorical sense, then, forming one body with the universe requires continuous effort to grow and to refine oneself. We can embody the whole universe in our sensitivity because we have enlarged and deepened our feeling and care to the fullest extent. However, there is no guarantee at the symbolic or the experiential level that the universe is automatically embodied in us. Unless we see to it that the Mandate of Heaven is fully realized in our nature, we may not live up to the expectation that "all things are complete in us."[39] Wang Fu-chih's refusal to follow a purely naturalistic line of thinking on this is evident in the following observation: "The profound person acts naturally as if nothing happens, but . . . he acts so as to make the best choices and remain firm in holding to the Mean."[40] To act naturally without letting things take their own course means, in Neo-Confucian terminology, to follow the "heavenly principle" (*t'ien-li*) without being overcome by "selfish desires" (*ssu-yü*).[41] Selfish desires are forms of self-centeredness that belittle the authentic human capacity to take part in the transformative process of heaven and earth. In commenting on the *Book of Change*, Ch'eng Hao observes:

> The most impressive aspect of things is their spirit of life. This is what is meant by origination being the chief quality of goodness. Man and heaven and earth are one thing. Why should man purposely belittle himself?[42]

Forming a trinity with heaven and earth, which is tantamount to forming one body with the myriad things, enjoins us from applying the subject-object dichotomy to nature. To see nature as an external object out there is to create an artificial barrier which obstructs our true vision and undermines our human capacity to experience nature from within. The internal resonance of the vital forces is such that the mind, as the most refined and subtle *ch'i* of the human body, is constantly in sympathetic accord with the myriad things in nature. The function of "affect and response" (*kan-ying*) characterizes nature as a great harmony and so informs the mind.[43] The mind forms a union with nature by extending itself metonymically. Its aesthetic appreciation of nature is neither an appropriation of the object by the subject nor an imposition of the subject on the object, but the merging of the self into an expanded reality through transformation and participation. This creative process, in Jakobson's terminology, is "contiguous," because rupture between us and nature never occurs.[44]

Chuang Tzu recommends that we listen with our minds rather than with our ears; with *ch'i* rather than with our minds.[45] If listening with our minds involves consciousness unaffected by sensory perceptions, what does listening with *ch'i* entail? Could it mean that we are so much a part of the internal resonance of the vital forces themselves that we can listen to the sound of nature or, in Chuang Tzu's expression, the "music of heaven" (*t'ien-lai*)[46] as our inner voice? Or could it mean that the all-embracing *ch'i* enables the total transposition of humankind and nature? As a result, the aesthetic delight that one experiences is no longer the private sensation of the individual but the "harmonious blending of inner feelings and outer scenes"[47] as the traditional Chinese artist would have it. It seems that in either case we do not detach ourselves from nature and study it in a disinterested manner. What we do is to suspend not only our sensory perceptions but also our conceptual apparatus so that we can embody nature in our sensitivity and allow nature to embrace us in its affinity.

I must caution, however, that the aesthetic experience of mutuality and immediacy with nature is often the result of strenuous and continual effort at self-cultivation. Despite our superior intelligence, we do not have privileged access to the great harmony. As social and cultural beings, we can never get outside ourselves to study nature from neutral ground. The process of returning to nature involves unlearning and forgetting as well as remembering. The precondition for us to participate in the internal resonance of the vital forces in nature is our own inner transformation. Unless we can first harmonize our own feelings and thoughts, we are not preapred for nature, let alone for an "interflow with the spirit of Heaven and Earth."[48] It is true that we are consanguineous with nature. But as humans, we must make ourselves worthy of such a relationship.

NOTES

1. Frederick F. Mote, *Intellectual Foundations of China* (New York: Alfred A. Knopf, 1971), pp. 17–18.

2. Ibid., p. 19.

3. For a thought-provoking discussion on this issue, see N. J. Girardot, *Myth and Meaning in Early Taoism* (Berkeley: University of California Press, 1983), pp. 275–310.

4. For a suggestive methodological essay, see William G. Boltz, "Kung Kung and the Flood: Reverse Euhemerism in the *Yao Tien*," *T'oung Pao* 67 (1981): 141–53. Professor Boltz's effort to reconstruct the Kung Kung myth indicates the possibility of an indigenous creation myth.

5. Tu Wei-ming, "Shih-t'an Chung-kuo che-hsüeh chung te san-ko chi-tiao" [A preliminary discussion on the three basic motifs in Chinese philosophy], *Chung-kuo che-hsüeh shih yen-chiu* [Studies on the history of Chinese philosophy] (Peking: Society for the Study of the History of Chinese Philosophy) 2 (March 1981): 19–21.

6. Mote, *Intellectual Foundations of China*, p. 20.

7. Ibid.

8. See Jung's Foreword to the *I Ching (Book of Changes)*, translated into English by Cary F. Baynes from the German translation of Richard Wilhelm, Bollingen Series, vol. 19 (Princeton, N.J.: Princeton University Press, 1967), p. xxiv.

9. Needham's full statement reads as follows: "It was an ordered harmony of wills without an ordainer; it was like the spontaneous yet ordered, in the sense of patterned, movements of dancers in a country dance of figures, none of whom are bound by law to do what they do, nor yet pushed by others coming behind, but cooperate in a voluntary harmony of wills." See Joseph Needham and Wang Ling, *Science and Civilization in China*, 6 vols. (Cambridge: Cambridge University Press, 1954-), 2:287.

10. Actually, the dichotomy of spirit and matter does not feature prominently in Chinese thought, see Tu, *Chung-kuo che-hsüeh shih yen-chiu*, pp. 21–22.

11. Wing-tsit Chan, trans. and comp., *A Source Book in Chinese Philosophy* (Princeton, N.J.: Princeton University Press, 1969), p. 784.

12. Ibid.

13. For a notable exception to this general interpretive situation in the People's Republic of China, see Chang Tai-nien, *Chung-kuo che-hsüeh fa-wei* [Exploring some of the delicate issues in Chinese philosophy] (T'ai-yuan, Shansi: People's Publishing Co., 1981), pp. 11–38; 275–306.

14. For a general discussion on this vital issue from a medical viewpoint, see Manfred Porkert, *The Theoretical Foundations of Chinese Medicine: Systems of Correspondence* (Cambridge, Mass.: MIT Press, 1974).

15. Tu, "Shih-t'an Chung-kuo che-hsüeh," pp. 19–24.

16. A paradigmatic discussion on this is to be found in the *Commentaries on the Book of Changes*. See Wing-tsit Chan, *Source Book in Chinese Philosophy*, p. 264.

17. See Chang Tsai's "Correcting Youthful Ignorance" in Wing-tsit Chan, *Source Book in Chinese Philosophy*, p. 501.

18. For this reference in the *Chou I*, see *A Concordance to Yi-Ching*, Harvard-Yenching Institute Sinological Index Series Supplement No. 10 (reprint; Taipei: Chinese Materials and Research Aids Service Center, Inc., 1966), 1/1.

19. The idea of the "dynastic cycle" may give one the impression that Chinese history is nondevelopmental. See Edwin O. Reischauer and John K. Fairbank, *East Asia: The Great Tradition* (Boston: Houghton Mifflin Co., 1960), pp. 114–18.

20. Chuang Tzu, chap. 7. See the Harvard Yenching Index on the *Chuang Tzu*, 20/7/11.

21. See William T. de Bary, Wing-tsit Chan, and Burton Watson, comps., *Sources of Chinese Tradition* (New York: Columbia University, 1960), pp. 191–92.

22. Wing-tsit Chan, *Source Book on Chinese Philosophy*, pp. 500–1.

23. Ibid., pp. 262–66. This idea underlies the philosophy of change.

24. Ibid., see. 14, p. 505. In this translation, *ch'i* is rendered "material force." The words *yin* and *yang* in parentheses are added by me.

25. Ibid., pp. 698–99.

26. Ibid., p. 496.

27. Wu Ch'eng-en, *Hsi-yu chi*, trans. Anthony C. Yü (Yü Kuo-fan) as *Journey to the West*, 4 vols. (Chicago: University of Chicago Press, 1977–), 1:67–78.

28. Ts'ao Hsüeh-ch'in (Cao Xueqin), *Hung-lou meng* [Dream of the Red Chamber], trans. David Hawkes as *The Story of the Stone*, 5 vols. (Middlesex, England: Penguin Books, 1973-), 1:47–49.

29. For two useful discussions on the story, see Fu Hsi-hua, *Pai-she-chuan chi* [An anthology of the White Snake story] (Shanghai: Shanghai Publishing Co., 1955) and P'an Chiang-tung, *Pai-she ku-shih yen-chiu* [A study of the White Snake story] (Taipei: Students' Publishers, 1981).

30. P. Ryckmans, "Les propos sur la peinture de Shi Tao traduction et commentaire," *Arts Asiatique* 14 (1966): 123–24.

31. Teng Shu-p'in, "Shan-ch'uan ching-ying—yü te i-shu" [The finest essence of mountain and river—the art of jade], in *Chung-kuo wen-hua hsin-lun* [New views on Chinese culture] (Taipei: Lien-ching, 1983), Section on Arts, pp. 253–304.

33. Ibid.

34. Ibid.

35. Ibid., p. 530.

36. Wang Ken, "Yü Nan-tu chu-yu" [Letter to friends of Nan-tu], in *Wang Hsin-chai hsien-sheng ch'üan-chi* [The complete works of Wang Ken] (1507 edition, Harvard-Yenching Library), 4.16b.

37. Wing-tsit Chan, *Source Book in Chinese Philosophy*, p. 98.

38. Ibid., p. 699.

39. *Mencius*, 7A4.

40. Wing-tsit Chan, *Source Book in Chinese Philosophy*, pp. 699–700.

41. For example, in Chu Hsi's discussion of moral cultivation, the Heavenly Principle is clearly contrasted with selfish desires. See Wing-tsit Chan, *Source Book in Chinese Philosophy*, pp. 605–6.

42. Ibid., p. 539.

43. For a suggestive essay on this, see R. G. H. Siu, *Ch'i: A Neo-Taoist Approach to Life* (Cambridge, Mass.: MIT Press, 1974).

44. Roman Jakobson, "Two Aspects of Language and Two Types of Aphasic Disturbances," in Roman Jakobson and Morris Halle, *Fundamentals of Language* ('sGravenhage: Mouton, 1956), pp. 55–82. I am grateful to Professor Yu-kung Kao for this reference.

45. *Chuang Tzu*, chap. 4. The precise quotation can be found in *Chuang Tzu ying-te* (Peking: Harvard-Yenching Institute, 1947), 9/4/27.

46. *Chuang Tzu*, chap. 2 and *Chuang Tzu ying-te*, 3/2/8.

47. For a systematic discussion of this, see Yu-kung Kao and Kang-i Sun Chang (Sun Kang-i), "Chinese 'Lyric Criticism' in the Six Dynasties," American Council of Learned Societies Conference on Theories of the Arts in China (June 1979), included in *Theories of the Arts in China*, eds. Susan Bush and Christian Murck (Princeton, N.J.: Princeton University Press, 1984).

48. *Chuang Tzu*, chap. 33 and *Chuang Tzu ying-te*, 93/33/66.

III. A Confucian Perspective on Learning to be Human[1]

In the modern pluralistic cultural context, the Confucian "faith" in the intrinsic meaningfulness of humanity may appear to be finite, historical, secular, and culturally specific. However, to the living Confucian, this faith is an articulation of truth, an expression of reality and, indeed a view of life so commonly accepted in East Asia for centuries and so obviously rational that it is singularly self-evident. In this essay, I intend to demonstrate, based upon my own understanding of the Confucian project, that this humanistic claim about faith is of profound significance to the study of religion as an evolving and developing discipline which may, in the long run, establish a unity of understanding and appreciation of ultimate concerns despite the seductiveness of sophisticated relativism currently espoused by some of our most brilliant and open-minded colleagues in social sciences and the humanities.

I. *Learning for the Sake of the Self.* The Confucian approach to perennial human questions has generally been considered finite, if not miserably parochial. In part, this is because Confucius, in response to the queries of his students, refused to speculate on the subjects of death and spirits on the grounds that our understanding of life and human beings should be of primary importance.[2] The Confucian point of departure which focuses on the person living here and now is, however, predicated on a broadly conceived notion of life and human beings in which death and spirits feature prominently as constitutive elements. In other words, a genuine appreciation of the Confucian perception of the living person necessarily involves sensitivity to death and spirits. The significance of this will be discussed later but it is important to note here that it is not only inadequate but misleading to assert that because Confucius did not overtly answer questions about death and spirits he was unmindful of those profound human concerns. In fact, it is difficult to imagine what shape the Confucian tradition would have assumed had the mourning rituals and the ancestor cult been left out.

Yet, despite the outsider's view that traditional Confucians were under their ancestors' shadow,[3] the Confucian commitment to the

51

human community is firm and comprehensive. This commitment may mean instrumentally that the whole Confucian enterprise begins with the person living here and now. It may also mean substantively that the person in ordinary daily existence is the basis for the full realization of humanity. The Confucian insistence that learning is for the sake of the self,[4] an end in itself rather than a means to an end, speaks directly to this. Learning, for the Confucian, is to learn to be human. We are, to be sure, inescapably human, and in a naturalistic sense it is our birthright to be so. But in an aesthetic, moral or religious sense, being human necessitates a process of learning. Learning to be human then means becoming aesthetically refined, morally excellent and religiously profound. I am critically aware that the terms and categories I have just used are not Confucian although they can be shown to be compatible with the original Confucian insight. Perhaps it is simply a matter of emphasis, but the primary concern of Confucian learning is character formation defined in ethical terms.

If the primary Confucian concern is to learn to become a good person, what does this entail? It is vitally important to know, from the outset, that learning to become a good person in the Confucian context is not only the primary concern but also the ultimate and comprehensive concern. Therefore, it does not make much sense to compare and contrast the idea of the good person with that of the wise, strong, sensitive, intelligent, or creative person. To the Confucian, the good person is necessarily wise, strong, sensitive, intelligent, creative, and more. If we prefer to use the word "good" to designate a quality that can be distinguished from other desirable qualities such as wise and creative, we may have to redefine the primary Confucian concern in more neutral terms such as "learning to become more authentically or more fully human." With due respect to the interpretive consensus among Sinologists that Confucianism is a form of social ethics, the word "authenticity" even with its modern existential implications seems to me more appropriate than narrowly conceived moralistic terms such as "honesty" and "loyalty" to convey the original Confucian sense of learning for the sake of the self.

To learn to become an authentic person in the Confucian sense is certainly to be honest with oneself and loyal to others, but it also entails a ceaseless process through which humanity in its all-embracing fullness is concretely realized. This dimension of Confucian learning is not reducible to any particular virtue; nor is it an aggregate of those that are distinctively Confucian. Yet, taking the living person here and now as a point of departure inevitably imposes constraints on the Confucian intention to universalize its project. How can a Confucian assume that learning to be human, a process which varies according to country, history, culture, social class, and a host of other factors, is a universally valid conception? Traditional Confucians were of course not aware of the significance of this question. They believed that the idea was sound; they put it into practice; they demonstrated its validity through exemplary teaching; they embodied it; indeed, they lived it.

II. *Understanding through Inquiry.* The living Confucian in the twentieth century, who responds to the challenge of pluralistic relativism, with heightened critical self-awareness, cannot take for granted that the Confucian message is self-evidently true. The idea of learning for the sake of the self may have been a reflection of the perceived privilege of the cultural elite in the later half of the Spring and Autumn period (722–481 B.C.).[5] It may have been an integral part of the ideology of the newly emerging feudal bureaucracy (or the declining slave-owning aristocracy) designed to monopolize the channel of upward social mobility. It may also have been a manifestation of the pecular Sinic predilection for moral education at the expense of scientific knowledge and institution building. It is difficult, after all, to determine whether the Confucian idea of humanity was really inclusive in a sense comparable to the idea of "all men are created equal" or whether it signified a rather exclusivistic "we Chinese" or even "we the educated classial scholars in the state of Lu."

Furthermore, the living Confucian is also aware that the idea of learning for the sake of the self could not have meant a quest for one's individuality. Even in the West, individualism as a positive doctrine is a relatively recent phenomenon.[6] Self, in the classical Confucian sense, referred to a center of relationships, a communal quality which was never conceived of as an isolated or isolable entity. Since the social basis, the cultural background, and the ethicoreligious context in which the Confucian idea of learning for the sake of the self emerged were all so radically different from what we experience in the modern West as "learning" and as "self," how can we retrieve its meaning without distorting its original intent in order to make it relevant to us here and now?

The task of trying to understand what Confucius meant when he said that true learning was for the sake of the self requires painstaking archaeological digging. Many disciplines—etymology, textual analysis, exegesis and commentary, just to mention a few of the traditional Sinological tools — will have to be brought to bear on the process. If we extend our task to include an appreciation of the traditional Confucian understanding of the Master's statement over the centuries, other disciplines such as cultural history, comparative religion, hermeneutics, and philosophy will also be required. Even then, we can never be sure that we have gotten it right. For the gap between the two radically different epistemic eras, to use a fashionable expression, may forever remain wide and open. However, the responsibility of the scholarly community is precisely to struggle against overwhelming odds in order to reach an understanding, no matter how partial and how imperfect that understanding turns out to be. For the living Confucian, such an intellectual endeavor is not only desirable but necessary for spiritual self-definition.

The matter, however, is complicated by the fact that what is at stake goes beyond the need of the scholarly community to extend its intellectual horizons and the desire of the Confucian to search for his or her meaning in life. The challenge all members of the scholarly community who are actively involved in comparative studies must face is whether or not, in principle, we can really understand such a deceptively simple Confucian statement as "learning is for the sake of the self" out of context. The answer, unfortunately, must be in the negative. We cannot know what it means if we do not situate it in its proper context: Why was the statement made? What did it want to affirm? Was it a response to a different kind of learning prevalent at the time? How central is it to the Confucian mode of thinking? Is it a code for something much more elaborate and significant? There is no guarantee that we can fully appreciate what Confucius meant to convey even after we have found satisfactory answers to these questions, for there will be numerous other questions that demand our attention, if we are serious about our inquiry.

These issues are also relevant to the Confucian living today. The sort of difficulty that scholars encounter in moving from one linguistic universe to the other pertains to modern Confucians as well. The age of certainty in which the educated person in China would be expected to know what it means to be a Confucian is forever gone. In today's pluralistic world, the Confucian, like his or her counterpart in the Buddhist, Jewish, Christian, Islamic, or Hindu community, must learn to live an ethicoreligious life as a deliberate choice. However, unlike those in other faith communities, all Confucians must also try to apprehend the meanings of the statements in the classical texts with the same kind of conscientiousness that critical scholars of Confucian learning display. This is partly due to the absence of a functional equivalent to the priesthood in the Confucian tradition; perhaps an even more significant factor is the lack of tangible religious institutions responsible for standardizing and transmitting Confucian precepts. It is therefore interesting to note that the Chinese term for Confucian, *ju,* generically means "scholar".[7]

It may not be far-fetched to suggest that the modern approximation of the traditional Chinese idea of *ju* is the scholar in the humanities. However, in the highly professionalized atmosphere of the academic setting, a scholar in the humanities captures only one aspect of what *ju* purports to stand for. The contemporary use of the term "intellectual," especially in the sense of one who is engaged in and concerned with the well-being of humanity, comes close to the idea of *ju.* In fact, this communal dimension of Confucianism is preeminently a social philosophy.[8] Understandably, Confucian learning is often characterized as altruistic, for its primary purpose is thought to be for the sake of others.

III. *Centrality of Self-Cultivation.* The prevalent view that Confucianism is a form of social ethics which particularly emphasizes human-relatedness is basically correct, but it fails to account for the centrality of self-cultivation as an independent, autonomous and inner-directed process in the Confucian tradition. Confucians do maintain that one becomes fully human through continuous interaction with other human beings and that one's dignity as a person depends as much on communal participation as on one's own sense of self-respect. But the Weberian characterization of the Confucian spiritual orientation as "adjustment to the world"[9] because of its alleged teaching of submission to established patterns of human relationships seriously undermines the Confucian capacity for psychological integration and religious transcendence. In fact, the ability of the Confucian tradition to undergo profound transformations without losing its spiritual identity lies in its commitment to the inner resources of humanity.

The self as the center of relationships has always been the focus of Confucian learning. One's ability to harmonize human relations does indeed indicate one's self-cultivation, but the priority is clearly set. Self-cultivation is a precondition for harmonizing human relations; if human relations are superficially harmonized without the necessary ingredients of self-cultivation, it is practically unworkable and teleologically misdirected. The common Chinese expression that the friendship of small-minded people is as sweet as honey and the friendship of profound persons is as plain as water suggests that the relationships dictated by need are far inferior to disinterested fellowship dedicated to moral growth. One enters into communication with other human beings for a variety of reasons, many of which are, to some modern sociologists, morally neutral and thus irrelevant to the inner lives of the persons involved. Confucians recognize that human beings are social beings, but they maintain that all forms of social interaction are laden with moral implications and that self-cultivation is required to harmonize each one of them.

The heuristic value of learning for the sake of the self can perhaps be understood as an injunction for self-cultivation. Since self-cultivation is an end rather than a means, learning motivated by reasons other than self-knowledge, such as fame, position and wealth, cannot be considered true learning. An archer who fails to hit the mark and turns around introspectively to rectify the mistake from within enacts the Confucian concern that to know oneself internally is the precondition for doing things right in the external world.

If human relations are harmonized, it is because the people involved have cultivated themselves. To anticipate a harmonious state of affairs in one's social interaction as a favorable condition for self-cultivation is, in the Confucian sense, not only unrealistic but illogical. Self-cultivation is like the root and trunk, and harmonious human relations are like the branches. Both temporally and in terms of importance, the priority is irreversible.[10] Strictly speaking, learning for the sake of others as a demonstration of altruism cannot be truly altruistic, unless it is built on the foundation of self-knowledge. The Confucian Golden Rule, "Do not do unto others what you would not want others to do unto you,"[11] does not simply mean that one should be considerate to others; it also means that one must be honest with oneself. It was perhaps for this reason that Confucius felt that some of his best disciples still had a great deal to learn in order to put the Golden Rule into practice.

What is the status of the Confucian Golden Rule in self-cultivation, if it cannot be uniformly applied? It is certainly not a categorical imperative in the Kantian sense; nor is it the guiding principle for action to which one is enjoined to conform. Rather, it is a standard of inspiration and an experienced ideal made meaningful to the students through the exemplary teaching of their master. Self-cultivation may mean different things to different people at different stages of moral development, and its realization may also assume many different forms. Yet, self-cultivation remains the locus of Confucian learning. Learning to be human, as a result, centers on the self, not the self as an abstract idea but the self as the person living here and now.

IV. *From a Personal Point of View.* One of the most intriguing insights of Confucian learning is that learning to be human entails learning for the sake of the self and that the self so conceived is not the generic self but I myself as an experiencing and reflecting person here and now. To turn the mode of questioning from the impersonal self to the personal I requires intellectual sophistication as well as existential commitment. The safe distance between what I as a person speculate about in propositional language and what I speak as a concrete human being is no longer there. I am exposed, for what I think I know is now inevitably intertwined with what I do know. If I am wrong, it is not simply because what I have proposed is untenable but also because of a defect in the way I live. However, the psychoanalytical procedure of allowing my deep-rooted private self to be scrutinized by another intelligence is not part of the Confucian tradition. Confucian self-cultivation presupposes that the self worth cultivating is never the private possession of a single individual but a sharable experience that underlies common humanity.

It is not at all surprising then that, despite the centrality of self-cultivation in Confucian learning, autobiographic literature exhibiting secret thoughts, private feelings, and innermost desires and drives is extremely rare in the Confucian tradition. Obviously, the cultivated self is not private property that we carefully guard against intrusion from outside. The ego that has to be protected against submersion in the waves of social demand is what the Confucians refer to as *ssu* (the privatized self, the small self, the self that is a closed system). The true self, on the contrary, is public-spirited, and the great self is the self that is an open system. As an open system, the self in the genuine sense of the word is expansive and always receptive to the world at large. Self-cultivation can very well be understood as the broadening of the self to embody an ever-expanding circle of human relatedness. However, it would be misleading to conclude that the Confucian self broadens horizontally only to establish meaningful social relations. The concentric circles that define the self in terms of family, community, country, and the world are undoubtedly social groups, but, in the Confucian perspective, they are also realms of selfhood that symbolize the authentic human possibility for ethicoreligious growth.

Ethicoreligious growth, for the Confucian, is not only a broadening process but also a deepening process. As I myself resonate with other selves, the internal resources inherent in me are multiplied. I acquire an appreciation of myself through genuine communication with the other; as I know more of myself, I apprehend more of the other. The Confucian dictum, "in order to establish myself, I establish others; in order to enlarge myself, I enlarge others,"[12] is therefore not only an altruistic idea but also a description of the self in transformation. The quest for inner spirituality as a lonely struggle belongs to a radically different rhetorical situation. Confucian self-cultivation is a deliberate communal act. Nevertheless, the self is not reducible to its social roles. The dramatic image of the modern person who assumes a variety of social roles is definitely unConfucian. The idea of my assuming the role of son in reference to my father and simultaneously assuming the distinct and separate role of father in reference to my son is unnatural, if not distasteful. From my own experience, as far as I can remember, I have always been learning to be a son. Since my son's birth, I have also been learning to be a father and my learning to be a son has to take a new significance as a result of becoming a father myself. Futhermore, my being a son and a father is also informed and enriched by being a student, a teacher, a husband, a colleague, a friend, and an acquaintance. These are ways for me to learn to be human.

Normally we do not talk about these matters in public. They are too personal. We should not reveal too much of our private feelings; they are not intellectually interesting. Yet, at the same time, we are obsessed with what we think, feel, and want. We often doggedly assert our opinions, nakedly express our emotions, and unabashedly demand our wants. We take rights seriously but we have to be persuaded by authority or law to accept our duties. We are estranged from our own cultural traditions and, as alienated humans in post-industrial societies, from our own communities. As we become increasingly subjectivistic, individualistic, and narcissistic, we can neither remember the old nor instruct the young. We are politically isolated and spiritually alone. Yet in our scholarly endeavors we assume that we have to take an impersonal stance in order to reason objectively in the abstract.

V. *Confucius as an Exemplar.* Confucius was willing to speak as a self-reflective human being. He opted for an intensely personal style of communication. And, by conscious choice, he shared his thoughts and feelings with those around him: "My friends, do you think I am secretive? There is nothing which I hide from you, my friends. There is Ch'iu (Confucius' first name) for you."[13] Confucius interacted openly with his students not by pedagogical design but as a reflection of his attitude toward life. We may suspect that he could afford to reveal himself thoroughly because he spoke from the lofty position of an accomplished sage. The truth of the matter, however, is quite different. Confucius never believed that he had attained sagehood. He was, like us, struggling to learn to be human. His self-image was that of a fellow traveller, committed to the task of realizing humanity, on the way of becoming fully human. As he continued to refine himself in living the life of a *ju*, he frankly confessed that he failed to learn to do the ordinary things that like-minded human beings ought to do:

> There are four things in the Way of the profound person, none of which I have been able to do. To serve my father as I would expect my son to serve me: that I have not been able to do. To serve my ruler as I would expect my ministers to serve me: that I have not been able to do. To serve my elder brother as I would expect my younger brothers to serve me: that I have not been able to do. To be the first to treat friends as I would expect them to treat me: that I have not been able to do.[14]

Confucius' humility is also shown in his clear perception of what he could do:

> There are presumably men who innovate without possessing knowledge, but that is not a fault I have. I use my ears widely and follow what is good in what I have heard; I use my eyes widely and retain what I have seen in my mind. This constitutes a lower level knowledge.[15]

By assigning himself to the "lower level knowledge," Confucius removed himself from "the best who are born with knowledge" and allied himself with "those who get through learning."[16] As a learner, Confucius took himself seriously as a concrete living person in transformation. He approached with sincerity and critical self-awareness his task as a witness to common humanity:

> In practicing the ordinary virtues and in the exercise of care in or-
> dinary conversation, when there is deficiency, the profound person
> never fails to make further effort, and when there is excess, never
> dares to go to the limit. His words correspond to his actions and his
> actions correspond to his words.[17]

As a seer and a listener, Confucius used his sensory perception wisely to reach a standard of moral excellence in which the virtue of modesty is taken for granted and the vital importance of constantly reflecting on things near at hand is fully recognized. Confucius' genuineness as a person is a source of inspiration to those who share his humanist wisdom not because of its abstract idealism but because of its concrete practicality.

VI. *Ultimate Meaning in Ordinary Existence.* The Confucian project, as exemplified by the lived reality of the Master, is a personal approach to human learning. Its message, simply put, is that we can realize the ultimate meaning of life in ordinary human existence. What we normally do on a daily basis is precisely the activity in which humanity manifests the highest excellence of itself. To initiate the whole process of learning to be human with the person living here and now is to underscore the centrality of self-cultivation at each juncture of moral growth. Implicit in this project is the injunction that we should take full responsibility for our humanity, not for any external reasons but for the very fact that we are humans.

The living person, in the Confucian order of things, is far more complex and meaningful than a mere momentary existence. The idea of an isolated individual who eventually dies a lonely death in the secularized biophysiological sense is not even a rejected possiblity in the Confucian perception of human reality. A human being is an active participant of an agelong biological line, a living witness of a historical continuum, and a recipient of the finest essences in the cosmos. Inherent in the structure of the human is an infinite potential for growth and an inexhaustible supply of resources for development. Ontologically a person's selfhood embodies the highest transcendence within its own reality; no external help is needed for the self to be fully realized. The realization of the self, in the ultimate sense, is tantamount to the realization of the complete unity between humanity and Heaven. The way to attain this, however, is never perceived as the establishment of a relationship between an isolated individual and God. The self as a center of relationships in the human community must recognize that it is an integral part of a holistic presence and, accordingly, work its way through what is near at hand.

Mencius, in a suggestive passage, observes:

> All the ten thousand things are there in me. There is no greater joy for me than to find, on self-examination, that I am true to myself. Try your best to treat others as you wish to be treated yourself, and you will find that this is the shortest way to humanity.[18]

The ontological assertion that one's selfhood is totally sufficient does not lead to the existential complacency that self-realization involves no more than the quest for inner spirituality. On the contrary, while through self-cultivation, I, as a person, can take great delight in realizing that I have been in touch with my genuine humanness, I must endeavor to relate conscientiously to others as the most efficacious way of apprehending our commonly shared humanity. The implied soteriology, if we dare employ such a loaded concept, is found in another Mencian statement:

> For a man to give full realization to his heart is for him to understand his own nature, and a man who knows his own nature will know Heaven. By retaining his heart and nurturing his nature he is serving Heaven. Whether he is going to die young or to live to a ripe old age makes no difference to his steadfastness of purpose. It is through awaiting whatever is to befall him with a perfected character that he stands firm on his proper destiny.[19]

Two terms in the quotation above, "steadfastness of purpose" and "proper destiny," deserve our special attention. First, however, a caveat must be noted: the Chinese text cannot be so neatly dissected as the English translation seems to permit us to do in this analysis. Since our goal is a general discussion of the sort of soteriological intent implicit in the Mencian conception of the human condition, the nuanced linguistic features should not concern us here. Mencius fully recognizes the distinctness of the person in his ontological assertion that through knowing one's own nature, one can know Heaven. People are unique. Just as there are no two identical faces, there are also as many paths of self-realization as there are human beings. There are numerous factors, internal as well as external, that determine the shape of a unique person. Yet, "steadfastness of purpose," as Mencius would have it, is the direct and immediate result of a person's will power and is, therefore, available to all members of the human community without reference to any differentiating factor. The example that Confucius used to illustrate a similar point is pertinent here: "The Three Armies can be deprived of their commanding officer, but even a common man cannot be deprived of his purpose."[20]

This "steadfastness of purpose" is all that is needed for self-cultivation. All human beings are equal so far as this dimension of human reality is concerned. A severely handicapped person may exert a great deal of effort to coordinate his physical movements, but his will power is absolutely independent, autonomous, and self-sufficient. We admire a Helen Keller not only for what she in fact managed to overcome but for the steadfastness of purpose that makes her awe-inspiring performance possible in the first place. Actually there are numerous cases where self-improvement in the physical sense is an unsurmountable task. Many people die before they can reach their potential. We are all, in this sense, fated to be unfulfilled. Confucius' best disciple, for example, died young and the Master lamented: "There was one Yen Hui who was eager to learn. . . . Unfortunately his alloted span was a short one and he died. Now there is no one. No one eager to learn has come to my notice."[21] Yet, one's steadfastness of purpose can not only transcend the structural limitations of one's existence but also transform them into instruments of self-realization. The case of Yen Hui is particularly suggestive here. His poverty, premature death, and lack of any tangible accomplishments by the perceived Confucian standards of public service did not at all deter the Master from praising, time and again, his eagerness to learn and his resolve to become a *ju*:

> How admirable Hui is! Living in a mean dwelling on a bowlful of rice and a ladleful of water is a hardship most men would find intolerable, but Hui does not allow this to affect his joy. How admirable Hui is![22]

In the light of this, one's "proper destiny" is inseparable from one's willingness and ability to take oneself to task inwardly. One's calling, as it were, is none other than the inner voice that enjoins one to become what one ought to be. This critical self-awareness, informed by one's openness to an ever-expanding circle of human-relatedness, is the authentic access to one's proper destiny. The reality of the human is such that an eagerness to learn in order to give full realization to one's heart, to know one's own nature and to appreciate the meaning of humanity is the surest way to apprehend Heaven. Since our nature is conferred by Heaven, it is our human responsibility to participate in the cosmic transformation so that we can form a trinity with Heaven and Earth.[23] Our proper destiny, personally and communally, is not circumscription. We are not circumscribed to be merely human. Rather, our proper destiny is an invitation, a charge to take care of ourselves and all the beings in the world that is our abode. We must learn to transcend what we existentially are so that we can become what we ontologically are destined to be. We need not depart from our selfhood and our humanity to become fully realized. Indeed, it is through a deepening and broadening awareness of ourselves as humans that we serve Heaven.

The underlying structure of this mode of thinking is analogically presented in a key passage in the Confucian classic, *Centrality and Commonality*, better known as the *Doctrine of the Mean*:

> The way of Heaven and Earth is extensive, deep, high, brilliant, infinite, and lasting. The heaven now before us is only this bright, shining mass; but when viewed in its unlimited extent, the sun, moon, stars, and constellations are suspended in it and all things are covered by it. The earth before us is but a handful of soil; but in its breadth and depth, it sustains mountains like Hua and Yüeh without letting them leak away, and sustains all things. The mountain before us is only a fistful of straw; but in all the vastness of its size, grass and trees grow upon it, birds and beasts dwell on it, and stores of precious things (minerals) are discovered in it. The water before us is but a spoonful of liquid, but in all its unfathomable depth, the monsters, dragons, fishes, and turtles are produced in them, and wealth becomes abundant because of it.[24]

By analogy, what we see in front of us is but the physical presence of a changing body. However, those who are absolutely sincere in the sense that they, through ceaseless learning to be human, have become witnesses of humanity as such, "can order and adjust the great relations of mankind, establish the great foundations of humanity, and know the transforming and nourishing operations of

Heaven and Earth." The reality that the perfect sage symbolizes is not a superhuman reality but genuine human reality: "all embracing and extensive, and deep and unceasingly springing, these virtues (wisdom, generosity, tenderness, firmness, refinement and so forth) come forth at all times. All embracing and extensive as heaven and deep and unceasingly springing as an abyss!"[25]

The Confucian "faith" in the intrinsic meaningfulness of humanity is a faith in the living person's authentic possibility for self-transcendence. The body, the mind, the soul, and the spirit of the living person are all laden with profound ethicoreligious significance. To be religious, in the Confucian sense, is to be engaged in ultimate self-transformation as a communal act. Salvation means the full realization of the anthropocosmic reality inherent in our human nature.

NOTES

1. This essay is intended to be a response from a Confucian point of view to Wilfred Cantwell Smith's recent treatise on *Faith and Belief* (Princeton: Princeton University Press, 1979). I am deeply impressed by Smith's assertion: "Thus it is faith, in a form appropriate to our day, that enables one to cope intellectually and personally with pluralistic relativism — with, for instance, truth as that to which all accounts of it approximate — so that acceptance of diversity enriches rather than undermines one's own apprehension of truth" (p. 170). Although I cannot claim to have understood the theological implications of his historical reflection, I find myself in sympathetic resonance with his thought-provoking observation: "Truth is ultimately one, although the human forms of truth and the forms of faith decorate or bespatter our world diversely. Our unity is real transcendently; whether history will so move that we approximate it more closely actually in the construction on earth of a world community, not merely a world society already virtually with us, is a question of our ability to act in terms of transcending truth, and love."

2. "Chi-lu asked how the spirits of the dead and the gods should be served. The Master said, 'You are not able even to serve man. How can you serve the spirits?' 'May I ask about death?' 'You do not understand even life. How can you understand death?'" *Analects*, XI:12. All translations from the *Analects* are based on D. C. Lau, trans., *Confucius: The Analects* (Middlesex, England: Penguin Classics, 1979).

3. The expression is borrowed from Francis L. K. Hsü, *Under the Ancestors' Shadow; Kinship, Personality, and Social Mobility in China* (Stanford: Stanford University Press, 1971).

4. *Analects*, XIV:24.

5. Hou Wai-lu, et al., eds., *Chung-kuo ssu-hsiang shih* (History of Chinese thought), 5 vols. (Peking: Jen-min Publishing Co., 196–59), vol. I, pp. 131–190.

6. See Steven Lukes, *Individualism* (Oxford: Blackwell, 1973).

7. For a discussion of the meaning of *ju*, see Hu Shih, "Shuo ju" (On the concept of *ju*) in *Hu Shih wen-ts'un* (Preserved works of Hu Shih; reprint, Taipei: Yüan-tung Publishing Co., 1953), IV, pp. 1–103. For a comprehensive treatment of the origins of *ju* in English, see D. B. Obenchain, *Ministers of the Moral Order: Innovations of the Early Chou Kings, the Duke of Chou, Chung-ni and Ju* (unpublished Ph.D. dissertation, Committee on the Study of Religion, Harvard University, 1984).

8. See Étienne Balazs, "La crise de fin des Han," in his *La bureaucratie céleste; Recherches sur l'économie et la société de la Chine traditionnelle* (Paris: Gallimard, 1968), p. 180.

9. Max Weber, *The Religion of China*, trans. Hans H. Gerth (New York: The Free Press, 1964), p. 235. For a general assessment of Weber's interpretation of Confucianism, see Wolfgang Schuluchter, ed., *Max Webers Studie über Konfuzianismus und Taoismus* (Frankfurt: Suhrkamp, 1983).

10. The *Great Learning* states in its main text: "From the Son of Heaven down to the common people, all must regard cultivation of the personal life as the root or foundation." See Wing-tsit Chan, trans. and comp., *A Source Book of Chinese Philosophy* (Princeton: Princeton University Press, 1969), p. 87.

11. *Analects*, XII:2; XV:24.

12. *Ibid.*, VI:30.

13. *Ibid.*, VII:23.

14. *The Doctrine of the Mean*, chap. 13. See Wing-tsit Chan, p. 101. A statement comparable in spirit is found in the *Analects*, XIV:28.

15. *Analects*, VII:28.

16. *Ibid.*, XVI:9.

17. *The Doctrine of the Mean*, chap. 13; Wing-tsit Chan, p. 101.

18. *Mencius*, VIIA:4.

19. *Mencius*, VIIA:1; D. C. Lau, p. 182.

20. *Analects*, IX:26.

21. *Ibid.*, VI:3.

22. *Ibid.*, VI:11.

23. *The Doctrine of the Mean*, chap. 22; Wing-tsit Chan, pp. 107–108.

24. *The Doctrine of the Mean*, chap. 26; Wing-tsit Chan, p. 109.

25. *The Doctrine of the Mean*, chap. 31; Wing-tsit Chan, p. 112.

IV. The Value of the Human in Classical Confucian Thought

The root metaphor in the Confucian classic, the *Analects*, is the Way (*tao*).[1] The Confucian Way suggests an unceasing process of self-transformation as a communal act. It is specified as a human way, a way of life. The Way of Heaven also features prominently in Confucian literature and an understanding of the meaning of death is essential for a comprehensive appreciation of the Confucian perception of humanity. But it seems that the ontic weight in the Confucian spiritual orientation falls on the lived experience of ordinary human existence.

The *Analects* places a great deal of emphasis on commonly shared human concerns. It characterizes the method of humanity as an analogical reflection on that which is near at hand as its point of departure. One's own existence, body and mind, provides the primary context wherein the Way is pursued concretely. Without this basic grounding, the Way can never be found and one's humanity can never be realized. The Way does not in itself give full expression to humanity; it is through human effort that the Way is manifest.

Analogy, in this sense, far from being an imperfect form of deductive reasoning, signifies a mode of inquiry significantly different from linear logic but no less rigorous and compelling. To think analogically is to develop self-understanding by a continuous process of appropriating insights into the human situation as a whole and one's particular "location" in it. This involves systematic reflection and constant learning.

As an integral part of a comprehensive quest for self-knowledge, Tseng Tzu, a disciple of Confucius, is recorded to have engaged in daily self-examination on three points: "Whether, in transacting business for others, I may have been not faithful; whether, in intercourse with friends, I may have been not truthful; whether I may have not mastered and practiced the instructions of my teacher."[2] This attempt to inform one's moral self-development by constantly probing one's inner self is neither a narcissistic search for private truth nor an individualistic claim for isolated experience. Rather, it is a form of self-cultivation which is simultaneously also a communal act of harmonizing human relationships.

By implication, the centrality of learning (*hsüeh*) in the *Analects* must also be interpreted as a process of training the self to be responsive to the world and culture at large. Thus, one studies *Poetry* (*Shih*) in order to acquire "language" (*yen*) as a necessary means of communication in the civilized world, and *Ritual* (*Li*) in order to internalize the "form of life" characteristic of one's own community. Accordingly, learning is a way to be human and not simply a program of making oneself empirically knowledgeable. The whole process seeks to enrich the self, to enhance its strength and to refine its wisdom so that one can be considerate to others and honest with oneself.

Needless to say, learning in the Confucian perspective is basically moral self-cultivation. It is a gradual process of building up one's character by making oneself receptive to the symbolic resources of one's own culture and responsive to the sharable values of one's own society. Thus, Confucius observes, "In order to establish oneself, one should try to establish others; in order to enlarge oneself, one should try to enlarge others."³ This sense of mutuality is predicated on the belief that learning to be human is by no means a lonely struggle to assert one's private ego. On the contrary, human beings come into meaningful existence through symbolic interchange and reciprocal relationship which affirms a commonly experienced truth.

Inherent in this belief is a deep-rooted concern for the human as a communicable and sharable value. It is inconceivable that one's humanity could be realized in insolation or expressed by a private language. Of course, periods of self-imposed moratorium, such as the observance of the mourning ritual, are a highly respected aspect of life in virtually all schools of Confucian thought. But even there, the primary focus is on social solidarity through an elaborate reenactment of commonly experienced roles and scenes. Indeed, the memory of the dead intensifies the care for the living.

The central concern of knowledge in this connection is to cultivate the human way and the way of life. Understandably, teaching and learning by example is considered the authentic and perhaps also the most effective method of education. One learns to be benevolent, truthful, courageous and firm not by following a set of abstract moral rules but by a continuous encounter with the multiplicity of existential situations exemplified in the life of the teachers. The teacher, who must also be a dedicated student, responds to specified questions about self, society, politics, history, and culture not merely as an informed elder but also as an experiencing and loving fellow wisdom-seeker on the way.

This is probably the main reason that the value of ritual assumes such a central significance in the *Analects*. Like language, ritual is a form of communication and self-expression. Without a growing awareness of the ritual language, one cannot become a fully participating member of one's own society. Maturation entails a creative appropriation of the prescribed values shared by the community at large. Ritual as a non-verbal mode of human interaction is particularly emphasized in Confucian literature because it involves a commitment not only synchronically to a form of life but also diachronically to a living tradition.

However, despite the apparent indication that the ontic weight of the *Analects* tends toward human sociality, it is misleading to characterize the Confucian perception of learning as sociological. For one thing, Confucius himself maintains that real learning is for the sake of the self (*wei-chi*) rather than for the sake of others (*wei-jen*).[4] Indeed, the learning of the profound person is a learning to gain personal knowledge, which implies a way of life that can never be completely objectified as a blueprint for behavior. Exemplary teaching so conceived necessitates a sense of discovery. After all, the dialogical encounter as an incessantly confirming and renewing process of self-understanding always involves creativity. The way of the profound person is therefore as much a process of internal self-transformation as a demonstrable communal act. The internality and immediacy of the way to be human is such a recognized value in the *Analects* that Confucius unequivocally asserts, "Is humanity (*jen*) indeed far away? If I wish to be human, and lo! humanity is at hand."[5]

It is also in this sense that ritual is thought to come afterwards because it has to be built upon humanity.[6] And without humanity, ritual practice easily degenerates into formalism. Confucius' response to Yen Hui's inquiry into the meaning of humanity is most instructive. Instead of characterizing humanity as loving and caring as he does in other contexts, Confucius explains to his best disciple that humanity consists in self-mastery and returning to ritual.[7] In the light of this seminal idea, it is vitally important to note that if ritualization is the Confucian way to be human, it is inseparable from a more fundamental Confucian concern for self-mastery.

A significant development of the Confucian concern for self-mastery is found in Mencius' philosophical anthropology. By conceptualizing learning as nothing other than the quest for the lost heart, Mencius underscores the centrality of heart in his thought.[8] To him, the way of learning to be human is primarily a purification and nourishment of the heart. But since the Chinese word *hsin* in *Mencius* connotes conative as well as cognitive and affective meanings, the cultivation of the heart involves not only harmonizing one's feelings but also refining one's consciousness and establishing one's will. Actually the Mencian heart, far from being merely a physiological or a psychological idea, is an ontological basis for moral self-cultivation. Mencius claims that it is because of the heart, which is also set forth as the "great body" (*ta-t'i*), that morality is not drilled into us from outside, but inherent in our nature.[9]

It is in this connection, I think, that Mencius insists upon a fundamental distinction between inability (*pu-neng*) and unwillingness (*pu-wei*).[10] While Mencius fully acknowledges differences in temperament, talent, intelligence, and environmental influences among human beings, he refuses to grant that the ability of learning to be human as a quest for moral self-development is not readily available to each member of the human community. The willing faculty itself, namely the inner decision of the heart, is not only the ultimate reason but also the actual strength for self-realization. Indeed, Mencius' moral philosophy further articulates the Confucian belief in the power of the human will: "Although the commander of the three armies can be snatched away, the will of even a commoner cannot be snatched away."[11] As I have noted elsewhere, Mencius' unflagging faith in human perfectibility through self-effort is a direct result of his commitment to the view that no matter how disturbed and destroyed the human heart has become, its inner strength for rejuvenation can never be subdued.[12] Actually this deceptively simple appeal to what may be called the indestructibility of the true self is closely related to a theory of human nature which emphasizes the commonality and universality of the value of the human.

By focusing his attention on "what is common in all our hearts," Mencius wishes to show that moral goodness is not merely a potential inherent in human nature but a universally experienced reality. Surely Mencius is critically aware of "all too human" atrocities against nature, mankind, and the self. After all his age is historically designated as the period of the "Warring States," known for its numerous cases of internecine struggles among those of the same surname and of the same family. The allegory of the Niu Mountain, denuded of trees by wood-cutters and even of buds and sprouts by browsing cattle and goats, clearly indicates that Mencius knows well the deprivation of the human condition. However, notwithstanding his realistic appraisal of the actual state of humanity, he propounds the thesis that "the sage and I are the same in kind."[13] Implicit in this assertion is the message that our existential situation, no matter how degenerate it has become, does not deny us the same reality that enables ordinary human beings to become sages.

This fiduciary commitment to the inner resources of the self is based upon an observation that common human feelings such as commiseration, shame, deference, and a sense of right and wrong, relative and feeble as they are at times, are the concrete foundations of moral self-cultivation.[14] The very fact that we, as ordinary human beings, can experience alarm and concern when we suddenly see a child about to fall into a well sufficiently demonstrates that we are endowed with an ability to sympathize with others. To be sure, our sympathy is sometimes latent, and occasionally it is no more than a "spark" buried in the dust of selfish worries. Yet, the nature and function of the heart is such that it can regain its vitality as soon as it is preserved and nourished. Although one can lose one's heart, it is inconceivable that one cannot find it upon willing. Needless to say, the act of willing itself is also an activity of the heart. The apparent circularity of thinking is subtle but not vicious. Mencius is absolutely serious in claiming that if anyone with moral feelings "knows how to give them the fullest extension and development, the result will be like fire beginning to burn or a spring beginning to shoot forth."[15] This is actually the way by which an ordinary human being can eventually become a sage, symbolizing humanity in its all-embracing fullness. The primary concern of learning in Mencius is thus the quest for self-knowledge. To seek the lost heart is a spiritual discipline whereby primordial feelings, such as commiseration, shame, deference, and a sense of right and wrong are transformed into moral qualities, such as humanity, righteousness, propriety, and wisdom.

However, it is misleading to conclude that in Mencius' thought knowledge has lost its objective validity and self-knowledge is no more than the self-awareness of an isolated self in transformation. For one thing, the prominence of "internality" (*nei*) as Mencius would have it is neither a concern for privacy nor an attachment to individuality. Rather, it intends to show that personal knowledge is an authentic way to genuine communication as well as to deep self-understanding. This is in accord with the Confucian instruction that learning for the sake of the self is the best way to manifest common humanity: the ability to take one's own feelings as a guide is the course of human-relatedness.[16]

Undeniably, strong human feelings are often associated with instinctual demands, such as appetite for food or sex. Although Mencius strongly recommends that the cultivation of the heart depends on making our desires few,[17] he never advocates asceticism. On the contrary, he not only recognizes but proposes that basic physiological and psychological needs be properly fulfilled. Actually he insists that it is the duty of the political leader to feed and enrich the people as a prior condition for educating them. Without an adequate livelihood, Mencius maintains, it is senseless to impose moral standards upon the people.[18] Yet it is vitally important to point out that the gratification of animal desires is no more than the minimum requirement of being human. If one is preoccupied with food and sex at the expense of one's "great body," one can hardly appreciate the value of the human in its full expression. This is like the short-sighted man who is fixated on nourishing his finger to the exclusion of rest of the body.[19] In response to the question, "Since we are all human beings, why is it that some follow their great body and others follow their small body?" Mencius states, "When our senses of sight and hearing are used without thought and are thereby obscured by material things, the material things act on the material senses and lead them away."[20]

By implication, it is "thinking" (ssu) that can free us from the limitation of the small body. Lest we should mistake this view for a kind of intellectualism, thinking in the Mencian context involves not only the heart and the mind but also the body. It signifies a holistic and integrated way of learning. Thus, Mencius observes that "if we first establish the great body in us, then the small body cannot overcome it. It is simply this that makes a person great."[21] It is also in this sense that Mencius maintains that only the sages can fully realize their "bodily designs" or their "human forms."[22] In other words, the development of the true self, as differentiated from the expansion of the privatized ego, is a process that opens oneself up to an ever broadening and deepening horizon of values shared by the enlarging community of like-minded moral persons. This is a concrete path leading towards a universalizable experience of personal identity and communication. Against this background, it seems fitting that Mencius concludes that if we can fully develop our hearts, we can completely realize our human nature; and if we completely realize our human nature, we will know Heaven.[23]

This seems on the surface no more than a naïve faith in the ability of the heart to fully develop itself and in so doing not only to realize humanity in general but also to know the ultimate reality, Heaven. However, a fundamental assumption in classical Confucian thought underlies this seemingly unbridled romantic assertion on the unity of the human way and the Way of Heaven. The prescriptive reason is given in a short but highly suggestive text, *Chung-yung,* commonly known as the *Doctrine of the Mean.* In my study on *Chung-Yung,* which I translate as "centrality and commonality," I have made the following observation:

> Professing the unity of man and Heaven, *Chung-yung* neither denies nor slights a transcendent reality. Actually, since human nature is imparted from and confirmed by Heaven, it is inconceivable in *Chung-yung's* view that man can be alienated from Heaven in any essential way. As an integral part of Heaven's creative process, man is not only endowed with the "centrality" (the most refined quality) of the universe but is charged with the mission of bringing the cosmic transformation to its fruition. Therefore the Way is nothing other than the actualization of true human nature. In a strict sense, the relationship between Heaven and man is not that of creator and creature but one of mutual fidelity; and the only way for man to know Heaven is to penetrate deeply into his own ground of being. Consequently, an inquiry into philosophy or religion must begin with a reflection on the problem of man here and now.[24]

This rudimentary formulation of *Chung-yung's* philosophical anthropology may give the impression that the Mencian line in the Confucian tradition, of which *Chung-yung* is a part, seems to advocate the thesis that "man is the measure of all things." But as I have further observed:

> One can [certainly] argue that learning and teaching in *Chung-yung* are basically concerned with the problem of how to become a person, and that doctrines such as the unity of man and Heaven and the harmony of man and nature are manifestations of this humanistic concern. Spiritualism and naturalism as such do not play a key role in *Chung-yung.* But we would be ill-advised to interpret *Chung-yung's* humanism as a form of anthropocentrism, ignoring its spiritualist and naturalist dimensions.[25]

Actually it is not difficult to see that in the perspective of *Chung-yung*, the realization of the deepest meaning of humanity entails a process transcending the anthropological realm. The logic is readily comprehensible: since human nature is imparted from Heaven, it shares a reality that underlies the myriad things. To actualize this underlying reality, therefore, is not to transcend humanity but to work through it. This is predicated on the belief that ontologically human nature is endowed with the "original ability" and the "original wisdom" to realize the ultimate meaning of Heaven in ordinary human existence. But the task of actualizing the ontological truth of humanity in concrete, everyday experience requires a continuous process of self-cultivation which is reminiscent of Tseng Tzu's description of the way and burden of the profound person: "For humanity (*jen*) is the burden he has taken upon himself; and must we not grant that it is a heavy one to bear? Only with death does his journey end; then must we not grant that he has far to go?"[26]

It is in this sense that the person who realizes his own nature to the full necessarily becomes a paradigm of authentic humanity. "What is being realized, then, signifies not only his personal humanness but humanity as such and as a whole. And since humanity is an integral part of the 'myriad things,' a complete realization of humanity must lead to the realization of things as well."[27] Against this background, the sincere, true, and real persons are thought, through their quests for self-knowledge, to have transformed the universe as well. The following statement from the *Chung-yung* can thus be taken as an articulation of the Confucian faith in human perfectibility.

> Only those who are absolutely *sincere* can fully develop their nature. If they can fully develop their nature, they can fully develop the nature of others. If they can fully develop the nature of others, they can then fully develop the nature of things. If they can fully develop the nature of things, they can then assist in the transforming and nourishing process of Heaven and Earth. If they can assist in the transforming and nourishing process of Heaven and Earth, they can thus form a trinity with Heaven and Earth.[28]

Indeed, "The profound person, through a long and unceasing process of delving into his own ground of existence, discovers his true subjectivity not as an isolated selfhood but as a true source of creative transformation."[29]

The apparent conflict between the search for inner spirituality and the commitment to social responsibility is no longer relevant.

Even the tension between self and society, one of the most salient characteristics of "religious" experience, also assumes a rather different shade of meaning. "Internality" in the Mencian tradition of Confucian thought denotes an experienced human value, a personal knowledge of the good. It is inconceivable that the ripening of one's inner moral sense of humanity and righteousness does not lead to a growing concern for social well-being. Indeed, the real threat to the maturation of the self is selfishness. A privatization of the self is, in Mencius' terminology, the frustration of the great body by the small one. The cultivation of the heart, then, is to make it receptive to the universal power of the self to communicate with other structures of being.

The humanist vision which first appeared in the *Analects*, then developed in the *Book of Mencius*, and eventually attained a remarkable fruition in *Chung-yung*, is a holistic approach to the perennial human concern for self-understanding and self-realization. Confucian humanism is therefore fundamentally different from anthropocentrism because it professes the unity of man and Heaven rather than the imposition of the human will on nature. In fact the anthropocentric assumption that man is put on earth to pursue knowledge and, as knowledge expands, so does man's dominion over earth is quite different from the Confucian perception of the pursuit of knowledge as an integral part of one's self-cultivation. To be sure, the belief that knowledge implies power is not totally absent in the Confucian tradition. Hsün Tzu, for example, strongly advocates the position that since culture is man-made, the human transformation of nature is not only necessary but also highly desirable. Yet, what Hsün Tzu proposes is hardly a form of aggressive scientism. Indeed, he is so painfully aware of the principle of scarcity that his general attitude towards natural resources is not manipulative but conservationist.[30]

The human transformation of nature, therefore, means as much an integrative effort to learn to live harmoniously in one's natural environment as a modest attempt to use the environment to sustain basic livelihood. The idea of exploiting nature is rejected because it is incompatible with the Confucian concern for moral self-development. Once our attention is focused upon the external, as the argument goes, our internal resources will be dissipated. In Mencius' words, the interaction between material things and material senses can form a vicious circle. As the things act upon the senses, the senses will demand more things for gratification. This will lead to an uncontrollable expansion of the "small body," a kind of inflated ego. As a result, the true self (the human heart), will be lost. This seems to support the modern sociological observation that the glorification of the technocratic power may produce a protean creature whose flexibility is disproportional to his miserably limited inner freedom. In other words, his adaptability is merely symptomatic of the brute fact that, having been shaped into many unnatural forms by man-made environments, he is no longer capable of experiencing his own selfhood.

However, it is helpful to note that the Confucian quest for a vision of the whole from a humanist point of view is by no means incongruous with the scientific spirit of acquiring empirical knowledge, although it is certainly in conflict with the dogmatic positivistic assertion that only verifiable knowledge is philosophically sound. Actually empirical knowledge is such a cherished value in the Confucian tradition that its way of learning to be human entails a comprehensive program of education which includes, among other subjects, the natural world of grass, trees, birds and animals. Also, it should be mentioned that the Confucian "six arts," prerequisites for the educated person, involve arithmetic, as well as ritual, music, archery, charioteering and calligraphy.[31] Furthermore, it is not difficult to see that the Five Classics are rich sources for the study of astronomy, geography, government, history, poetry and art. Understandably the *Great Learning*, a highly compact essay on Confucian education, begins its instruction with the precept of "investigating things."[32] To be sure, the extension of knowledge in the Confucian sense is always conceived as an integral part of a holistic way of humanization. But the value of knowledge is absolutely irreducible in Confucian humanism; it is inconceivable that one can become fully human without going through a conscious process of learning to do so.

Implicit in this spiritual orientation is a concerted effort to maintain a delicate balance between freedom as an inner moral direction and knowledge as a self-disclosure to the cosmos as a whole. It rejects both an introspective affirmation of the self as an isolable and complacent ego and an unrestrained attachment to the external world for the sake of a limitless expansion of one's manipulative power. The myth of the Faustian drive or of the unbound Prometheus, symbolizing the human passion to know, to change, and to conquer, is alien to the Confucian concept of man not because it dramatizes self-transcendence but because it glorifies a complete destruction of the primordial order. When Mencius observes that the great man does not lose his childlike heart, he is perhaps also making a general statement about knowledge and its relationship to human nature.[33] To him, the value of knowledge lies in its contribution to the wisdom of self-fulfillment, of communality, and of union with Heaven. In other words, knowledge helps us to realize our original nature. If knowledge is pursued for its own sake to the extent that it becomes completely beyond human self-understanding, it will turn out to be a serious threat to our inner freedom.

On the other hand, the appropriation of knowledge in the Confucian tradition never intends to be a possession, as a way of controlling nature. Rather, it implies a movement of opening up the self to nature. To live a full life, then, requires the willingness and the courage to transform the limited and limiting structure of the ego into an ever deepening and broadening self. It is in this sense that true subjectivity is not only compatible with but also essential for the development of an experienced universality. The real challenge to self-realization is not the external world but self-ignorance and egoism. The Confucian Way, suggesting an unceasing process of self-transformation as a communal act,[34] is therefore an attempt to show that knowledge, properly understood as a humanist value, can ultimately free us from the constrictions of the privatized ego.

This approach to the problem of the self naturally leads us to a comparative observation: the Confucian tradition either omits or rejects a large category of Western ideas which is thought to have been the necessary outgrowth of a more refined philosophical understanding of humanity. The category includes ideas of self-interest, private property, spiritual loneliness, and psychological egoism as positive contributions to the formulation of respectively political, economic, religious, and ethical individualism. Indeed, it can be further pointed out that a conflicting, if not contradictory, category of ideas assumes great prominence in Confucian thought: for example, duty-consciousness, public service, mutuality between man and Heaven, and a sense of community. Of course, we need to examine the different stages of Chinese history to determine the genetic reasons found in economic conditions, political organizations, social structures, and other relevant constraints for the seeming asymmetry, mainly from the Western viewpoint, between ideas of individualism and their social practices.

Does this imply that the Confucian perception of the dignity of man is separable from the individual's autonomy, privacy, and self-development? Surely, equality in Confucianism is defined in terms of man's inner worth, his inherent ability to attain moral excellence.

Since the ontological basis as well as the actual strength of self-realization is considered to be anchored within the structure of human nature and mind, respect for the dignity of man, as a corollary, is believed to be egalitarian in a universal sense. However, it does not necessarily follow that since respect is equally due to all persons in virtue of their being persons, there is no way of criticizing autonomy as self-centeredness, privacy as self-isolation, and self-development as an expression of egoism.

It is difficult to argue that a man's dignity can be preserved if he does not decide and choose in a self-determined way. Yet, to say that his dignity depends on the fact that his actions are solely determined by his conscious "self" is not without serious ambiguity. Specifically when and how a person acts autonomously is often problematic. More intriguing is the ethicoreligious question: What kind of person can really experience a sense of inner freedom and thus claim to be autonomous? Similarly, to define privacy as freedom from interferences and obstacles is predicated on the belief that, in Isaiah Berlin's words, "a frontier must be drawn between the area of private life and that of public authority." Unfortunately the notion of "frontier" is morally debatable and can be easily abused in the political sphere. Even in the case of self-development, although the practice of egoism does not seem to us as dangerous as the inculcation of ideologically-controlled collectivistic ideas in the unsuspecting mind, it is nevertheless a perversion of human growth.

Historically, the emergence of individualism as a motivating force in Western society may have been intertwined with highly particularized political, economic, ethical, and religious traditions. It seems reasonable that one can endorse an insight into the self as a basis for equality and liberty without accepting Locke's idea of private property, Adam Smith's and Hobbes' idea of private interest, John Stuart Mill's idea of privacy, Kierkegaard's idea of loneliness, or the early Sartre's idea of freedom. While I am sympathetic to Steven Luke's conclusion that "the only way to realize the values of individualism is through a humane form of socialism,"[35] I suspect that the task may have to begin with an inquiry into the value of the human with all its far-reaching philosophical implications.

NOTES

1. For a general discussion on this root metaphor, see Herbert Fingarette, *Confucius — The Secular as Sacred* (New York: Harper & Row, 1972), pp. 18–36. I have

also written on the subject in reference to Confucius' spiritual self-identification, see my essay on "The Confucian Perception of Adulthood," *Daedalus: Journal of the American Academy of Arts and Sciences*, 105:2 (Spring 1976), 109–123. This essay is included in *Adulthood*, ed. Erik H. Erikson (New York: W. W. Norton & Company, 1978), pp. 113–127. I wish to note that Paul Ricoeur's "multi-disciplinary studies of the creation of meaning in language" have been most inspiring to me in my research on this particular aspect of Confucian thought; see his *The Rule of Metaphor*, trans. by Robert Czerny (Toronto: University of Toronto Press, 1977).

2. *Analects*, 1:4.

3. Ibid., 6:28.

4. The statement in the *Analects* reads: "The scholars of antiquity studied for the sake of the self; nowadays scholars study for the sake of others" (14:25). Arthur Waley correctly interprets this to mean that "[i]n old days men studied for the sake of self-improvement; nowadays men study in order to impress other people." See *The Analects of Confucius*, trans. by Arthur Waley (London: George Allen & Unwin, 1938), p. 187.

5. *Analects*, 7:29.

6. The statement in the *Analects* reads: "Tzu-hsia asked, saying, what is the meaning of 'Oh the sweet smile dimpling,/The lovely eyes so black and white!/Plain silk that you would take for colored stuff.' The Master said, The painting comes after the plain groundwork. Tzu-hsia said, Then ritual comes afterwards? The Master said, Shang [Tzu-hsia] it is who bears me up. At last I have someone with whom I can discuss the Songs!" (3:8). For this translation see Waley, pp. 95–96. It should be noted that "the Songs" here refers to the *Book of Poetry*, which symbolizes the natural expression of basic human feelings.

7. *Analects*, 12:1. For a consideration of the philosophical significance of this passage in Confucian thought, see my paper "The Creative Tension between *Jen* and *Li*," *Philosophy East and West*, 12:1–2 (January–April 1968), 29–39.

8. *Mencius*, 6B:11.

9. For a discussion of Mencius' moral philosophy, see my paper "On the Mencian Perception of Moral Self-Development," *The Monist*, 61:1 (January 1978), 72–81. Also see *Mencius*, 6A:15.

10. *Mencius*, 1A:7.

11. *Analects*, 9:25.

12. "On the Mencian Perception of Moral Self-Development," p. 76.

13. *Mencius*, 6A:7.

14. The term "fiduciary commitment" is here used in Michael Polanyi's sense; see his *Personal Knowledge: Towards a Post-Critical Philosophy* (New York: Harper & Row, 1962), pp. 30–31. See *Mencius*, 6A:6.

15. *Mencius*, 2A:6.

16. *Analects*, 6:28.

17. *Mencius*, 7B:35.

18. Ibid., 1A:7.20: 3A:3.

19. Ibid., 6A:14.

20. Ibid., 6A:15.

21. Ibid., 6A:15.

22. Ibid., 7A:38.

23. Ibid., 7A:1.

24. Tu Wei-ming, *Centrality and Commonality: An Essay on Chung-Yung* (Honolulu: The University Press of Hawaii, 1976), p. 9.

25. Ibid., p. 10.

26. *Analects*, 8:7.

27. Tu Wei-ming, *Centrality and Commonality*, p. 118.

28. *The Doctrine of the Mean*, chapter 22. For this translation, see Wing-tsit Chan, trans., *A Source Book in Chinese Philosophy* (Princeton: Princeton University Press, 1973), pp. 107–108.

29. Tu Wei-ming, *Centrality and Commonality*, p. 140.

30. For a brief account of Hsün Tzu's political and social thought, see Fung Yu-lan. *A History of Chinese Philosophy*, trans., Derk Bodde (Princeton: Princeton University, 1952), vol. I, pp. 294–302.

31. This refers to the famous "six arts" in Confucian education, see the "Ta-ssu-t'u" section of the "Ti-kuan" chapter in the *Chou-li*.

32. The precept of *ko-wu* ("investigation of things") was one of the most important foci of intellectual debate in Neo-Confucian thought. It is the first of the "eight steps" of education in the *Great Learning*. See Wing-tsit Chan, *A Source Book*, pp. 84–94.

33. *Mencius*, 4B:12.

34. For a more comprehensive treatment of this point, see my paper on "Ultimate Self-Transformation as a Communal Act: Comments on Modes of Self-Cultivation in Traditional China," *Journal of Chinese Philosophy* (1979), 237–246.

35. Steven Lukes, *Individualism* (New York: Harper & Row, 1973), p. 157.

V. *Jen* as a Living Metaphor in the Confucian *Analects*

In an article surveying Chinese and Western interpretations of *jen* (humanity), Wing-tsit Chan maintains that Confucius in the *Analects* was the first to conceive of *jen* as the general virtue "which is basic, universal and the source of all specific virtues." "Although Confucius' concept of *jen* as the general virtue is unmistakable," Chan further observes, "he never defined it."[1] Chan's position that in the hierarchy of values in Confucian symbolism *jen* occupies the central position around which other cardinal virtues are ordered, although *jen* in itself is never specified, seems self-evidently true in light of traditional Chinese and Japanese exegeses.

To my knowledge, the only serious challenge to this interpretive consensus is Herbert Fingarette's focused investigation on *li* as the "holy rite" in the human community. In *Confucius — The Secular as Sacred*, Fingarette argues that the metaphor of an inner psychic life is not even a "rejected possibility" in the *Analects* and that the way of Confucius' *jen* should be understood as "where reciprocal good faith and respect are expressed through the specific forms defined in *li*."[2] The purpose of the present article is to conduct a new inquiry into *jen* as a living metaphor, while bearing in mind Fingarette's highly provocative reflections.

I. *The Rhetorical Situation.* To the modern inquirer who has been steeped in the art of argumentation, Confucius may appear to be "a prosaic and parochial moralizer," his collected sayings "an archaic irrelevance."[3] This initial response is likely to become an unreflective fixity, if the inquirer is mainly concerned with philological issues as matters of fact.[4] Needless to say, a study geared only to explicating the stylistic nuances of the original text leaves many questions unasked. And since "unasked questions are unlikely to be answered,"[5] the impression that Confucius was an outmoded ethical teacher, the study of whom is only *historically significant*,[6] will remain persistent. In what sense can Confucius be understood and appreciated as, for example, in Fingarette's words, "a thinker with profound insight and with an imaginative vision of man equal in its grandeur to any I know"?[7]

To begin, I would suggest that the mode of articulation in the *Analects* is a form of what Wayne C. Booth has forcefully argued for as "the rhetoric of assent."[8] In such a rhetorical situation, the internal lines of communication are predicated on a view of human nature significantly different from that of the pseudo-scientific assertion that ideally man is a rational atomic mechanism in a universe that is value-free. Rather, the basic assumptions are as follows: human beings come into existence through symbolic interchange. We are "created in the process of sharing intentions, values, meanings; in fact more like each other than different, more valuable in our commonality than in our idiosyncrasies: not, in fact, anything at all when considered separately from our relations."[9] Viewed from this perspective, the whole world defined in terms of the polarities "individual" and "society" shifts: "even usage of words like *I, my, mine, self,* must be reconsidered, because the borderlines between the self and the other have either disappeared or shifted sharply."[10]

It is in this connection that Fingarette's perceptive observation becomes singularly pertinent:

> The images of the inner man and of his inner conflict are not essential to a concept of man as a being whose dignity is the consummation of a life of subtlety and sophistication, a life in which human conduct can be intelligible in natural terms and yet be attuned to the sacred, a life in which the practical, the intellectual and the spiritual are equally revered and are harmonized in the one act—the act of *li.*[11]

Indeed, intent on underscoring the commonality, communicability, and community of the human situation, the rhetoric of assent affirms not only the malleability of human nature but also the perfectibility of undivided selves through group sharing and mutual exhortation. Yet this is neither a license for unbridled romantic assertion nor a belief in dogmatic scientistic manipulation, but an attempt to establish "a commonsensical defense of the way we naturally, inescapably, work upon each other,"[12] without resorting to the "clean linearity" of an argumentative procedure. Elsewhere, I have used the notion of "fiduciary community" as opposed to an "adversary system" in describing this kind of psychic as well as social ethos.[13]

The philosophical anthropology predicated on this rhetorical insight maintains that "man is essentially a self-making-and-remaking, symbol-manipulating [worker], an exchanger of information, a communicator, a persuader and manipulator, an inquirer."[14] The symbolic exchange wherein self-identification and group awareness in both cognitive and affective senses take place thus becomes the primary human milieu. Against this background, the dialogical encounters couched in analogical reasoning are by no means "an unsound form of the inductive argument."[15] For their persuasive power lies not in the straightness of a logical sequence devoid of emotion but in its appeal to common sense, good reasons, and a willingness to participate in the creation of sharable values.

Of course, as Wayne Booth observes, "we have no reason to assume that the world is rational in the sense of harmonizing all our 'local' values; in fact we know that at every moment it presents . . . sharp clashes among good reasons."[16] Actually, there is no assumption in the *Analects* like the one found in the objectivists' claim that "all truly reasonable men will always finally agree."[17] On the contrary, it is taken for granted that reasonable men of diverse personalities will have differing visions of the Way. As I have pointed out in my reflection on the Confucian perception of adulthood, "[s]ince the Way is not shown as a norm that establishes a fixed pattern of behavior, a person cannot measure the success or failure of his conduct in terms of the degree of approximation to an external ideal."[18] Consequently, "[e]ven among Confucius' closest disciples, the paths of self-realization are varied. Between Yen Hui's premature death and Tseng Tzu's longevity, there are numerous manifestations of adulthood."[19]

However, the multiplicity of paths in realizing the Way is not at all in conflict with the view that the pursuit of the Way necessitates a continuous process of symbolic exchange through the sharing of communally cherished values with other selves. The self as a center of relationships rather than as an isolable individual is such a fundamental premise in the *Analects* that man as "an ultimately autonomous being" is unthinkable, and the manifestation of the authentic self is impossible "except in matrices of human converse."[20]

The conversations in the *Analects* so conceived are not merely instructive sayings of the Master but intersubjectively validated ideas, communal values exemplified by life experiences of the speakers in the act of *li*. Since the act of *li* entails the participation of the others, the rhetorical situation in the *Analect* is, in an existential sense, characterized not by the formula of the teacher speaking to the student but by the ethos in which the teacher answers in response to the student's concrete questioning. And the exchange as a whole echoes

a deep-rooted concern, a tacit communal quest, for self-realization
as a collaborative effort. Understandably, in the Confucian tradition, teaching (*chiao*) and learning (*hsüeh*) for both the teacher and
the student are inseparable, indeed interchangeable.

II. *The Semiotic Structure: Jen as a Sign.* It is commonly accepted
that etymologically *jen* consists of two parts, one a simple ideogram
of a human figure, meaning the self, and the other with two horizon-
tal strokes, suggesting human relations.[21] Peter Boodberg, obviously
following this interpretive tradition in "Semasiology of Some
Primary Confucian Concepts," proposes that *jen* be rendered as "co-
humanity." And, based upon a phonological analysis of related
words in ancient Chinese pronunciation, he further proposes that a
root meaning of *jen* should be softness, weakness, and, I presume by
implication, pliability.[22]

Boodberg's claims, far from being a novel reading of the classics,
can be substantiated by the vast lore of Chinese and Japanese
scholarship on the subject. In a recent study on the evolution of *jen* in
pre-Confucian times, the author summarizes her findings by identifying the original meanings of *jen* in terms of two semiotic foci: (1) as
the tender aspect of human feelings, namely, love and (2) as an
altruistic concern for others, and, thus a mature manifestation of
humanity.[23] But in either case, *jen* functions as a particular virtue,
often contrasted with other equally important virtues, such as *li*
(propriety), *hsin* (faithfulness), *i* (righteousness), *chih* (intelligence),
and *yung* (bravery). Therefore, it is quite conceivable that a man of
jen could be neither brave nor intelligent, for his tenderness may
become a sign of weakness and his altruistic concern for others, an
obstacle in achieving a realistic appraisal of the objective conditions.

The author then concludes that the concept of *jen* in the *Analects*
seems to have been a crystallization of these two trends in the early
Spring and Autumn period. In her words, the creative synthesis of
Confucius skillfully integrates *jen* as "*ai-jen*" (love and care for others)
and *jen* as "*ch'eng-jen*" (fully human or adult in the ethical sense).[24]
Thus, in the *Analects, jen* is elevated to a general virtue, more embracing than any of the other core Confucian virtues. Surely, "love"
remains a defining characteristic of *jen*, but as the scope of *jen*
becomes qualitatively broadened, it is no longer possible to conceive
of *jen* merely as a localized value. Indeed, a man of *jen* is necessarily
brave and intelligent, although it is not at all impossible that a brave
man or an intelligent man falls short of being a *jen* man. In a deeper

sense, through the general virtue of *jen*, such values as bravery and intelligence are being transvalued. Bravery and intelligence as contributing elements in the symbolic structure of *jen* must now be understood as courage and wisdom.

Genetic reasons aside, this quantum leap of intellectual sophistication is perhaps the main reason *jen*, in the *Analects*, appears to be discouragingly complex. Methodologically, it seems that one problem is particularly germane to the complexity of the semiotic structure of *jen*: let us call it the problem of linkage. Before undertaking a brief analysis of this problem, however, it should be noted from the outset that the lack of a definitional statement about what *jen* is in itself in the *Analects* must not be construed as the Master's deliberate heuristic device to hide an esoteric truth from his students: "My friends, I know you think that there is something I am keeping from you. There is nothing at all that I keep from you. There is nothing which I do that is not shown to you, my friends" (7:23). On the contrary, Confucius seems absolutely serious in his endeavor to transmit the true sense of *jen*, as he understood and experienced it, to his students. After all, as numerous scholars have already stated, it is *jen* rather than *chih, yung*, or *li* that really features prominently and uniquely in the *Analects*.

Although Confucius "rarely spoke of profit, fate, or *jen*," (9:1) his recorded remarks on *jen* by far surpass his comments on any other virtues in the *Analects*. Of course, each recorded articulation on the subject is but a clue to the all-inclusive virtue, or in Waley's words, the "mystic entity."[25] Among the hundred and five references to *jen* in 58 out of 498 chapters of the *Analects*,[26] there are, to be sure, statements that appear to be conflicting or paradoxical assertions. A mechanistic catologuing of these statements is not likely to develop a coherent interpretation of *jen*. A more elaborate strategy is certainly required.

First, we must not pass lightly over what seem to be only cliché virtues ascribed to those who are thought to manifest *jen*: "courteous," "diligent," "faithful," "respectful," "broad," and "kind" (13:19, 14:5, 17:6). For these traditional virtues provide the map of common sense and good reasons on which *jen* is located.[27] However, the tenderness of *jen* is also closely linked with such virtues as "brave," "steadfast," and "resolute." Accordingly only those of *jen* know how to love men and how to hate them (4:3), for the feelings of love and hate can be impartially expressed as fitting responses to concrete situations only by those who have reached the highest level of morality.[28] This is predicated on the moral principle that those who sincerely strive to become *jen* abstain from evil will (or, if you wish, hatred); as a result, they can respond to a value-laden and emotion-charged situation in a disinterested but compassionate manner. The paradox, rather than obscurity, is quite understandable in terms of Confucius' characterization of the accommodating and compromising hyperhonest villager as the spoiler of virtue (17:13). A man of *jen* refuses to tolerate evil because he has no evil will toward others; his ability to hate is thus a true indication that he has no penned up hatred in his heart.[29]

The problem of linkage is particularly pronounced when *jen* is connected with two other important concepts, *chih* and *li*. Our initial puzzlement over the precise relationship of *jen* to *chih* or *li* can be overcome, if *jen* is conceived of as a complex of attitude and disposition in which the other two important concepts are integral parts or contributing factors. In other words, *jen* is like a source in which symbolic exchange comes into existence. By implication, it is in *jen's* "field of influence"[30] that the meanings of *chih* and *li* are shaped. They in turn enrich *jen's* resourcefulness. Without stretching the point, I would suggest that the relationship of *jen* to *chih* or to *li* is analogous to the statement that "a man of *jen* certainly also possesses courage, but a brave man is not necessarily *jen*" (14:5). To be sure, in the courts of communal exchange, as exemplified in the rhetorical situation of the *Analects*, the presence of *jen* without *li* and *chih* is illegitimate. Furthermore, the examples of *li* as ritualism and *chih* as cleverness clearly indicate that *li* or *chih* without *jen*, easily degenerates into formalism or insensitivity. Thus, a man who is not *jen* can have nothing to do with *li* (3:3), because the true spirit of *li* is always grounded in *jen*.

Whether or not *jen* and *chih* are like "two wings, one supporting the other,"[31] in the Confucian ethical system, the two frequently appear as a pair (4:2, 6:21, 9:28, 12:22, 15:32, 14:30). The contrast between mountain, tranquility, and longevity symbolizing the man of *jen* on the one hand, and water, movement, and happiness symbolizing the man of *chih*, on the other (6:21), gives one the impression that *jen* and *chih* seem to represent two equally significant styles of life. Confucius' preference, however, becomes clear when he asserts that without *jen*, a man cannot for long endure either adversity or prosperity and that those who are *jen* rest content in *jen*; those who are *chih* pursue *jen* with facility (4:2). The necessity for *jen* to sustain *chih* and the desirability for *chih* to reach *jen* is shown in a crucial passage which states that "even if a man's *chih* is sufficient for him to attain it, without *jen* to hold it, he will lose it again" (15:32).

Chih in the *Analects* may occasionally be put in a negative light to mean fragmented or nonessential knowledge (15:33); sometimes the absence of *chih* can convey a sense of receptivity and flexibility (9:7), and even its opposite, *yü* (stupidity or folly), may in extraordinary situations be applauded as a demonstration of inner strength (5:20). *Jen*, by contrast, is always understood as "Goodness" (Arthur Waley), "Human-heartedness" (E. R. Hughes), "Love" (Derk Bodde), "Benevolent Love" (H. H. Dubs), "Virtue" (H. G. Creel), and "Humanity" (W. T. Chan). The practice of qualifying *jen* with such adjectives as "false" (*chia*) and "womanish," (*fu-jen chih jen*) which appear in later writings in ancient China, is completely absent in the *Analects*. In the light of the preceding discussion, it seems that, while *jen* and *chih* appear as mutually complementary virtues in Confucian symbolism, *jen* is unquestionably a more essential characterization of the Confucian Way.

Therefore, it may not be far-fetched to suggest that *jen* is in a subtle way linked up with virtually all other basic Confucian concepts. Yet its relation to any of them is neither obscure nor mystical. I believe that a systematic inquiry into each occurrence of the linkage problem should eventually yield the fruit of a coherent semiotic structure of *jen*. The matter involved is no less complex than what the scholarly tradition of *ko-i* has demonstrated. But through "matching concepts" or more dramatically, through a series of wrestlings with the meanings of each pair of ideas in terms of comparative analysis, *jen's* true face should not be concealed for long.

At the present juncture, we may tentatively conclude: Confucius refused to grant *jen* to Tzu-lu despite his talents in political leadership and to Jan Ch'iu despite his virtuosity in state rituals (5:7); he also resisted the temptation to characterize the loyalty (*chung*) of Tzu-wen and the purity (*ch'ing*) of Ch'en Wen Tzu as *jen* (5:18), not because *jen* implies "an inner mysterious realm" but because *jen* symbolizes a holistic manifestation of humanity in its commonest and highest state of perfection.

III. *The Semantic Locus: Jen as a Symbol.* When we shift our attention from the linkage problem to focus on *jen* as a problem in itself, we are easily struck by the assurance that *jen* is immediately present if desired: "Is *jen* far away? As soon as I want it, there it is right by me" (7:29). Also, we are told that although it is difficult to find one who really loves *jen*, each person has sufficient strength to pursue its course without relying upon external help (4:6). This sense of immediacy and infallibility assumes a new shade of meaning when, in Tseng Tzu's imagery, *jen* becomes a heavy burden to be shouldered throughout one's life (8:7). Indeed, *jen* can be realized only after one has done what is difficult (6:20).

The paradoxical situation in which *jen* presents itself both as a given reality and as an inaccessible ideal is further complicated by a group of passages in the *Analects*, orienting our thoughts to the absolute seriousness with which *jen* is articulated. Thus, the *chün-tzu* (profound person) is instructed never to abandon *jen* "even for the lapse of a single meal;" instead, "he is never so harried but that he cleaves to this; never so tottering but that he cleaves to this" (4:5). *Jen* must come before any other consideration (4:6); it is a supreme value more precious than one's own life and therefore an idea worth dying for (15:8).

Yet the pursuit of *jen* is never a lonely struggle. It is not a quest for inner truth or spiritual purity isolable from an "outer" or public realm. From the *jen* perspective, "a man of humanity, wishing to establish his own character, also establishes the character of others, and wishing to fully manifest himself, also helps others to fully manifest themselves. The ability to take what is near at hand as an example may be called the method of realizing *jen*" (6:28). The task of *jen*, far from being an internal, subjectivistic search for one's own individuality, depends as much on meaningful communal inquiry as on self-scrutiny.

Tseng Tzu's daily self-examination is a case in point. The effort of personal cultivation certainly suggests a spiritual-moral dimension not reducible to social considerations, but the three areas of concern—loyalty to others, faithfulness to friends and commitment to learning (1:4), are so much an integral part of the "symbolic interchange" mentioned earlier that Master Tseng's message is clearly in the realm of human relations. The self so conceived is a kind of value-creating field in which the fiduciary community exists and is realized by a tradition of selves in continuous interaction with selves. It is in this connection, I believe, that Confucius insisted that true learning be specified as learning for the sake of the self (14:25).

However, an essential characterization of *jen* impels us to go beyond the behavioristic approach, no matter how comprehensive it purports to be. In fact, the reason *jen* seems to be "surrounded with paradox and mystery in the *Analects*"[32] is also relevant here. The four-word phrase, *"ke-chi fu-li,"* wrongly rendered by Arthur Waley as "he who can himself submit to ritual,"[33] clearly shows that the attainment of *jen* involves both self-mastery and returning to ritual. The interpretation that "the man who can submit himself to *li* is *jen*" misses the point in a fundamental way.[34] And, by implication, the portrayal of *jen* as a disposition "after one has mastered the skills of action required by *li*" is probably an inadequate view of the linkage problem.[35] *Jen* is not simply "a matter of the person's deciding to submit to *li* (once he has the objective skill to do so);"[36] rather, it is a matter of inner strength and self-knowledge, symbolizing an inexhaustible source for creative communal expression.

The primacy of *jen* over *li* and the inseparability of *li* from *jen*, a thesis I tried to develop in my study "*Li* as Process of Humanization,"[37] can be substantiated by Confucius' response to Lin Fang who asked about "the foundation of li." After having noted the importance of the question, the Master recommended that "in ceremonies, be thrifty rather than extravagant, and in funerals, be deeply sorrowful rather than shallow in sentiment" (3:4). Obviously the emphasis is not on role performance but on "the raw stuff of humanity." Therefore, it is not at all surprising that the Master was very pleased with Tzu-hsia when he understood that "just as the painting comes from the plain groundwork, ritual comes afterwards" (3:8).

The centrality of self-mastery to the practice of *jen* can be shown in Confucius' remark that "a man who is strong, resolute, simple, and slow to speak is near to *jen*" (13:27). In fact, notwithstanding the danger of psychologizing the *Analects*, it is important to note that the text contains many ideas specifying that the mature personal stance is determined not merely by social approval but more importantly by personal integrity, as in freeing oneself from arbitrariness of opinion, dogmatism, obstinacy, and egoism (9:4). Accordingly, dispositional qualities resulting from spiritual-moral cultivation, such as cordiality, frankness, courteousness, temperance, and deference, are thought to be bases upon which proper human intercourse should be conducted (1:10). This particular concern for self-improvement clearly underlies Confucius' suggestion that looking out for faults is a way of recognizing *jen* (4:7). The vigilant way of overcoming one's moral and spiritual "sickness" is nothing other than constantly "looking within" (12:4).

It is in this sense, I think, that the controversial notion of *yu* (sorrow, worry, trouble, anxiousness) in the *Analects* does signify a "subjective state" not provable or demonstratable by ordinary hard tests.[38] In fact it is a reflection of personal knowledge or inner awareness, comparable to what Michael Polanyi calls a kind of in-dwelling.[39] Surely, *yu* is related to "the notion of objective uncertain-ty and unsettledness with possible ominous import,"[40] but it is much more than a matter of objective comportment. The characterization that the man of *jen* is not *yu* (9:28, 14:30) suggests, at least on the surface, that *yu* is the opposite of *jen*.[41] However, Confucius makes it clear that virtue without proper cultivation, ignorance of the task of learning, inability to change according to the words of the righteous, and failure in rectifying faults are example of *yu* (7:3).

The context in which "the man of *jen* is not *yu*" occurs should put the issue in proper perspective. Two passages conveying essentially the same idea have a parallel syntactical structure: The wise are not perplexed; the brave are not fearful; the *jen* are not *yu*. To be sure, the brave are not fearful, but Confucius instructed the fearless Tzu-lu that his "associate must be able to approach difficulties with a sense of fear and eventually manage to succeed by strategy" (7:10). Similarly, since the person who is aware of his ignorance really knows (2:17), the wise is he who can put aside the points of which he is in doubt (2:18). Along the same line of thinking, Confucius can speak of himself as so joyful and eager in learning and teaching that he forgets *yu* and ignores the onset of old age (7:18), precisely because he is *yu* with regard to the *Tao* and not to his private lot (15:31).[42]

The absence of the language and imagery of a purely psycholog-ical nature, or for that matter of a purely sociological nature, should not trouble us in the least. After all, recent developments in psychology and sociology as well as in philosophy in the West have already rendered the sharp contrast between "individual" and "socie-ty" not only undesirable but empirically unsound.

IV. *The Interpretive Task.* It should become obvious by now that "the deepest meaning of the thought of Confucius and, paradoxi-cally, its application to our time" is yet to be discerned by a sys-tematic and open-minded inquiry into the *Analects*. Fingarette is certainly right in concluding that "[t]he noble man who most perfectly [has] given up self, ego, obstinacy and personal pride (9:4) follows not profit but the Way."[43] Nevertheless, I cannot help wondering whether such a man, having come to fruition as a person, is really a "Holy Vessel."[44] I would rather contend that it is precisely in the recognition that "the profound person is not a vessel" (2:12) that the interpretive task of true humanity in the *Analects* begins.

NOTES

1. Wing-tsit Chan, "Chinese and Western Interpretations of *Jen* (Humanity)," *Journal of Chinese Philosophy* 2 (1975), 109.

2. Herbert Fingarette, *Confucius — The Secular as Sacred* (New York: Harper & Row, 1972), p. 42.

3. Ibid., vii. Of course, Fingarette makes it clear that this initial response of his to the *Analects* was short-lived.

4. The word "philological" is used here simply to designate the methods of linguistic analysis in the Ch'ien-Chia tradition of Ch'ing scholarship. I am aware that "philology" in terms of the principles of Böckh's *Philologie*, signifying "the recognition of that which was once cognized," can be philosophically meaningful. I am indebted to Masao Maruyama for this insight. See his *Studies in the Intellectual History of Tokugawa Japan*, trans. Mikiso Hane (Princeton: Princeton University Press, 1974), xx.

5. Fingarette, *Confucius*, ix.

6. It is important to note that "historically significant" in the Levensonian sense is comparable to the idea of "traditionalistic," which means that the "heritage" in question has little modern relevance, because it is no longer a living tradition.

7. Fingarette, *Confucius*, vii.

8. Wayne C. Booth, *Modern Dogma and the Rhetoric of Assent* (Chicago: The University of Chicago Press, 1974). I am indebted to my colleague, Leonard Nathan, for calling my attention to this seminal work.

9. Ibid., p. 134.

10. Ibid. Also, cf. Fingarette, pp. 72–73.

11. Fingarette, *Confucius*, p. 36.

12. Booth, *Modern Dogma*, p. 141.

13. Tu Wei-ming, *Centrality and Commonality: An Essay on Chung-yung* (Honolulu: The University Press of Hawaii, 1976), pp. 52–99.

14. Booth, *Modern Dogma*, p. 136.

15. Based on Monroe C. Beardsley's *Thinking Straight: Principles of Reasoning for Readers and Writers* (Englewood Cliffs, N.J.: Prentice-Hall, 1966), pp. 130–36; 284, quoted in Booth, *Modern Dogma*, p. 141.

16. Booth, *Modern Dogma*, p. 110.

17. Ibid., p. 111.

18. Tu Wei-ming, "The Confucian Perception of Adulthood," *Daedalus* 105, no. 2 (Spring, 1976), 110.

19. Ibid., 121.

20. Booth, *Modern Dogma*, p. 132. Also, see Fingarette, *Confucius*, p. 34.

21. I am aware that this etymological reading of the sign, traceable to the Han lexicographer Hsü Shen, may itself have been influenced by the Confucian tradition. See Wing-tsit Chan, "Chinese and Western Interpretations," 108–109.

22. Peter Boodberg, "The Semasiology of Some Primary Confucian Concepts," *Philosophy East and West* 2, no. 4 (October, 1953), 317–332. For Chan's critical

remarks on Boodberg's phonological analysis of *jen*, see Wing-tsit Chan, "Chinese and Western Interpretations," 125.

23. Fang Ying-hsien, "Yüan-jen lun—tzu Shih Shu chih K'ung Tzu shih-tai kuan-nien chih yen-pien," (On the origins of *jen*—the transformation of the idea from the time of the *Poetry* and the *History* to the time of Confucius) *Ta-lu tsa-chih* 52, no. 3 (March, 1976), 22–34.

24. Ibid., 33.

25. Arthur Waley, *The Analects of Confucius* (London: Allen & Unwin, 1938), p. 28.

26. Based upon Wing-tsit Chan, "Chinese and Western Interpretations," 107.

27. Cf. Fingarette, *Confucius*, p. 41.

28. Ibid., p. 40.

29. Thus, I cannot go along with Fingarette's observation that "it becomes all too evident that the concept *jen* is obscure." See ibid.

30. Booth, *Modern Dogma*, p. 126n.

31. Wing-tsit Chan, *A Source Book in Chinese Philosophy* (Princeton: Princeton University Press, 1973), p. 30.

32. Fingarette, *Confucius*, p. 37.

33. Waley, p. 162. See my critique of Waley's interpretive account, "The Creative Tension between Jen and Li," *Philosophy East and West* 18, no. 2 (April, 1968), 30–31.

34. Fingarette, *Confucius*, p. 42.

35. Ibid., p. 51.

36. Ibid.

37. "Li as Process of Humanization," *Philosophy East and West* 22, no. 2 (April, 1972): 188.

38. Booth, *Modern Dogma*, p. 116.

39. Michael Polanyi, *Personal Knowledge: Towards a Post-Critical Philosophy* (New York: Harper & Row, 1964), pp. 173, 344, 378.

40. Fingarette, *Confucius*, p. 46.

41. Ibid., p. 43.

42. It is in this sense that I must take issue with Figarette's interpretive position, see ibid., pp. 45–47.

43. Ibid., p. 79.

44. Ibid.

VI. The Idea of the Human in Mencian Thought: An Approach to Chinese Aesthetics

In his *Chung-kuo i-shu ching-shen* (Spirit of Chinese aesthetics), Hsü Fu-kuan states that Confucians and Taoists share the belief that self-cultivation is basic to artistic creativity.[1] This is contrary to the trite and commonplace observation that the essential purpose of art is to assist in the perfection of the moral and spiritual personality. It suggests a way of perceiving what art is rather than what its function ought to be. Art, in this sense, becomes not only a technique to be mastered but also an articulation of a deepened subjectivity. It moves and touches us because it comes from a source of inspiration which humanity shares with heaven, earth, and the myriad things. Proponents of this view assert that the manifestation of true subjectivity depends on a complete transformation of the self, which they attempt to achieve by various methods: the establishing of the will, the emptying of the mind, the fasting of the heart, and the nourishing of the great body. Deepened subjectivity centers upon the "great foundation" (*ta-pen*) of the cosmos. As a result, it harmonizes different forms of life and brings humanity into tune with nature, so that the distinction between subject and object is dissolved.

Hsü Fu-kuan adds that a root idea in Chinese aesthetics is precisely this insistence that the dichotomies of subject/object, self/society, and man/nature are unreal and thus transformable.[2] True subjectivity opens up the privatized ego so that the self can enter into fruitful communion with others. The ultimate joy of this communicability allows us, in Chuang Tzu's phrase, to roam around with the Creator.[3] Since even the gap between Creator and creature is bridgeable,[4] when human beings create art they participate "in the transforming and nourishing process of heaven and earth."[5]

Hsü maintains that philosophically and historically the *Chuang Tzu* text epitomizes the emergence of aesthetic subjectivity in China. He is aware, of course, that the moral subjectivity established in Confucian teachings is also laden with far-reaching aesthetic implications, and he alludes to Confucius' fascination with music and the relevance of the six arts to the development of Chinese aesthetics.[6] However, he says little about Mencius. In the present

chapter, I would like to examine the ways that the Mencian perception of self-cultivation is pertinent to theories of art in China.

My purpose is twofold: to explore the idea of the human in
classical Confucian thought with particular emphasis on Mencius,
and to suggest that such an exploration could be fruitful for an
understanding of Chinese aesthetics. I intend neither to offer a
thorough analysis of the Mencian image of man nor to argue that
Mencius, rather than Chuang Tzu for example, is particularly relevant to Chinese aesthetics. I do hope to show, however, that in
China philosophical anthropology has provided much of the symbolic resources for the development of theories of art. As I focus on
some of the insights found in a text which is central to ethics and
hitherto ignored with regard to aesthetics, my immediate concern is
simply to present an orientation or a method of analysis. It is possible
that such an approach will eventually lead us to belief that Chinese
arts have deep humanist roots.

I. *Tao (The Way)*. The principle of the human way in its all-embracing fullness underlies Mencian thought.[7] As a metaphor in
Mencian language, the Way is never a static category, signifying
something external and objective. It is a process, a movement, and,
indeed, a dynamic unfolding of the self as a vital force for personal,
social, and cosmic transformation. Rather than a norm to be con-
formed to, Mencius sees the Way as a standard of inspiration that
must be reenacted by ceaseless effort. We do not achieve humanity
purely and simply by being alive. We must learn to cultivate
ourselves so that we can fully realize those humane possibilities inherent in our nature. Only then can we say that we are on our way
to becoming authentically human. This unending process led Tseng
Tzu to describe the mission of a resolute scholar as a long road and a
heavy burden: "For humanity (*jen*) is the burden he has taken upon
himself; and must we not grant that it is a heavy one to bear? Only
with death does his journey end; then must we not grant that he has
far to go?"[8]

What will we become, if we commit ourselves to this long and
strenuous task of learning to be human? There must be people who
have no interest whatsoever in this sort of effort. Is there really any
serious deficiency in their lives, if they never entertain the possibility
of self-improvement? Mencius does not speculate on what kind of
miserable creatures human beings can degenerate into. The rampant inhumanity among men during the period of the Warring

States was probably indication enough of the lower end of the scale. Mencius is acutely aware of the internecine struggle for wealth and power throughout the country, but he maintains that ordinary human beings can become sages by directly applying the inner resources of their hearts (*hsin*) for their own moral and spiritual cultivation. He asserts that the sages and we are the same in kind.[9] Even if we learn to become sages, we do not ascend to a different kind of being. We are still human to the core. Even though Mencius denounces those who choose not to improve themselves as committing inexcusable self-abasement,[10] he fully recognizes their right to be human. Between sagehood and self-deprivation, the range of humanity is truly vast.

A defining characteristic of Mencian thought is the belief that human beings are perfectible through self-effort.[11] He appeals neither to the existence of God nor to the immortality of the soul, but sees the spontaneous feelings of the heart as sufficient for the task. It seems that there is a moral "deep structure" inherent in human nature that can be fully developed, without forcing, as a natural process of growth.[12] This deceptively simple and easy way of self-development is, however, not a quest for isolated inner spirituality. Rather, it is a holistic process of learning through which the privatized ego is transformed into a feeling and caring self. We have here, in addition to the idea of a deep structure, also the image of natural growth. Learning so conceived not only encompasses the sudden emergence of one's innate qualities but also unhurried nourishment of "buds" and "sprouts" of humanity. For example, we are all capable of feelings of commiseration when suddenly confronted with the tragedies and misfortunes of other human beings, as seen in our immediate response to a child who falls into a well.[13] But unless we cultivate our sense of commiseration, it will be limited in its capacity and it will not flow beyond a small circle of close associates. Often, it takes an unusually powerful impact from outside to awaken us from our ordinary insensitivity. Developing the deep structure, like learning a moral language or acquiring a ritual form, requires a balanced ("neither forgetting nor assisting")[14] approach. Just as the usefulness of the five kinds of grain depends upon their ripeness, "the value of humanity depends upon its being brought to maturity."[15]

Even the mature person does not cease to learn, for the development of our innate qualities necessitates continuous refinement. To learn a moral language proficiently or to acquire a ritual form thoroughly is a perpetual challenge. Just as we require daily practice in order to develop the ability to generate new linguistic patterns or to create new modes of human interaction, we must constantly cultivate the capacity of the self in order to enter into fruitful communion with others. Maturity, as a value in human learning, thus includes an authentic possibility for further growth. There is a multiplicity of paths to be pursued in the process of moral development, but they converge at various states to give us standards of inspiration that we can look up to, not as fixed models but as ways of witnessing the excellence in humanity.[16] This leads us to the following characterization in *Mencius*:

> He who commands our liking is called good (*shan*).
> He who is sincere with himself is called true (*hsin*).
> He who is sufficient and real is called beautiful (*mei*).
> He whose sufficiency and reality shine forth is called great (*ta*).
> He whose greatness transforms itself is called sagely (*sheng*).
> He whose sageliness is beyond our comprehension is called spiritual (*shen*).[17]

From the good to the spiritual there are numerous degrees of subtleties. A sophisticated appreciation must also take into consideration the dynamic process that underlies all of them, as a more detailed explanation of the idea of the human in classical Confucian thought will make clear.

II. *Shen (Body)*. It is often assumed that the Confucian method of self-cultivation (*hsiu-shen*) is sociological, since it teaches a child to be obedient to his parents, to respect authority, and to accept societal norms. This common-sense observation fails to account for a large amount of literature in the Confucian tradition that repeatedly stresses the importance of taking care of one's body as a necessary condition for learning to be human. Tseng Tzu's symbolic gesture of showing his hands and feet to his disciples shortly before he died clearly indicates the reverence he had for what was given to him by his parents.[18] It is not merely out of a sense of filial piety that one must respect one's physical body as a sacred vessel, to borrow an image from the *Analects*.[19] The self as a concrete living reality is inseparable from the body. Since self-cultivation in its literal meaning refers to the cultivation of the body, there is a rich reservoir of body-related language in the Confucian classics. Indeed, without an awareness of the importance of the body, we can hardly appreciate the significance of the six arts (*liu-i*)[20] in classical Confucian thought.

Etymologically the character "*i*," which is commonly rendered as "art," signifies the activity of planting, of cultivating fields.[21] It seems that the agricultural origin of the character later gave rise to its meaning of acquired skills. Thus a man of *i* is a talented person capable of performing unusual tasks.[22] The Confucian emphasis on literary accomplishments may have provided the impetus to define *i* in terms of fine arts.[23] In the classical educational context, however the six arts are disciplines that have particular reference to physical exercises. They are activities to be performed as well as subjects to be mastered mentally. The learning of the six arts seems to be a deliberate attempt to allow civilizing influences to work through our bodies as well as our minds. Of course, we are not necessarily aware of the underlying philosophical import of these disciplines. But the idea that the arts implant prosocial attitudes in us as a one-way sub-jugation is misleading. We are not simply being socialized; we are actively engaged in our own socializing by planting and cultivating the "buds" and "sprouts" within us. This is part of the reason for Mencius' insistence that "rightness" is not drilled into us but is in-herent in the deep structure of our human nature.[24]

Accordingly, ritual, the first of the six arts, is a discipline of the body. It is intended to transform the body into a fitting expression of the self in our ordinary daily existence. The practice of ritual, which involves such simple activities as sweeping the floor and answering short questions,[25] trains us to perform routine functions in society as fully participating members. We learn to stand, sit, walk, and eat properly so that we can live in harmony with those around us. We do so not to seek their approval but to respond to the standards that have inspired us to become an integral part of the community. Some of those around us may use ritual language in a clumsy way. That should not discourage us from trying to perfect our own arts, however, because we ourselves are primarily responsible for what we can and ought to become. On the other hand, if we fail to live up to the expectations of our community, it should be a grave concern for us, because we cherish the reciprocal relationship as a necessary con-dition for our own moral and spiritual self-cultivation. Thus, we emulate those who are worthy of our admiration and turn our gaze within to scrutinize ourselves in the presence of a bad man.[26] The Confucian golden rule—"Do not do to others what you would not want others to do to you!"[27]—supports the attitude of altruism as a corollary of being honest with oneself.

Confucian thought values the heuristic function of ritual so highly that it seems to have characterized ritualization as the concrete process whereby we learn to become mature human beings.[28] In fact, even though verbal instructions are common in Confucian teachings, the preferred method is to conduct them in an atmosphere suffused with nonverbal forms of communication. Exemplary teaching (*shen-chiao*), which is superior to teaching by words (*yen-chiao*), literally means to teach by one's body. Finely executed ritual acts as performative demonstrations of what one should do in given situations have greater educational force than verbal descriptions of them can ever have. The *Analects* is full of vivid examples of Confucius in action. The "Hsiang-tang" chapter, for instance, portrays in delightful detail how the Master dressed, sat, stood, bowed, walked, and ate. The care with which it depicts even the slightest gestures of the Master on solemn occasions is particularly illustrative:

> When carrying the tablet of jade, he seems to double up, as though borne down by its weight. He holds it at the highest as though he were making a bow, at the lowest, as though he were proffering a gift. His expression, too, changes to one of dread and his feet seem to recoil, as though he were avoiding something. When presenting ritual-presents, his expression is placid. At the private audience his attitude is gay and animated.[29]

If ritualization disciplines the body, music (the second of the six arts) is intended to harmonize the body so that it can appropriately express our emotions in tune with the rhythm of life. The importance of music in Confucian education cannot be exaggerated. Together with ritual it symbolizes the civilizing mode, the proper way of learning to be human. Since all authentic music is said to arise from the human heart,[30] it can shape the movements of the body into a graceful manifestation of the inner self. In Confucian literature, not only the performances of the court dancers but also the demeanors of cultured men are thought to be melodious.[31] Musical instruments, ranging from weighty stone chimes to the delicate lute, produce an infinite variety of sound patterns to channel all our "seven feelings" into their proper courses.[32]

One learns to play the lute or to sing lyric songs in order to communicate with others and, more importantly perhaps, to experience the internal resonance one shares with nature. Far from being a mere fleeting impression on our senses, the sound of the great music that we hear is an enduring virtue (*te*).[33] As harmony of heaven and earth, it brings us into accord with the primordial order. Music —

the right kind of music, and not the excessively sensuous songs of the state of Cheng[34] — can transform the human body into an articulation of beauty. As the *Analects* reports, after being exposed to the charming music of Shao, Confucius was in such a state of beatific enchantment that he did not notice the taste of meat for three full months.[35]

Although the arts of archery and charioteering may not have comparable cosmic significance, the physical exercises involved are, nevertheless, laden with far-reaching implications. An exemplary archer, for example, is not merely a skillful marksman but a "profound person" (*chün-tzu*) who, having mastered all the techniques of the art, constantly turns inward to examine himself, especially when he fails to hit the target.[36] If the case of Wang Liang in *Mencius* is any indication, the art of charioteering also involves complex rituals of self-mastery.[37] The discipline required builds one's sense of the proper forms of conduct as well as developing physical strength. By analogy, calligraphy and arithmetic can also be conceived as ways of refining one's body by acquiring the necessary dexterity with the brush or abacus to use it resourcefully.[38]

The "six arts" are therefore ways of cultivating the body. They transform the body from its original state where, like the rustic Shun before he was exposed to good words and good deeds,[39] it has merely the "buds" and "sprouts" of human possibility, into a center of fruitful relationships. As a center, a person never loses his proper location whenever and wherever he happens to be: the profound person always feels at home.[40] At the same time, he is sensitive and responsive to the human network around him. Through dialogical encounters, he deepens his self-awareness and enriches the lives of those who have entered into communion with him: "A man of humanity, wishing to establish himself, establishes others; wishing to enlarge himself, enlarges others."[41] To him, the "six arts" are not merely acquired skills; they are instrumental in establishing and enlarging himself. In the Mencian perspective, the person whose body is transformed by ritual, music, archery, charioteering, calligraphy, and arithmetic has created truth and beauty in and for himself. And as he is both a producer and an appreciator of the idea of human, he is eminently qualified to be called a "good," "true," and "beautiful" person.

Yet, self-cultivation involves much more than the transformation of the body. It is true that Mencius explicitly states, "Form and color (our body) are nature endowed by Heaven. It is only the sage who can fully realize his physical form."[42] But "physical form" (*hsing*) here symbolizes the self as a whole. The body is often a limited figure of speech in which the subtler and finer aspects of the self are deliberately relegated to the background. Paradoxically the sage can fully realize his physical form precisely because he has transformed and transcended it. The possibility of self-transformation and self-transcendence leads us to the language of the heart.

III. *Hsin (Heart)*. If the body is a spatial concept, occupying a specific location, a distinctive character of the heart is its remarkable ability to wander: "It comes in and goes out at no definite time and without anyone's knowing its direction."[43] Since the body is observable, it is possible for us to establish behavioral criteria to describe it. Exemplary teaching is, in a sense, model learning. The student learns proper ritual, right music, or good calligraphy by imitating the movements of the hands, feet, and body of the master. An outsider observing a Confucian student's learning the six arts may easily conclude that he is engaged in a sort of mimetic dance. But, presumably, the Confucian master is interested not only in the correctness of the form but also in the mental attitude behind it. He is keenly aware of the difference between a rote performer and an active participant, even though both follow instructions correctly. There is something missing in the rote performer. We might say that his heart is not in it. How does the master know that form-likeness is not the real thing? If the student knows exactly how ritual acts are to be performed and does so proficiently, how can we not conclude that his heart is in it all the time? Yet the master, with his discerning attentiveness, is able to pick up signs here and there that enable him to conclude that the student still lacks the intensity necessary for a virtuoso execution of the ritual. This seems to imply that form itself can be a sufficient basis for judging the truth and beauty of a performer. The Confucian master does not focus solely on the result, however, but also on the whole process by which the result is attained. His primary concern is the well-being of the student as a total person in transformation.[44]

In moral education, knowing manifests itself in acting, and through action one authenticates one's knowledge. It is inconceivable for one to will oneself to be polite, courteous, respectful, and humble, yet not have the inner strength to learn to be so. The Mencian distinction between "inability" (*pu-neng*) and "unwillingness" (*pu-wei*) is particularly relevant here. One may excuse oneself for one's inability to move a mountain single-handedly, but one cannot say that one is incapable of showing deference to an elder.[45] Since behavioral criteria are deficient in matters of intention, the master is never content simply to show his students the correct form. He tries to enable the student to create his own style and his own interpretation. A truly inspired student should be like Yen Hui, who perceived Confucius' teaching in mystic terms:

> The more I strain my gaze up towards it, the higher it soars. The deeper I bore down into it, the harder it becomes. I see it in front; but suddenly it is behind. Step by step the Master skillfully lures me on. He has broadened me with culture, restrained me with ritual. Even if I wanted to stop, I could not. Just when I feel that I have exhausted every resource, something seems to rise up, standing out sharp and clear. Yet though I long to pursue it, I can find no way of getting to it at all.[46]

As words (*yen*) can never fully explain the hidden meanings of intentions (*i*), the body can hardly express the inner feelings of the heart.

Although the body, no matter how ritualized, melodious, strong, and dexterous, is not able to encompass the activities of the heart, it is the proper place for the heart to reside. Mencius emphatically states that the way of learning consists of nothing other than the quest for the lost heart.[47] In this sense, the six arts are efforts to "preserve the heart" (*ts'un-hsin*). They are training for the heart as well as discipline for the body. While the body requires a long and gradual process to assume a proper form, the transformation of the heart appears to be swift, since the heart is amorphous: "Hold it fast and you preserve it. Let it go and you lose it."[48] It is misleading, however, to believe that an act of willing is by itself sufficient to preserve the heart. Mencius does appeal time and again to the king's "unbearing heart" (*pu-jen chih hsin*) to establish "humane government" (*jen-cheng*), as if we could solve the problem of tyranny by a natural extention (*t'ui*) of the king's inability to bear the suffering of others.[49] But we must not confuse this strategic attempt to pinpoint a basic feeling shared by all members of the human community, even by an insensitive king, with Mencius' philosophy of the heart. As the parable of the farmer in the state of Sung points out, the cultivation of the heart is a delicate matter. If we exert too much artificial effort to help a plant grow, it will soon wither. In the same way there is a natural course for the development of the heart. One should neither forget (*wang*) nor assist (*chu*) in one's daily effort to preserve it.[50]

"Hold it fast and you preserve it" should therefore be understood as the art of steering, involving a process of adjusting and balancing on unpredictable currents.

Despite its changing configuration, Mencius asserts that the structure of the heart is knowable through direct experience. He tells the story of I Ch'iu, a superior chess player who failed to instruct an absent-minded student, to show that the mere presence of "buds" and "sprouts" of humanity in us cannot guarantee our actually knowing and preserving our hearts.[51] Since "even a plant that grows most readily will not survive if it is placed in the sun for one day and exposed to the cold for ten," without sustained effort of cultivation, nothing much can be done with the few new shoots that come out.[52] To use a different analogy, the spring that is about to dry up can hardly overflow a small pond. On the other hand, in times of flooding, water can be extremely powerful. It is a matter of quantity as well as quality. Here lies a unique Mencian insight about the structure of the heart: if cultivated, it is capable of virtually unlimited expansion. This is the reason that, to Mencius, the heart is the "great body" (ta-t'i), whereas our physical form is only the "small body" (hsiao-t'i).[53] To know and preserve the heart is therefore to hold fast to a dynamic and ever-enlarging structure. The growth of the heart, unlike the maturation of the body, is infinite. Between self-deprivation and sagehood, the range of humanity is indeed vast. It is not the body but the heart that makes the real difference. Just as we eat to nourish the whole body rather than just a small portion of the belly, Mencius claims, self-cultivation allows the development of the "great body" rather than just the small.[54]

Mencius suggests that we can best nourish the heart by making our desires few.[55] What he advocates is not a kind of asceticism but a sense of priority. He fully recognizes the importance of such instinctual demands as the appetite for food and sex, but he insists that human fulfillment requires a holistic vision in which other equally compelling propensities—notably humanity, rightness, the rites and wisdom—ought to be satisfied as well. While the same instinctual demands we share with other animals define us in terms of what we are born with, the moral propensities inherent in our nature make us uniquely human.[56] This observation leads to two interrelated ideas: (1) the uniqueness of being human is a moral and spiritual question which cannot be properly answered if it is reduced to biological or social considerations; and (2) the actual process of self-development, or the nourishment of the heart, far from being a quest for pure morality or spirituality, necessarily involves the biological and social realities of human life. Consequently, if we satisfy only our instinctual demands, we can never realize the potential of the human heart. If we cultivate the "great body," however, our physical form will also be fulfilled:

> That which a profound person follows as his nature, that is to say, humanity, rightness, the rites and wisdom, is rooted in his heart, and manifests itself in his face, giving it a sleek appearance. It also shows in his back and extends to his limbs, rendering their message intelligible without words.[57]

The sage dwells in the peaceful abode of humanity and walks on the path of rightness.[58] Mencius claims that we learn to appreciate the greatness of such a person by an analogical reflection of the germinations of the four basic human feelings inherent in our own hearts: commiseration, shame and dislike, deference and compliance, and right and wrong. The germinating power of these feelings provides us with an intellectual intuition to perceive truth and beauty in ourselves as well as in sages and worthies.[59] The body-language must now ascend to the language of the heart to explain the educational functions of moral excellence in the human community: "A profound person transforms where he passes, and works wonders where he abides. He is in the same stream as Heaven above and Earth below."[60]

This cosmic reference opens up a new vista, adding a transcending perspective to the heart. Indeed, the Mencian heart is both a cognitive and an affective faculty, symbolizing the functions of conscience as well as consciousness. It not only reflects upon realities but, in comprehending them, shapes and creates their meaningfulness for the human community as a whole. In this way, the person who realizes his "great body" and "whose sufficiency and reality shine forth is called great." However, Mencius also maintains that "the great man does not lose his child-like heart"[61] and that the "great body" is, in the last analysis, our original nature. This twofold assertion that the great man has become a spiritlike being flowing with the cosmic transformation of heaven and earth and that, at the same time, what he manifests is no more than authentic humanity gives rise to what some Sinologists call mysticism in Mencian thought.

IV. *Shen (Spirit)*. We may recall that Mencius characterizes those whose greatness transforms itself as "sagely" and those whose sageliness is beyond our comprehension as "spiritual." Sageliness and spirituality are therefore, like goodness, truth, and beauty, symbols of human perfection. These are standards of inspiration to be continuously enacted as we learn to realize ourselves. In the Mencian perspective, they are not objective criteria for judging human worth but aesthetic appraisals of what human beings can attain and, by implication, what we ought to learn to become. Since sages and we are the same in kind, we should applaud Yen Hui's courage: "What sort of man was Shun (a sage-king)? And what sort of man am I? Anyone who can make anything of himself will be like that."[62] Indeed, it is not only the great man whose sufficiency and reality shine forth, for we possess the same internal resources:

> All the ten thousand things are there in me. There is no greater joy for me than to find, on self-examination, that I am true to myself. Try your best to treat others as you would wish to be treated youself, and you will find that this is the shortest way to humanity.[63]

Profound insight into the human condition, rather than naïve moral optimism, prompts Mencius to articulate his philosophical anthropology. Human beings "survive in adversity and perish in ease and comfort."[64] We learn to mend our ways only after we have made mistakes. "It is only when a man is frustrated in mind and in his deliberations that he is able to innovate. It is only when his intentions become visible on his countenance and audible in his tone of voice that others can understand him."[65] We learn to know ourselves, to communicate with others, and to assume responsibility for humanity through endeavor. Mencius observes that many of the ancient sages and worthies experienced personal ordeals before they emerged as spiritual models:

> That is why Heaven, when it is about to place a great burden on a man, always first tests his resolution, exhausts his frame and makes him suffer starvation and hardship, frustrates his efforts so as to shake him from his mental lassitude, toughen his nature and make good his deficiencies.[66]

In addition to the mandate of heaven, Mencius fully acknowledges that both the social and the psychological environments play important roles in human growth, but his faith in the possibility of moral and spiritual self-development leads him to perceive the matter in a hopeful light:

> For a man to give full realization to his heart is for him to understand his own nature, and a man who knows his own nature will know Heaven. By retaining his heart and nurturing his nature he is serving Heaven. Whether he is going to die young or to live to a ripe old age makes no difference to his steadfastness of purpose. It is through awaiting whatever is to befall him with a perfected character that he stands firm on his proper destiny.[67]

The profound person, accordingly, steeps himself in the Way in order to be able to find it within his own heart. "When he is at ease with it, he can draw deeply upon it; when he can draw deeply upon it, he finds its source wherever he turns."[68] The spring that did not have enough water to overflow a small pond before is now in a state of abundance: "Water from an ample source comes tumbling down, day and night without ceasing, going forward only after all the hollows are filled, and then draining into the sea."[69]

To continue the water analogy, self-cultivation in Mencian terms is an attempt to cultivate one's "floodlike *ch'i*." At this level it does not consist merely of developing the proper form or the right mental attitude. It aims, rather, at nourishing the inner resources, enhancing the power of the will and building up the reserve of one's psychic energy. The character *ch'i*, variously rendered as "material force" (W. T. Chan), "matter-energy" (H. H. Dubs), and "vital spirit" (F. W. Mote), denotes a kind of psycho-physiological power associated with breathing and the circulation of the blood. In the Mencian usage, it refers to a "strong, moving power" generated by moral and spiritual self-cultivation.[70]

Mencius' discourse on the "floodlike *ch'i*" was occasioned by Kung-sun Ch'ou's question about the method of attaining the state of the "unperturbed heart" (*pu-tung-hsin*). At the outset, Mencius asserts that "the will is commander over the *ch'i* while the *ch'i* is that which fills the body." Ordinarily the *ch'i* follows where the will directs. It is therefore important to "take hold of your will and do not abuse your *ch'i*." However, it is conceivable that when the *ch'i* is blocked, it also affects the will. Even though "the *ch'i* rests where the will arrives," nourishing the *ch'i* is essential to the well-being of the heart. What, then, is this floodlike *ch'i*?

It is difficult to explain. This is a *ch'i* which is, in the highest
degree, vast and unyielding. Nourish it with integrity and place no
obstacle in its path and it will fill the space between Heaven and
Earth. It is a *ch'i* which unites rightness and the Way. Deprive it of
these and it will collapse. It is born of accumulated rightness and
cannot be appropriated by anyone through a sporadic show of
rightness. Whenever one acts in a way that falls below the standard
set in one's heart, it will collapse. . . . You must work at it and
never let it out of your mind. At the same time, while you must
never let it out of your mind, you must not forcibly help it grow
either.[71]

As we can see, even in this brief passage, Mencius claims that within
the structure of the human body and the human heart, there is the
real potential and great possibility of enlarging the self to become
one with heaven and earth. Humanity so conceived is not an
unrealizable ideal but an inexhaustibly abundant power of moral
and spiritual transformation. To use an image found in *Chung-yung*,
since humanity can assist in the transforming and nourishing process of heaven and earth, it can form a trinity with them.[72]

Does such an approach to self-perfection suggest that there was a
deep humanist base for the arts in China? Since neither Mencius nor
Chuang Tzu was interested primarily in aesthetics, we must resort
to interpretive reconstruction to discover what theory of art, if any,
lies in these rich sources. Hsü Fu-kuan's successful effort to show by
recontextualizing the text that there are indeed aesthetic insights in
Chuang Tzu has encouraged me to raise questions about truth and
beauty in terms of the human self-images in works such as *Mencius*.
This kind of endeavor may ultimately broaden the scope of aesthetic
studies. But my real purpose has not been to explore the possibility
of a Confucian aesthetics, in contrast with or complementary to, a
Taoist aesthetics. Rather, I have sought to tap those symbolic
resources that are common to both traditions. To pursue Hsü's
analysis further, self-cultivation as a mode of thinking may have
predated any systematic attempt to formulate a tradition later identified as either Taoist or Confucian. In one of the most significant
events in classical Chinese intellectual history, Mencius creatively
appropriated some of these early insights to develop his integrated
idea of the human.

We can easily see how the use of Mencius' definition of the human way affects aesthetic terminology. The body and "the sentience that infuses the human frame"[73] become primary points of reference in conceptualizing the idea of beauty, and any impulse to objectify a norm of beauty as a static category is relegated to the background. Beauty, like all good and true qualities of human growth, exists as a standard of inspiration. It forms our sense of sufficiency and reality not as a fixed principle but as a dynamic interplay between the experiencing self and the perceived entity. We see beauty in things. In describing it, we move from its physical existence to its underlying vitality and, eventually, to its all-embracing spirit. The thing can be a tree, a stream, a mountain, or a stone. Its aesthetic effect on us, however, is not that of a silent object, but a living encounter and, indeed, a "spiritual communion" (*shen-hui*). This is not simply a form of anthropomorphism, and to interpret such encounters as the imposition of human characters on the external world limits and distorts the dialogical relationship that underlies the aesthetic experience. The idea of the human in *Mencius* is not anthropocentric. It does not subscribe to Protagoras' principle that man is the measure of all things. Instead, it intends to show that self-realization, in an ultimate sense, depends on a mutuality between man and nature. As Hsü Fu-kuan points out, a basic assumption in Confucian thought is that the completion of the self (*ch'eng-chi*) necessitates the completion (*ch'eng*), rather than the domination (*ts'ai*), of things (*wu*).[74]

Perhaps this is the reason that auditory perception features so prominently in classical Confucian thought. As I have noted in a different context, the Confucian Way is not perceptible if we cast our gaze outward;[75] the objectifying act of visualization alone cannot grasp the subtle manifestations of cosmic transformation. To be sure, the brilliant insight of a sage-king, such as that of the great Shun, is capable of penetrating the incipient activation of the universe by probing into minute signs of nature.[76] But, it is through the art of hearing that we learn to participate in the rhythm of heaven and earth. The "virtue of the ear" (*erh-te*), indeed the "virtue of hearing" (*t'ing-te*)[77] enables us to perceive the natural process in a nonaggressive, appreciative, and mutually supportive mode. Through the mental as well as physical discipline of listening, we open ourselves up to the world around us. By broadening and deepening our nonjudgmental receptivity, rather than by projecting our limited visions onto the order of things, we become co-creators of the cosmos.

Mencius' choice of music as a metaphor to characterize the sageliness of Confucius, in the light of the above discussion, seems to have been a deliberate attempt to present the Master's form of life in auditory images:

> Po Yi [Po I] was the sage who was unsullied; Yi Yin [I Yin] was the sage who accepted responsibility; Liu Hsia Hui [Liu-hsia Hui] was the sage who was easygoing; Confucius was the sage whose actions were timely. Confucius was the one who gathered all that was good. To do this is to open with bells and conclude with jade tubes. To open with bells is to begin in an orderly fashion; to conclude with jade tubes is to end in an orderly fashion. . . .[78]

Bells and jade tubes, or chimes, are musical instruments symbolizing the proper way of opening and concluding a ritual performance. A performance that accords with the highest standard of excellence requires both the "strength" to carry it out and the "skill" to make it right. It is not only the power and ability to complete the whole process but also the "timing" at each moment as the music unfolds that gives the quality of "an orderly fashion" to the performance. Thus Mencius further comments:

> To begin in an orderly fashion is the concern of the wise while to end in an orderly fashion is the concern of a sage. Wisdom is like skill, shall I say, while sageness is like strength. It is like shooting from beyond a hundred paces. It is due to your strength that the arrow reaches the target, but it is not due to your strength that it hits the mark.[79]

To return to the earlier metaphor, the perfect "timing" of Confucius' sageness goes beyond the unsullied, the responsible, and the easygoing, precisely because it symbolizes a great concert, "gathering together all that is good." If the single note properly produced can enlighten the mind — "Hence, hearing of the way of Po I, a covetous man will be purged of his covetousness and a weak man will become resolute" or "hearing of the way of Liu-hsia Hui, a narrow-minded man will become tolerant and a mean man generous"[80] — how much more so can a great concert inspire us?

The followers of this kind of approach would consider analogical thinking and the lyric mode, with their emphases on internal resonances, to be the supreme forms of aesthetic communication.

They would deliberately deprecate the art of argumentation, seeking beauty in understanding. A smile between two resonating hearts or an encounter between two mutually responding spirits cannot be demonstrated to the insensitive eye or the unattuned ear. Aesthetic language is not merely descriptive: it suggests, directs, and enlightens. It is not the language itself that is beautiful. Indeed, words need not be eloquent or ingenious, for they merely carry and convey (*ta*) the meaning (*i*).[81] It is the extralinguistic referent — the inner experience, the joy of the heart, or the transforming spirit — that is the real basis of beauty, either in artistic creativity or in aesthetical appreciation.

NOTES

1. Hsü-Fu-kuan, *Chung-kuo i-shu ching-shen* (Taichung: Tunghai University Press, 1966), p. 132.

2. Ibid.

3. *Chuang Tzu* 6. See Wing-tsit Chan, trans., *A Source Book in Chinese Philosophy* (Princeton: Princeton University Press, 1973), pp. 196–198.

4. F. W. Mote observes: "The basic point which outsiders have found so hard to detect is that the Chinese, among all peoples ancient and recent, primitive and modern, are apparently unique in having no creation myth; that is, they have regarded the world and man as uncreated, as constituting the central features of a spontaneously self-generating cosmos having no creator, god, ultimate cause or will external to itself." Even if we believe that this claim is too strong, it is undeniable that the perceived gap between man and heaven is bridgeable. See Mote, *Intellectual Foundations of China* (New York: Alfred A. Knopf, 1971), pp. 17–18.

5. *Chung-yung*, 22.

6. Hsü Fu-kuan, *Chung-kuo*, pp. 1–40, 48–49.

7. See Tu Wei-ming, "On the Mencian Perception of Moral Self-Development," *The Monist* (January, 1978), 61 (1): 72–81.

8. *Analects,* 8:7.

9. "The sage and I are of the same kind" and "The sage is simply the man first to discover this common element in my heart" (*Mencius* 6A:7). For this translation, see D. C. Lau, trans., *Mencius* (Middlesex, England: Penguin Classics, 1970), p. 164.

10. *Mencius*, 4A:10.

11. For a critical reflection on this Mencian claim, see Donald J. Munro, *The Concept of Man in Early China* (Stanford: Stanford University Press, 1969), pp. 72–77.

12. For a classical formulation of this belief in the goodness of human nature, see *Mencius* 6A:6.

13. *Mencius*, 2A:6.

14. Ibid., 2A:2.

15. Ibid., 6A:19.

16. Tu, "On the Mencian Perception of Moral Self-Development," pp. 80–81.

17. *Mencius*, 7B:25.

18. *Analects*, 8:3.

19. For a perceptive analysis of this, see Herbert Fingarette, "A Confucian Metaphor—the Holy Vessel," in his *Confucius—The Secular as Sacred* (New York: Harper & Row, 1972), pp. 71–79. See *Analects*, 2:12, 5:3.

20. *Chou-li chu-chu* (Shih-san-ching chu-shu ed., 1815), 10:24b and 14:6b.

21. This is the original meaning found in Hsü Shen's *Shuo-wen*. See Morohashi Tetsuji, *Dai Kan-wa ji-ten*, 13 vols. (Tokyo: Daishū Kan Book Co., 1955–1960), 9:987.

22. *Analects*, 6:6.

23. For example, the early Yüan scholar Liu Yin (1249–1293) observes that the meaning of the "arts" has undergone a fundamental change since the time of Confucius: While the Master used it to refer to the practices of ritual, music, archery, charioteering, calligraphy, and arithmetic, nowadays the arts mainly include poetry, prose, calligraphy, and painting. See "Hsü-hsüeh", in *Ching-hsiu hsien-sheng wen-chi* (1897 ed.) 1:3b–10b.

24. *Mencius*, 6A:6.

25. For a vivid description of some of the daily ritual practices, see Wang Meng-ou, *Li-chi chin-chu chin-i*, 2 vols. (Taipei: Commercial Press, 1970), 1:1–39.

26. *Analects*, 4:17.

27. Ibid., 15:23.

28. For an interpretation of ritual from this point of view, see Tu Wei-ming, "Li as Process of Humanization," *Philosophy East and West* (April, 1972), 22(2): 187–201. For a thought-provoking analysis of ritual, see Erik H. Erikson, *Toys and Reasons: Stages in the Ritualization of Experience* (New York: W. W. Norton & Company, 1977), pp. 67–113.

29. *Analects*, 10:5. For this translation, see Arthur Waley, *The Analects of Confucius* (London: George Allen & Unwin, 1953), p. 147.

30. See the beginning line of the "Yüeh-chi", in Wang Meng-ou, *Li-chi chin-chu chin-i*, 2:489.

31. For an interesting description of the demeanors of the *chün-tzu* by using jade as a metaphor, see Wang Meng-ou, *Li-chi chin-chu chin-i*, 2:827.

32. See Hsü Fu-kuan, *Chung-kuo*, pp. 1–8.

33. Ibid., pp. 12–33.

34. *Analects*, 15:10.

35. Ibid., 7:13, 3:25.

36. *Chung-yung*, 14.

37. *Mencius*, 3B:I.

38. Of course, there is no historical evidence to support the view that the abacus, or a kind of calculating machine, was actually used then. This apparently anachronistic observation is intended to note that it is highly likely that arithmetic was not conceived of only as a mental activity but also as a technique to be

mastered. The term *suan-shu* "technique of calculating"—to be sure, a later coinage—seems to convey this sense well. A form of finger exercise may have been involved in the study of arithmetic.

39. *Mencius*, 4B:1, 7A:16.

40. *Analects*, 9:13; *Chung-yung*, 14.

41. *Analects*, 6:28.

42. *Mencius*, 7A:38.

43. Ibid, 6A:8.

44. For a relevant study on this subject, see Herbert Fingarette, *The Self in Transformation* (New York: Harper & Row, 1965), pp. 244–293.

45. *Mencius*, 1A:7.

46. *Analects* 9:10 (see Waley, p. 140).

47. *Mencius*, 6A:11.

48. Ibid., 6A:6.

49. Ibid., 1A:7.

50. Ibid., 2A:2.

51. Ibid., 6A:9.

52. Ibid.

53. Ibid., 6A:14, 15.

54. Ibid., 6A:14.

55. Ibid., 7B:35.

56. Ibid., 6A:3.

57. Ibid., 7A:21.

58. Ibid., 6A:11.

59. Ibid., 2A:6.

60. Ibid., 7A:13 (see D. C. Lau, p. 184).

61. Ibid., 4B:12.

62. Ibid., 3A:1.

63. Ibid., 7A:4.

64. Ibid., 6B:15.

65. Ibid.

66. Ibid.

67. Ibid., 7A:1.

68. Ibid., 4B:14.

69. Ibid., 4B:18.

70. See Wing-tsit Chan, *Source Book*, p. 784, and F. W. Mote, *Intellectual Foundations*, p. 60.

71. *Mencius*, 2A:2 (see D. C. Lau, pp. 77–78).

72. *Chung-yung*, 22.

73. Huston Smith, *Forgotten Truth: The Primordial Tradition* (New York: Harper & Row, 1976), p. 63.

74. Hsü Fu-kuan, *Chung-kuo*, pp. 132–133.

75. Tu Wei-ming, "The Confucian Perception of Adulthood," *Daedalus* (April, 1976), 105(2):110.

76. *Mencius*, 4B:19.

77. It should be noted that these two terms do not appear in *Mencius*; they are found in the so-called "Lost Confucian Text" in the newly discovered Ma-wang-tui silk manuscripts. However, a preliminary investigation indicates that the "Lost Confucian Text" may very well have been in the Mencian tradition. For a brief reference, see Tu Wei-ming. "The 'Thought of Huang-Lao': A Reflection on the Lao Tzu and Huang Ti Texts in the Silk Manuscripts of Ma-wang-tui," *The Journal of Asian Studies* (November, 1979), 34(1), 96, n. 5.

78. *Mencius*, 5B:1 (D. C. Lau, p. 150).

79. Ibid. (D. C. Lau, pp. 150–151).

80. Ibid. (D. C. Lau, pp. 149–150).

81. *Analects*, 15:50.

VII. Selfhood and Otherness: The Father-Son Relationship in Confucian Thought

This chapter is an inquiry into the idea of the self in the Confucian tradition, the Confucian tradition as a mode of thinking and a way of life that still provides a standard of inspiration for people in East Asian societies. In presenting such an inquiry, I am aware that it must take place within a complex historical landscape and an equally complex modern intellectual discourse. I am also aware that the elasticity of Confucianism, as it has undergone the vicissitudes more than two millennia, inhibits generalizations about its views on perennial issues such as the idea of the self. Notwithstanding the special problems one encounters in articulating a particularly "Confucian" idea of the self, I shall nevertheless try to show that a characteristic Confucian selfhood entails the participation of the other and that the reason for this desirable and necessary symbiosis of selfhood and otherness is the Confucian conception of the self as a dynamic process of spiritual development.

I have elsewhere defined the Confucian quest for sagehood, in the ethicoreligious sense, as ultimate self-transformation as a communal act.[1] This definition involves two interrelated assumptions: (1) the self as a center of relationships and (2) the self as a dynamic process of spiritual development. Since the former has been more fully studied by cultural anthropologists, social psychologists, and political scientists in subjects such as family, socialization, and authority patterns in premodern and contemporary China,[2] our attention here will be focused on the Confucian idea of the self as development.

To differentiate the Confucian project from a variety of psychological technologies — transcendental meditation, holistic healing, rebirthing, dynamic living, and the like, currently in vogue throughout North America — which also claim self-development as an underlying assumption, it is helpful to note that, in the Confucian sense, self as development is a lifelong commitment which necessitates a ceaseless process of learning. Furthermore, Confucian learning is not only book-learning, but also ritual practice. It is through the disciplining of the body and mind that the Confucian acquires a taste for life, not as an isolated individual, but as an active participant in the living community—the family, the province, the state, and the world. The idea of "ritualization," which implies a dynamic process of self-cultivation in the spirit of filiality, brotherhood, friendship, discipleship, and loyalty, seems to capture well this basic Confucian intention.[3]

A distinctive feature of Confucian ritualization is an ever-deepening and broadening awareness of the presence of the other in one's self-cultivation. This is perhaps the single most important reason that the Confucian idea of the self as a center of relationships is an open system. It is only through the continuous opening up of the self to others that the self can maintain a wholesome personal identity. The person who is not sensitive or responsive to the others around him is self-centered; self-centeredness easily leads to a closed world, or, in Sung-Ming terminology, to a state of paralysis.[4] Therefore, to encounter the other with an open-minded spirit is not only desirable; it is as vital to the health of the self as is air or water to one's life. The well-known statement in the *Analects*, "Wishing to establish oneself, one establishes others; wishing to enlarge oneself, one enlarges others,"[5] enjoins us to help others to establish and enlarge themselves as a corollary of our self-establishment and self-enlargement. Strictly speaking, to involve the other in our self-cultivation is not only altruistic; it is required for our own self-development.

It is commonly assumed that by stressing the importance of social relations, Confucian thought has undermined the autonomy of the individual self. In this view, a Confucian self devoid of human-relatedness has little meaningful content of its own. Since the self in Confucian literature is often understood in terms of dyadic relationships, a Confucian man's self-awareness of being a son, a brother, a husband, or a father dominates his awareness of himself as a self-reliant and independent person. If we pursue this line further, the Confucian man is seen predominantly as a social being whose basic task is to learn the science and art of adjusting to the world.[6] If this is accepted as the reason that the presence of the other is significant in Confucian self-cultivation, Confucian ethics would hardly be differentiable from the common-sense notion that we are inescapably bound in a human community.

That the Confucian tradition has attached great importance to sociality, both in its formative years and in its subsequent developments, is beyond dispute. Surely a defining characteristic of

Confucian thought is its concern for social ethics.[7] But underscoring the significance of this particular dimension of Confucian thought should not lead to the conclusion that social ethics is all-embracing in the Confucian mode of thinking. In actuality, the evidence seems to show that, in a comprehensive understanding of the Confucian project, the social dimension is, on the one hand, rooted in what may be called a Confucian depth psychology and, on the other, must be extended to a realm of Confucian religiosity in order for its full significance to unfold. In other words, if we choose to employ terms derived from disciplines established in modern secular universities to characterize the Confucian idea of learning to be human, it is vitally important to realize that notions such as social adjustment hardly tell us the whole story. Concepts such as personal integration, self-realization, and ultimate concerns must also be used. It is outside the scope of this chapter to further pursue the art and strategy of interpreting Confucianism. Let it suffice to suggest that the Confucian emphasis on sociality is laden with fruitful ambiguities and that, if we do not prematurely tie up loose ends, Confucian sociality is laden with profound psychological and religious implications.[8]

We now return to our earlier question, what is the significance of the other in the Confucian project of self-cultivation? Since it is no longer satisfactory simply to note that the Confucian approach to ethics is sociological, we need to explore another track. To begin, let us examine in some detail the father-son relationship in the context of self-cultivation. The conventional belief is that since "filial piety" is a cardinal value in Confucianism, a salient feature of the father-son relationship is the unquestioned obedience of the son to the authority of the father. For the son to cultivate himself, in this view, he must learn to suppress his own desires, anticipate the wishes of his father, and take his father's commands as sacred edicts. His receptivity to his father is thus the result of his concerted effort to internalize his "superego," to the extent that his conscience automatically dictates that he do what his father wishes. Latent aggressiveness toward, not to mention hatred of, his father is totally repressed in belief and attitude as well as suppressed in behavior. Understandably, the Confucian son, overpowered by the authority of the father, evokes images of weakness, indecision, dependency, and conformity.

However, even if we accept this one-sided interpretation of the father-son relationship, the subjugation of the son involves a mobilization of internal resources which implies a complex process of internal adjustment, as well as accommodation and harmonization. For one thing, it is the willing participation of the son, socialized by a long and strenuous education supported by the community and sanctioned by the political leadership, that underlies the whole enterprise. Imagine, in Freudian terms, the complicated mechanism required to transform, indeed purify, the Oedipus complex in the Confucian son. The common impression that traditional Chinese society, steeped in Confucianism, managed to impose the unquestioned authority of the father on generation after generation of submissive sons is predicated on the false assumption that since the Confucian son had little choice, there was no opportunity for him to exhibit any voluntarism on matters of filial piety. One wonders if the control, even in its most efficacious phase, could really accomplish this without turning the so-called filial sons into hypocrites and psychopaths. Can a society survive, let alone provide a healthy environment for personal growth, if a large portion of its population is instructed to follow the dictates of gerontocratic dogmatism with no appeal to any transcendent authority?

Furthermore, the son's obedience to his father is not only restricted to the world of the living. For example, in the *Analects*, filial piety is attributed to a son because he chooses to follow his father's will for three years after the father's death.[9] But even this is only the beginning of a continuous reenactment of a memorial ritual in which the presence of the father, through the art of imagining, is made real throughout the rest of one's life. The *Book of Rites* describe in some detail the psychological state of the filial son in mourning:

> The severest vigil and purification is maintained and practised in the inner self, while a looser vigil is maintained externally. During the days of such vigil, the mourner thinks of the departed, how and where he sat, how he smiled and spoke, what were his aims and views, what he delighted in, and what he desired and enjoyed. By the third day he will perceive the meaning of such exercise. On the day of sacrifice, when he enters the apartment [of the temple], he will seem to see [the deceased] in the place [where his spirit-tablet is]. After he has moved about [to perform his operations], and is leaving by the door, he will be arrested by seeming to hear the sound of his movements, and will sigh as he seems to hear the sound of his sighing. . . .[10]

As Fung Yu-lan notes, "to gain communion with the dead through abstraction in this way, hoping that '*peradventure* they could enjoy his offerings,' is nothing more than to give satisfaction to the emotions of 'affectionate longings.'"[11]

The commitment of the son to the father is therefore a lifelong commitment and a comprehensive one at that. If the father, or at least the image of the father, is forever present, what symbolic act does the son employ to "kill" his father so that he can eventually declare his independence? Normally one would think that when the son begins to care for his aged father, he can then take the comfort of realizing himself as a provider, a giver. However, the ability to support one's father is classified as the lowest among the three degrees of filial piety in the *Book of Rites*, the other two being honoring him and not disgracing him.[12] After all, it is not only the father in the flesh that the son must learn to obey and respect. The father's ego-ideal must also be realized. It is precisely in this sense that Fung Yu-lan explains:

> On the spiritual side, filial piety consists, during the lifetime of our parents, in conforming ourselves to their wishes, and giving them not only physical care and nourishment, but also nourishing their wills; while should they fall into error, it consists in reproving them and leading them back to what is right. After the death of our parents, furthermore, one aspect of it consists in offering sacrifices to them and thinking about them, so as to keep their memory fresh in our minds.[13]

This normative view of filial piety seems incompatible with the well-known Confucian proverb: "There are no erroneous parents under Heaven." If what the proverb conveys is simply that, in the obedient eyes of the son, the father is incapable of committing mistakes, then its meaning is certainly in conflict with the idea of "reproving him" and even "leading him back to what is right." However, since Confucians do recognize that it is human to err, a corollary of the Confucian belief in human perfectibility,[14] they can certainly accept the plain truth that their fathers do sometimes fall into error. The "erroneous parents" then must be taken to mean wrong parents in the sense that they do not fit our ideals of parenthood. Surely the Confucians recognize that there are unfit parents. Common observation as well as legal judgment helps us to detect that this is not at all unusual. Traditional China certainly had a fair share of this kind of human tragedy also, and Confucians have not been blind to the blatant reality of unfit parents. However, what is one to do if one's father

falls short of being fatherly? It is not at all difficult to condemn unfit
fathers, but when and how can I say that my own father is unfit for
me? Indeed, what is the significance of committing myself to the
value that my father, no matter what he is or does, is always my
father?

The Confucian perception of this matter deserves our attention
because the "reality principle" applied to the father-son relationship
addresses not only the question of the superego but also that of the
ego-ideal in a thought-provoking way. Especially noteworthy, in this
connection, is the underlying assumption that a social dyad is not a
fixed entity, but a dynamic interaction involving a rich and ever-
changing texture of human-relatedness woven by the constant participation of other significant dyadic relationships. Methods of
analysis based upon either the theory of conflict resolution or a sort
of hydraulic mechanism of damming and releasing only scratch the
surface manifestation of the father-son dyad. Usually these methods
do not address the embedded meaning structure, let alone the
spiritual values that sustain it.

The Confucian approach takes as its point of departure that the
father-son relationship is absolutely binding. Unlike the minister in
the ruler-minister relationship, whose overriding concern for
righteousness may compel him to openly criticize, indeed remove
himself from the relationship as public protest, the son ought not to
sever his ties to his father under any circumstances. The trite and
commonplace observation that one cannot choose one's father is here
maintained as a core value. The Confucian proverb that there are no
erroneous parents clearly indicates that since we owe our origins to
our parents and since our existence itself is inextricably linked to our
parental relationships, we must recognize the continuous presence of
our parents in every dimension of our lived reality. Our bodies, for
instance, are not our own possessions pure and simple; they are
sacred gifts from our parents and thus laden with deep
ethicoreligious significance:

> The body is that which has been transmitted to us by our parents.
> Dare anyone allow himself to be irreverent in the employment of
> their legacy? If a man in his own house and privacy be not grave,
> he is not filial; if in serving his ruler he be not loyal, he is not filial;
> if in discharging the duties of office he be not serious, he is not
> filial; if with friends he be not sincere, he is not filial; if on the field
> of battle he be not brave, he is not filial. If he fail in these five

things, the evil [of the disgrace] will reflect on his parents. Dare he
but be serious?[15]

Filial piety so broadly conceived as the source of all virtues may be
the result of politicized Confucian ethics,[16] but the idea of continuing a biological reality because of its spiritual meaning as well as its
social and political significance is unmistakably an original Confucian insight.

An important feature of this insight is the recognition that the
father's ego-ideal, his wishes for himself as well as what he has created
as standards of emulation for his family, is an integral part of the legacy
that the son receives. The idea of continuity must not be taken
literally to mean the continuity of a biological line. An un-
broken genealogy for several generations surely calls for celebration,
not to mention the happy outcome of establishing and enlarging the
family fortune to include numerous talented and prosperous descen-
dants. Yet it is the scholarly achievements, the cultural attainments,
and the quality of life of the family that really define a successful
Confucian father. Enhancing the father's reputation entails a set of
conditions beyond the cherished value of allowing the family line to
continue. Mencius is perhaps misinterpreted as having subscribed to
the simple view that producing male progeny is the most important
duty of the filial son.[17] In a patriarchal society, the birth of a son may
have been conceived as a minimum requirement for continuing a
family line, but the transmission of the father's legacy clearly involves a much more complex process of symbolic interaction.

The plight of the legendary Sage-King Shun is a case in point.[18]
Born as the son of a brutish man in the Eastern Barbarian region,
Shun, in response to the exemplary teachings of the Sage-King Yao,
became a paradigm of filial piety through self-development. He was
able to do so against overwhelming odds. For one thing, his father
colluded with his stepmother and his half-brother in a series of plots
to murder him. Due to divine intervention, or in Confucian terminology, his extreme sincerity that reached to Heaven, he escaped
each threat of calamity unscathed. Never was his filial love for his
undeserving father compromised. For this exceptionally inspiring
expression of virtue, not to mention inner strength and personal
dignity, he was offered the throne by Yao to rule the Middle
Kingdom as an exemplar. For our purpose, it is illuminating to note
that in this legend Shun does not appear merely as an obedient son,
for had he been unquestioningly submissive to the brutality of his

father, he would have endangered his life, which in turn would have implicated his father in further unworthiness. It is precisely in this sense that in the *Sayings of the Confucian School*, Confucius instructs the filial son to endure only light physical punishment from an enraged father.[19] To run away from a severe beating, the argument goes, is not only to protect the body which has been entrusted to him by his parents but also to respect the fatherliness in his father that may have been temporarily obscured by rage.

The dilemma by which Shun was confronted was, of course, much more difficult to escape. There was hardly any indication that the old brute was a caring person. Shun's strategy was to do what his moral sense judged the best possible course of action at the moment. On the solemn matter of marriage, for example, he chose not to inform his father beforehand. Mencius, in defense of this apparently unfilial act, suggested to his students that allowing the father to interfere could have brought about more serious consequences.[20] Shun, in Mencius' view, appealed to a personality ideal for guidance which transcends all ordinary rules of civilized conduct and provides ultimate justification for the meaningfulness of any particular rule of conduct in the human community. He was deemed a paradigm of filial piety because, even though he was not submissive and by established convention might even be thought disobedient, his action showed concern and respect for what must have been the wishes of this father's ego-ideal. In this sense, Shun never challenged his father's authority, nor did he ignore it; he conscientiously rectified it and thus restored it. The continuous presence of the father, both actual and ideal, in Shun's moral consciousness enabled him to develop his inner strength through a constant symbolic interaction with this significant other. Shun could not have realized his filial love alone. For this, he was grateful not only to his father but also to his step-mother and half-brother.

The legend of Shun can be conceived of as the worst possible case for maintaining that filial piety is a natural expression of the son's spontaneous love and care for his father. The Confucian interpretation stresses the possibility of self-realization even if involved in the most unwholesome dyadic relationship. The moral is clear: we should all be inspired by Shun's example in adjusting himself to an extremely difficult relationship, harmonizing himself with it in his own quest for moral excellence, and using it to transform creatively himself and those around him. Thus the legend of Shun conveys the twofold message that the father-son relationship is inescapable and that it engenders an inexhaustible supply of symbolic resources for self-cultivation. Implicit in this message is a typical Confucian paradox. The father-son tie is a constraint, a limitation, and a bondage; yet through its constraining, limiting, and binding power, it provides a necessary means for self-cultivation for the father as well as the son. This seemingly arbitrary imposition of the superego upon the individual is rooted in a perception of the human condition as one in which the father-son relationship itself implies a transcendence beyond the psychosocial dynamics that envelops it. Shun's actions clearly show a realized possibility for the Confucian son to appeal to his father's ego-ideal, an appeal which in turn informs his own conscience of the best course of action.

In a thought-provoking essay, "Father and Son in Christianity and Confucianism," Robert Bellah remarks on the "truly heroic loyalty" of an unwavering minister in demonstrating the supreme value of filial piety in political protest as an indication of "the roots of the strength and endurance of a great civilization."[21] However, he also observes that in

> the Confucian attitude toward political and familial authority, there does not seem to be any point of leverage in the Confucian symbol system from which disobedience to parents could be justified. This does not mean parents could not be criticized. When they did not live up to the pattern of their ancestors there was indeed a positive duty to remonstrate, but they could not be disobeyed.[22]

This observation leads him to conclude:

> [T]he Confucian phrasing of the father-son relationship blocks any outcome of Oedipal ambivalence except submission — submission not in the last analysis to a person but to a pattern of personal relationships that is held to have ultimate validity. An outcome that could lead to creative social innovation as in the Protestant case was precluded by the absence of a point of transcendent loyalty that could provide legitimation for it. In the West, from the time of the Mosaic revelation, every particular pattern of social relations was in principle deprived of ultimacy. In China filial piety and loyalty became absolutes. In the West it was God alone who in the last analysis exercized power. In China the father continued to dominate.[23]

If we follow Bellah's insightful observation, the Confucian orientation clearly fails to account for the multilayered meaning of the
Oedipus complex: the sentiments and pathos of love and fear,
respect and guilt, and obedience and rebellion generated in man's
relationship to his father. The reason for its alleged failure, however,
is quite subtle. As Bellah notes in the beginning of his essay, "in
Chinese religious symbolism familial figures are far from central.
Though there is no civilization that has placed greater emphasis on
the father-son tie, it is not reflected in the ultimate religious symbolism."[24] This apparent asymmetry between social structure and
religious symbolism can serve as a reference point for a more focused
investigation of the father-son relationship in Confucian thought.
Again, it is helpful to take Bellah's essay as a point of departure.
"Having sampled briefly some of the implications of the father-son
symbolism in Christian belief and ritual," Bellah warns us against a
literal reading of the Freudian thesis:

> Nevertheless it becomes obvious upon reflection that the Christian
> symbolism is not explained by the Oedipus complex. If it were
> simply a direct projection of the Oedipus complex, then since the
> Oedipus complex is universal so would be Christian symbolism.
> But this is clearly far from the case. Christian symbolism is in fact
> highly unique, emerging from a particular historical context and
> bearing a particular historical role, a fact that Freud seems to have
> recognized. The particular qualities of the Christian symbolism
> emerged in the first instance from the Christian notion of God,
> around which the whole symbolic structure hangs.[25]

It seems that the explanatory power of the Oedipus complex as
Freud envisioned it was greatly enhanced by Christian symbolism
both as a background understanding and as a particular manifestation, if not direct projection, of a unique perception of the father-son
relationship. To be sure, Christian symbolism can hardly be *explained*
by the simple notion of a direct projection of the Oedipus complex.
The very fact that the Oedipus complex makes a great deal of sense
for the analysis of basic Christian motifs in psychodynamic terms
seems to suggest that its own conceptualization may have been deeply
influenced by Judaeo-Christian symbolism in the first place. The
Oedipus complex may not be as universal as Freud supposed it to
be. It is neither "the nucleus of all neurosis," nor the "origin" of the
major aspects of human society and culture as he asserted in *Totem*

and Taboo.[26] Nevertheless, the Oedipal situation, the highly charged emotional ambivalence inherent in the father-son relationship, does appear to have universal significance. The projection theory, however, is too simple-minded a causality to account for the tremendous power and influence that cultural symbolism exerts upon social structure.

Despite the centrality of the family in Confucian society, it is not conceived as an end in itself. The Confucians regard the family as the natural habitat of humans; it is the necessary and the most desirable environment for mutual support and personal growth. The father-son relationship, viewed in this context, is a defining characteristic of the human condition: it is human to have a father. The ultimate purpose of life is neither regulating the family nor harmonizing the father-son relationship, but self-realization. Indeed, only through self-cultivation can one's family be regulated and, by implication, one's relationship to one's father harmonized. Understandably the *Great Learning* takes self-cultivation as the root and regulating the family, governing the state, and bringing peace to the world as the branches.[27] The implicit logic that self-cultivation can eventually bring about universal peace under Heaven, as branches are the natural outcome of a healthy root, need not concern us here. It will suffice to note that, while there is no evidence that cultural symbols such as *T'ien* (Heaven) and *Tao* (Way) in Confucianism are projections of familial values, the father-son relationship and the other "five relationships" must be understood in terms of a transcendence that gives meaning to this particular social structure.

Unlike Christian symbolism, which tends to undermine the significance of familial relationships in its soteriology, with Jesus as saviour, Confucian salvation, as it were, takes the basic dyadic relationships in the family as its point of departure. The emphasis is on the concrete path by which one learns to be human rather than on the final goal of self-realization. The idea of the *Analects* that filiality and brotherliness are the bases of humanity, properly interpreted, means that being filial and brotherly is the initial step towards realizing one's humanity.[28] Mencius, in criticizing Moist universalism, argues against the ethics of treating people on the street as dearly as one would treat one's father.[29] It is not the ethical idealism that bothers Mencius but the impracticality of the whole procedure. If we reduce the richness, including the fruitful ambiguities, of the father-son relationship to the one-dimensional encounters we normally have with people on the street, our good intention of caring for strangers as dearly as we care for our parents may result in treating our dear ones as indifferently as we treat strangers. The insistence that we begin our tasks of self-realization in the context of the immediate dyadic relationships in which we are inevitably circumscribed is a basic principle underlying the father-son relationship in Confucian symbolism.

An equally basic principle governing the father-son relationship is reciprocity.[30] The impression of the father as the socializer, the educator, and thus the authoritarian disciplinarian is superficial, if not mistaken. It is true that the Confucian son is not permitted to express his rebellious feelings toward his father, but to describe the explosion of age-long repressed aggression of sons against fathers as a central problem in modern as well as traditinal Confucian society is misleading. According to the norm, the father should act fatherly so that the son can follow in a manner most appropriate to his self-identification. The son's filiality is conceived as a response to the father's kindness. The father must set an example for the son as a loving and respectable person before he can reasonably expect his son to love and respect him. Indeed, he should, in his son's mind, be seen as an exemplary teacher. On the other hand, he is not encouraged to instruct his son personally for fear that the intimacy between father and son be damaged as a result.[31] For this reason, exchanging sons for the purpose of formal instruction has been a common practice in Chinese society.

The sternness of the father image in Confucian culture must not be confused with aloofness or indifference. The father is not supposed to be physically close to the son. Physical closeness seems to be a prerogative of mother and son. Nevertheless, the father remains intimate with the son as his constant companion in the most critical stages of his development. The caring father guides the son's education, oversees his maturation, assists in his marriage arrangements, and prepares him for his career. The son in turn endeavors to fulfill his father's aspirations by internalizing them as goals in his own life. Reciprocity so conceived seems common in many other societies. A peculiar justification in the Confucian symbolism is that this reciprocal intimacy is not only absolutely necessary but also highly desirable for personal spiritual growth. This is diametrically opposed to the idea that the quest for inner spirituality requires that one transcend or forsake all primordial ties. The centrality of the father-son relationship in Confucian thought can thus be seen as a paradigmatic expression of the Confucian perception that selfhood entails the participation of the other.

Does this mean that since in Confucian symbolism there is no obvious shift of the ultimacy (e.g., Heaven or Way) from the natural
social order to a transcendent reference point (such as God), there is
no resultant capacity to ask ultimate questions? If this is the case,
Confucian selfhood is, in the last analysis, a category in social ethics
and one which does not seem to have any profound religious import.
On the other hand, if Confucian selfhood is itself a transcendent
reference point, a line of thought I intend to pursue further here,
how are we to understand its linkages with ultimate ideas such as
Heaven and Way?

The answer lies in the Confucian conception of the self not only as
a center of relationships but also as a dynamic process of spiritual
development. Ontologically, selfhood, our original nature, is endowed by Heaven.[32] It is therefore divine in its all-embracing
fullness. Selfhood, in this sense, is both immanent and transcendent.
It is intrinsic to us; at the same time, it belongs to Heaven. So far,
this conception may appear to be identical to the Christian idea of
humanity as divinity circumscribed. By analogy, Confucian
selfhood, or original human nature, can be seen as God's image in
man. However, the transcendence of Heaven is significantly different from the transcendence of God. The Mencian thesis that a full
realization of our minds can lead us to a comprehension of our
nature and eventually to an understanding of Heaven is predicated
on the belief that our selfhood is a necessary and sufficient condition
for us to appreciate in total the subtle meanings of the Mandate of
Heaven. To translate this into Christian terms, it means that
humanity itself, without God's grace, can fully realize its circumscribed divinity to such an extent that the historical Jesus as God
incarnated symbolizes no more than a witness of what people ought
to be able to attain on their own. After all, Christ is also called the
Great Exemplar. However, this claim exhibits a family resemblance
to the notorious Confucian pelagianism: the denial of original sin,
the assertion that we are endowed with the freedom of will not to sin,
and the avowal that we as human beings have the unassisted initiating power to appropriate the necessary grace for salvation. Indeed, the Confucian position does not even consider grace relevant
to self-realization.

Though we do not take transcendence to mean an external source
of authority, not to mention a "wholly other," there is still a distinctly
transcendent dimension in Confucian selfhood, namely that Heaven
resides in it, works through it and, in its optimal manifestation, is

also revealed by it. Selfhood so conceived maintains a tacit communication with Heaven. It is the root from which great cultural
ideals and spiritual values grow. Understandably, subjectivity in the
Confucian sense is not particularistic and is, paradoxically, the concrete basis for universality.

Since I have elsewhere elaborated on this point,[33] let us here in-
quire only into the significance of transcendence in selfhood for the
idea of dynamic spiritual development. If goodness is intrinsic to
human nature, why is there any need for self-realization? A direct
response is simply to note that the intrinsic goodness in our nature is
often in a latent state: only through long and strenuous effort can it
be realized as an experienced reality. In a deeper sense, however, a
distinction between ontological assertion and existential realization
must be made. Self-realization is an existential idea, specifying a
way of bringing into existence the ontological assertion that human
nature is good. Precisely because human nature is good, the
ultimate basis for self-realization and the actual process of initiating
self-cultivation are both located in the structure of the self. Pelagian
fallacy notwithstanding, Confucian selfhood contains the necessary
inner resources for its own dynamic spiritual development.

There is an implicit circularity in this conception of the self:
human nature is good so that there is an authentic possibility for
dynamic spiritual development and vice versa. If we accept that the
above-mentioned distinction of ontological assertion and existential
realization also involves a dialectic relationship, the circularity is no
longer a vicious one. Rather, we can well see that inherent in the
structure of the self is a powerful longing for the transcendent, not
for an external supreme being but for the Heaven that has bestowed
on us our original nature. This longing for the transcendent, in a
deeper sense, is also an urge for self-transcendence, to go beyond
what the self existentially is so that it can become what it ought to be.
Although we are, in ontological terms, never deficient in our
internally-generated capacity for spiritual development, we must
constantly open ourselves up to the symbolic resources available to
us for pursuing the concrete paths of self-realization. The participation of the other is not only desirable but absolutely necessary. For
as centers of relationships, we do not travel alone to our final
destiny; we are always in the company of family and friends, be they
remembered, imagined, or physically present.

The ultimate question for the Confucians then is, how can I, in
the midst of social relations, realize my selfhood as the Heaven-

endowed humanity? The reason that the father-son relationship is so central to Confucian symbolism is itself a reflection of this mode of questioning. Since I can never realize myself as an isolated or even isolable individual, I must recognize as a point of departure my personal locus with reference to my father among other dyadic relationships. My relationship to my father is vitally important for my own salvation, because if it is ignored, I can no longer face up to the reality of who I am in a holistic sense. After all, my Heaven-endowed nature can only be manifested through my existence as a center of relationships. For my own self-cultivation, I cannot but work through, among other things, my relationship to my father with all its fruitful ambiguities. The Sage-King Shun certainly had a more difficult task than most, but he, like us, could not bypass his social relationships in order to establish an intimate connection with Heaven directly. He was able to reach Heaven in the sense of fully realizing his selfhood precisely because he courageously faced up to the challenge of his social relationships near at hand. Social relationships are not in themselves ultimate concerns. They become prominent in Confucian symbolism because they are, on the one hand, rooted in one's depth psychology and, on the other, extended to one's religiosity.

The father-son relationship, in this sense provides a context and an instrumentality for self-cultivation. It is not because our fathers dominate or because we dare not disobey them that we cultivate our sense of respect for them. We respect them for our own projects of self-realization and, with gentle persuasion, they may be convinced that it is also for theirs. Indeed, our ego ideals come into existence as a result of our discipleship, friendship, ministership, brotherhood, and a host of other social roles. The father-son relationship, central as it is, constitutes but one among them. Like Shun, we take our relationships to our fathers as absolutely binding, but we do not submit ourselves to their arbitrary rule. For their own sake as well as ours, we must appeal to our Heaven-endowed nature, our conscience, for guidance. After all, it is for the ultimate purpose of self-realization that we honor our fathers as the source of the meaningful life that we have been pursuing. Indeed, there is a sense of a "creative fidelity"[34] in our relationships to our fathers. We are all involved in a joint venture to bring about the good life for our society. We know that we have to rise above the self-centeredness of our limited world views really to appreciate the universal Mandate of Heaven inherent in our human nature. We take our dyadic relationships seriously because they, in concrete ways, help us to enrich our supply of internal resources with symbolic content. Filiality, brotherliness, friendship, and the like are thus integral parts of our spiritual development. It is in this sense that Confucian selfhood entails the participation of the other.

Lest we should misconstrue the symbiosis of selfhood and otherness as a still-undifferentiated organismic notion, it is important to note that the Confucian perception of the self, without ideas of original sin and God's grace, is far from being an assertion of prelapsarian naïveté. The lack of a myth of the Fall notwithstanding, human frailty, fallibility, and diabolism are fully recognized in Confucian symbolism. The Confucians are acutely aware of the human propensity for self-destruction, not to mention slothfulness, wickedness, arrogance, and the like. Indeed, it is this deep sense of the tremendous difficulty that one encounters in one's self-cultivation that prompts the Confucians to define personal spiritual development as a communal act. The idea of a loner trying to search for salvation in total isolation, without the experiential support of a community, is not inconceivable in Confucian society. The more cherished approach, however, is self-cultivation through communication with and sharing in an ever-expanding circle of human-relatedness. Even at the risk of losing one's individual autonomy, the Confucian chooses fellowship of companionable people and "like-minded friends" to develop themselves jointly through mutual exhortation. In this connection, the father-son relationship, not unlike the teacher-student relationship, or for that matter the husband-wife relationship, is in the last analysis a "covenant" based upon a fiduciary commitment to a joint venture. Through the significant other, one deepens and broadens one's selfhood. This is the meaning of the Confucian self not only as center of relationships, but also as a dynamic process of spiritual development.

NOTES

1. Tu Wei-ming, "Ultimate Self-Transformation as a Communal Act," *Journey of Chinese Philosophy* 6 (1979), 237–246.

2. For representative works in these areas, see Emily M. Ahern, *Chinese Ritual and Politics* (Cambridge: Cambridge University Press, 1981); Francis L. K. Hsü, *Americans and Chinese: Purpose and Fulfillment in Great Civilizations* (Garden City, N.Y.: Doubleday Natural History Press, 1970) and *Under the Ancestral Shadow: Kinship, Per-*

sonality, and Social Mobility in China (Stanford: Stanford University Press, 1971); Lucian W. Pye, *The Spirit of Chinese Politics; A Psychocultural Study of the Authority Crisis in Political Development* (Cambridge, Mass.: M.I.T. Press, 1968); Arthur P. Wolf, *Religion and Ritual in Chinese Society* (Stanford: Stanford University Press, 1974) and A. P. Wolf, ed., *Studies in Chinese Society* (Stanford: Stanford University Press, 1978).

3. Tu Wei-ming, "Li as Process of Humanizatin," *Philosophy East and West*, XXII:2 (April 1972), 187–201. For "ritualization" in a psychoanalytical sense, see Erik H. Erikson, *Toys and Reasons; Stages in the Ritualization of Experience* (New York: W.W. Norton & Company, 1977).

4. Wing-tsit Chan, trans., *A Source Book of Chinese Philosophy* (Princeton: Princeton University Press, 1969), p. 530.

5. *Analects*, 6:30.

6. Max Weber, *The Religion of China: Confucianism and Taoism*, trans. Hans H. Gerth (Glencoe, Ill.: Free Press, 1951), p. 235.

7. Étienne Balazs, *Chinese Civilization and Bureaucracy; Variations on a Theme*, trans. H.M. Wright and ed. Arthur F. Wright (New Haven: Yale University Press, 1964), p. 195.

8. Huston Smith, "Transcendence in Traditional China," *Religious Studies*, 2 (1967), 185–196.

9. *Analects*, 1:11.

10. Fung Yu-lan, *A History of Chinese Philosophy*, trans. Derk Bodde (Princeton: Princeton University Press, 1952), I, pp. 351–352.

11. Ibid., p. 352.

12. Ibid., p. 359.

13. Ibid.

14. Donald J. Munro, *The Concept of Man in Early China* (Stanford: Stanford University Press, 1969), pp. 49–83; also see his *The Concept of Man in Contemporary China* (Ann Arbor: University of Michigan Press, 1977), pp. 15–25.

15. Fung Yu-lan, p. 360.

16. Hsü Fu-kuan, "Chung-kuo hsiao-tao ssu-hsiang te hsing-ch'eng yen-pien chi-ch'i tsai li-shih chung te chu-wen-t'i" ("The formation, development and historical issues of filial thought in China"), in his *Chung-kuo ssu-hsiang shih lun-chi* (collected essays on Chinese thought; Taichung, Taiwan: Tunghai University Press, 1968), pp. 155–200. Although Professor Hsü later significantly modified his historical interpretation, his claim that a broadly conceived notion of filial piety as the source of all virtues may have been the result of politicized Confucian ethics is still valid.

17. *Mencius*, 4A:26, 4B:30.

18. Ibid., 5A:2.

19. *K'ung Tzu chia-yü* (Sayings of the Confucian school), comp. Wang Su (reprint of the Shu edition of the Sung dynasty; Taipei: Chung-hua Book Co., 1968), 4:5a–6a.

20. *Mencius*, 5A:2.

21. Robert N. Bellah, *Beyond Belief: Essays on Religion in a Post-Traditional World* (New York: Harper & Row, 1976), p. 95.

22. Ibid., p. 94.

23. Ibid., p. 95.

24. Ibid., p. 78.

25. Ibid., p. 82.

26. S. Freud, *Totem and Taboo*, trans. James Strachey (New York: W.W. Norton & Company, 1952), p. 157.

27. Wing-tsit Chan, pp. 86–87.

28. *Analects*, 1:2.

29. *Mencius*, 3B:9.

30. Lien-sheng Yang, "The Concept of *Pao* as a Basis for Social Relations in China," in *Chinese Thought and Institutions*, ed. John K. Fairbank (Chicago: University of Chicago Press, 1957), pp. 291–309, 395–397.

31. *Mencius*, 4A:19.

32. Wing-tsit Chan, p. 98.

33. Tu Wei-ming, *Centrality and Commonality: An Essay on Chung-yung* (Honolulu: The University Press of Hawaii, 1976), pp. 100–141.

34. Gabriel Marcel, *Creative Fidelity*, trans. Robert Rosthal (New York: Farrar, Strauss & Co., 1964).

VIII. Neo-Confucian Religiosity and Human-Relatedness

The primary purpose of Neo-Confucian learning is "for the sake of one's self" (*wei-chi*).[1] One learns to be human not to please others or to conform to an external standard of conduct. Indeed, "learning to be human" (*hsüeh tso-jen*) is a spontaneous, autonomous, fully conscious, and totally committed intentional act, an act of self-realization. It gives its own direction and generates its own form and creates its own content. Virtually all root precepts in Neo-Confucian thought, in both the Ch'eng-Chu and the Lu-Wang traditions, take self-realization as a background assumption. Ch'eng I's "Self-cultivation requires reverence; the pursuit of learning depends on the extension of knowledge";[2] Chu Hsi's "dwelling in reverence and fathoming principle";[3] Lu Hsiang-shan's "establishing first that which is great in us";[4] Wang Yang-ming's "full realization of one's primordial awareness";[5] and Liu Tsung-chou's "effort of vigilant solitariness"[6] are paradigmatic examples. Yet, even though Neo-Confucianism asserts that the center of creativity in the ethicoreligious realm is human subjectivity, it is neither subjectivistic nor individualistic.

For one thing, the self in Neo-Confucian thought, instead of being the private possession of an isolated individual, is an open system. It is a dynamic center of organismic relationships and a concrete personal path to the human community as a whole. In this essay I intend to explore the ethicoreligious significance of this insight by addressing some of the perennial issues of religion and family from the perspective of Neo-Confucian philosophical anthropology.

A defining characteristic of Neo-Confucian thought is its reenactment of the classical Mencian learning of the mind as a ceaseless process of deepening and broadening self-knowledge. This involves an ontological justification for the enterprise of personal cultivation and an existential description of how to pursue it. In Neo-Confucian terminology, learning for the sake of one's self involves two inseparable dimensions: "original substance" (*pen-t'i*) and "moral effort" (*kung-fu*). On the level of original substance, the justification for learning of the mind is predicated on the Neo-Confucian perception of humanity as "sensitivity."[7] Human beings, like any other modalities of being in the cosmos, are endowed with the reality known as the

131

"principle" (*li*). Human beings are thus an integral part of the "chain of being," encompassing Heaven, Earth, and the myriad things. However, the uniqueness of being human is the intrinsic capacity of the mind to "embody" (*t'i*) the cosmos in its conscience and consciousness. Through this embodying, the mind realizes its own sensitivity, manifests true humanity and assists in the cosmic transformation of Heaven and Earth.[8]

Far from being a romantic assertion about the unity of all things, this Neo-Confucian commitment to the unlimited sensitivity of the mind is a deliberate attempt to accord human nature a kind of godlike creativity.[9] In theological terms, although Neo-Confucians do not believe in a transcendent personal God who is sometimes characterized as the "wholly other," they have faith in the ultimate goodness and all-embracing divinity of human nature, which is decreed by Heaven to be fully realized through the conscious and conscientious activity of the mind. An obvious background assumption here is what may be called the idea of the "continuity of being."

The reality of Heaven so conceived is by no means radically alien and therefore incomprehensible to the willing, feeling, and knowing functions of the mind. The mind may never understand the subtlety of the workings of Heaven through its intellectual faculty alone, but the nourished and cultivated mind, like the attuned ear, can perceive even the most incipient manifestations of the voice of God. Of course, Neo-Confucianism, being significantly different from any style of theologizing, depicts the course of Heaven as devoid of sound and fragrance.[10] Furthermore, following the Mencian tradition, it insists that Heaven sees as the people see and Heaven hears as the people hear.[11] This mutality of Heaven and man defines Neo-Confucian religiosity.

Wilfred Cantwell Smith, in his seminal study on the meaning and end of religion, makes a helpful distinction between "a religion" as an institution characterized by a set of objectifiable dogmas and "being religious" as spiritual self-identification of the living members of a faith community.[12] Accordingly, the problem of whether Neo-Confucianism is a religion should not be confused with the more significant question: what does it mean to be religious in the Neo-Confucian community? The solution to the former often depends on the particular interpretive position we choose to take on what constitutes the paradigmatic example of a religion, which may have little to do with our knowledge about Neo-Confucianism as a spiritual tradition; the question of being religious is crucial for our appreciation of the "inner dimension" of the Neo-Confucian project. For the sake of expediency, being religious in the Neo-Confucian sense can be understood as being engaged in *ultimate self-transformation as a communal act*.[13] Since the self, as already mentioned, is an open system, this process entails a continuous enlargement of the self.

We can perhaps envision the enlargement of the self diagrammatically as a series of constantly expanding concentric circles which symbolize the unplumbed sensitivity of the mind to embrace Heaven, Earth, and the myriad things. To enlarge oneself is therefore to purify, enlighten, and bring to fruition the ultimate capacity of the mind to "embody" the cosmos. The self so conceived is not a static structure but a dynamic process. It is a *center* of relationships, not an enclosed world of private thoughts and feelings. It needs to reach out, to be in touch with other selves, and to communicate through an ever-expanding network of human-relatedness. Yet, even though the Neo-Confucian self can be understood very well in terms of social roles, it is primarily an ethicoreligious idea with far-reaching cosmological and ontological implications.

The concrete path to actualize human nature through the learning of the mind involves a dynamic interplay between contextualization and decontextualization. This unique feature of Neo-Confucian ethics and religiosity can be further characterized as a dialectic of structural limitation and procedural freedom which emerges at each stage of self-cultivation. The necessity of recognizing the interrelated conditions, the context, in which the self as a center of relationships initiates its own realization is based on the aforementioned "continuity of being." Self-transformation is by definition not simply a departure from but is also a return to one's "locale." It is not a quest for pure spirituality nor is it a liberation from the flesh, the mundane, or the profane. The dichotomy of secular and sacred, or for that matter of body and mind, is rejected as heuristically misleading. The real task, perceived by the Neo-Confucians, is to manifest the ultimate meaning of life in ordinary human existence.[14]

The Neo-Confucian universe is certainly not without locale and date. Time and space experienced by the "self in transformation"[15] provide an inalienable context — thus the centrality of primordial ties in Neo-Confucian self-definition. Surely, the sense of being situated in a definite place at a particular moment involves more than the awareness of one's physical presence. The human mind may resemble a *tabula rasa*, but a person is always born to a complex social network. The self, not as an abstract concept but as a lived reality, must be aware of the others around it as integral parts of its own existence. The situation of the self requires not only a passive acceptance but also an active recognition. Once the fact of human-relatedness is recognized, one can begin to assume personal responsibility for one's social role. The structural limitation that we are inevitably contextualized need not be perceived merely as an external imposition on our freedom of choice; it also provides us the nourishment for survival, the environment for growth, and the symbolic resources for creativity.

In a deeper sense, however, the meaning of the self in Neo-Confucian thought cannot be determined by the social roles that contextualize it. At any particular juncture of one's development, no matter how coercive one's structural limitation is or is perceived to be, there is always the possibility to transcend it and overcome its negative influence. The self is situated, but neither enclosed nor enslaved, in its sociality. The texture of the dyadic relationships that define its social roles is never fixed. It has to be constantly interwoven with the changing configuration of disappearing and emerging threads which the self encounters in its life situations. To be sure, there are underlying permanent webs, such as the father-son relationship, that must endure all contingencies. Even this, however, is by no means fixed because as it shapes other relationships, it is also being shaped by them. The interaction of a variety of dyadic relationships generates the dynamism for personal integration earlier referred to as procedural freedom.

To pursue this further, the enlargement of the self, with its eventual union with Heaven as the most generalized universality, travels the concrete path of forming communions with a series of expanded social groups. The *locus classicus* for this ethicoreligious insight is the *Great Learning*:

> When the personal life (*shen*) is cultivated, the family (*chia*) will be regulated; when the family is regulated, the state (*kuo*) will be in order; and when the state is in order, there will be peace throughout the world (*t'ien-hsia*).[16]

The Neo-Confucian reading of the text, true to the spirit of learning for the sake of self-realization, puts great emphasis on the issues directly relevant to the cultivation of one's personal life. Thus, much hermeneutic effort is focused on the "inner dimension" of the enlargement of the self. This consists of the "investigation of things" (*ko-wu*), "extension of knowledge" (*chih-chih*), "sincerity of the will" (*ch'eng-i*), and "rectification of the mind" (*cheng-hsin*).[17] A kind of archaeological digging, with the expressed purpose of acquiring a deep understanding of the self, features prominently in the writings of virtually all major Neo-Confucian thinkers.

The Neo-Confucian faith in the perfectibility of the self is extended to the family, the state, and the world. Cultivation of the self as the "root" (*pen*) conveys not only personal but also social, political, and religious import. The corollary to this belief in the great transformative potential of the self is an awareness of the necessary form for its manifestation. Implicit in the statement that "when the personal life is cultivated, the family will be regulated" is an assertion that, as long as the family is not yet regulated, the cultivation of the personal life must be continued. By analogy, if the body politic is not yet in order or if peace has not yet pervaded all under Heaven, the effort of self-cultivation should not be interrupted. Learning (*hsüeh*), in the Neo-Confucian sense, requires an ultimate and a continuous commitment.

Robert N. Bellah has argued that Neo-Confucian religiosity is limited by the lack of transcendent leverage in Confucian symbolism. As a result, "there is no basis for a structurally independent religious community."[18] Since there is little in the Confucian position which justifies going beyond socially sanctioned norms, the authentic possibility for creative social innovation is often "precluded by the absence of a point of transcendent loyalty that [can] provide legitimation for it."[19] Recent scholarship, including Bellah's own reflection on the matter, has significantly revised this broadly conceived Weberian interpretation of Confucian ethics. Thomas Metzger, for example, argues with energy that there is indeed a functional equivalent to the Puritan ethic in Neo-Confucianism.[20] Max Weber's claim that the spiritual orientation of Confucianism is adjustment to the world, rather than mastery over the world, is no longer tenable. Nor is his overall assessment of the Confucian life-orientation:

> A well-adjusted man, rationalizing his conduct only to the degree requisite for adjustment, does not constitute a systematic unity but rather a complex of useful and particular traits. . . . Such a way of life could not allow man an inward aspiration toward a "unified personality," a striving which we associate with the idea of personality. Life remained a series of occurrences.[21]

However, even though Weber was misinformed when he insisted that in the Confucian ethic "there was no leverage for influencing conduct through inner forces freed of tradition and convention,"[22] his basic thesis still merits our attention. Weber argues that by harmonizing the conflict between the self and society, Confucian ethics lacks

> any tension between nature and deity, between ethical demand and human shortcoming, consciousness of sin and need for salvation, conduct on earth and compensation in the beyond, religious duty and socio-political reality.[23]

Whether or not the Neo-Confucian masters themselves managed to overcome the conflict between their commitment to moralizing politics through spiritual self-transformation and the autocratic demand for loyal participation in the political order, it was not conceivable to them, as it was taken for granted in Christianity, that "every particular pattern of social relations was in principle deprived of ultimacy."[24] And, historically, it is undeniable that under the influence of highly politicized Confucian symbolism, "filial piety and loyalty became absolutes."[25] The inability of even the most brilliant minds in Confucian China to develop a soteriology beyond politics clearly indicates that the idea of transcendence, as radical otherness, was not even conceived as a rejected possibility in Neo-Confucian thought.

To criticize Neo-Confucian symbolism for lack of transcendent leverage is to impose a Christian and, therefore, alien perspective. It would be indeed difficult for modern Confucians to appreciate fully the idea of the "wholly other," the sentiment of absolute dependency, or the justification for total faith in an unknowable God. However, within the symbolic resources of the Neo-Confucian tradition, the authentic possibility exists for developing a transcendent leverage which can serve as the ultimate basis for an intellectual community, or the community of the like-minded followers of the Way, structurally independent of the political order and functionally inseparable from the lived realities of society and politics. Despite the difficulty of conceptualizing transcendence as radical otherness, the Confucian commitment to ultimate self-transformation necessarily involves a transcendent dimension. The idea of going beyond the usual limits of one's existential self so that one can become true to one's Heavenly endowed nature entails the transformative act of continuously excelling and surpassing one's experience here and now. This transformative act is predicated on a transcendent vision that ontologically we are infinitely better and therefore more worthy than we actually are. In the ultimate sense we, as persons, form a trinity with Heaven and Earth. From this transcending perspective, it is not at all inconceivable that every particular pattern of social relations is only instrumentally important and is therefore deprived of ultimacy.

We can perhaps restate Neo-Confucian religiosity in terms of a twofold process: a continuous deepening of one's subjectivity and an uninterrupted broadening of one's sensitivity. Ultimate self-transformation as a communal act, in this connection, entails a series of paradoxes. The cultivation of the self assumes the form of mastering the self; for the self to realize its original nature, it must transform its self-centered structure. Accordingly, to deepen one's subjectivity requires an unceasing struggle to eliminate selfish and egoistic desires. By inference, just as cultivation of the personal life impels us to go beyond egoism, regulation of the family, governing the state and bringing peace throughout the world impel us to transcend nepotism, racism, and chauvinism. The Neo-Confucians may not have been as sensitive to the bigotry of these limited and limiting collective consciousnesses as we are in our pluralistic global village. Yet, it is vitally important to note that, in their perception, broadened sensitivity should also enable one to rise above anthropocentrism. To them, the real meaning of being human lies in the mutuality of Heaven and man and the unity of all things.

From this anthropocosmic perspective, the Neo-Confucian idea of the family is laden with ethicoreligious as well as social and political implications. Chang Tsai's (1020–1077) *Western Inscription,* which Wing-tsit Chan describes as "the basis of Neo-Confucian ethics," speaks directly to this:

> Heaven is my father and Earth is my mother, and even such a small creature as I finds an intimate place in their midst. Therefore that which fills the universe I regard as my body and that which directs the universe I consider as my nature. All people are my brothers and sisters, and all things are my companions.[26]

The family and, by extension, the state and the world are integral parts of the "fiduciary community" where organismic connections unite all modalities of being in a common bond. A natural application of this anthropocosmic vision to human society recognizes that:

> Even those who are tired, infirm, crippled, or sick; those who have
> no brothers or children, wives or husbands, are all my brothers
> who are in distress and have no one to turn to.[27]

However, as Chu Hsi (1130–1200) points out, the underlying
assumption in Chang Tsai's all-embracing humanity is not undifferentiated "universal love," but the Neo-Confucian thesis: "principle
is one but its particularizations are diverse" (*li-i fen-shu*).[28] Without
going into the technical issues, this thesis means that, from the
perspective of the "original substance," the organismic unity per-
vades everything. There is absolute equality among things and the
mind's sensitivity can and should embody all of them without
discrimination. From the functional viewpoint, on the other hand,
the exertion of "moral effort" necessitates a concrete analysis of a
given situation. As a result, the diversity in which the principle is
particularized becomes the central concern. Since it is thought to be
humanly impossible for one to care for a stranger in the same degree
and to the same extent that one cares for one's closest kin, a proper
way to express one's sensitivity requires a differentiated manifestation.

The "five human relations" (*wu-lun*), understood in this light,
point to five structurally and functionally distinct dyadic relationships.[29] A sense of priority or an order of hierarchy can be assigned
to the five relations. The prominence of the father-son dyad seems
indicative of a prioritized or hierarchical pattern which underlies all
the relationships. It is misleading, however, to suggest that the
father-son dyad provides a model for the other four. Rather, each
has a uniqueness which cannot be reduced to or subsumed under
any other. A common mistake in interpreting traditional Chinese
political culture, presumably under the influence of Neo-
Confucianism, is to assume that the ruler-minister relationship is
modelled on that of the father-son. The father-son or, generally
speaking, the parent-child relationship is a primordial tie, absolutely
binding and inescapably given. While one cannot choose one's
parents, the freedom not to enter a ruler-minister relationship and
the choice to sever a political obligation is always available. Thus,
the guiding principle between father and son is "affinity" (*ch'in*),
whereas the governing virtue between ruler and minister is
"righteousness" (*i*). It may be more appropriate to understand the

ruler-minister in terms of the father-son and the friend-friend relationships combined.

Another common mistake in analyzing the five relations is to exaggerate the importance of asymmetry in all the dyads. This gives rise to the general impression that the "three bonds" (*san-kang*),[30] emphasizing the one-dimensional dependency of the minister on the ruler, the son on the father and the wife on the husband, are defining characteristics of Neo-Confucian ethics. Historically, Neo-Confucianism as a political ideology may have contributed to despotic, gerontocratic, and male-oriented practices in premodern Chinese society; however, the value that underlies the five relations is not dependency but "reciprocity" (*pao*).[31] The filiality of the son is reciprocated by the compassion of the father, the obedience of the minister reciprocated by the fair-mindedness of the ruler and so forth. Friendship, in this connection, is a reciprocal relation *par excellence*. It is mutuality rather than dependency that defines "trust" (*hsin*) between friends.

The fiduciary community which friends enter into is not a "trust" created to achieve a narrowly defined economic or social goal. The modern idea of a religious fellowship, rather than a professional association or an academic society, comes close to the Neo-Confucian "way of the friend" (*yu-tao*), which is intimately connected with the "way of the teacher" (*shih-tao*). Friendship as well as the teacher-student relationship exists for the sake of communal self-transformation. Its purpose is moral education:

> Master Lien-hsi (Chou Tuni-i, 1017–1073) said: Righteousness, uprightness, decisiveness, strictness, and firmness of action are examples of strength that is good, and fierceness, narrow-mindedness, and violence are examples of strength that is evil. Kindness, mildness, and humility are examples of weakness that is good, and softness, indecision, and perverseness are examples of weakness that is evil. Only the Mean brings harmony. The Mean is the principle of regularity, the universally recognized law or morality, and is that to which the sage is devoted. Therefore the sage institutes education so as to enable people to transform their evil by themselves, to arrive at the Mean and to rest there.[32]

This idea of moral education "for the sake of one's self" also features prominently in the relationship between brothers. The application of the principle of reciprocity in the pursuit of self-knowledge involves altruism as well as fairness. The pervading spirit is empathetic understanding of the other which implies considerateness and forgivingness (*shu*).³³ The idea of vengeance is diametrically opposed to the Neo-Confucian value of reciprocity. To the question: "Suppose the older brother is respectful toward his younger brother but the younger brother is not reverent toward the older brother. Should the older brother imitate his brother's lack of reverence and stop being respectful?" Chu Hsi emphatically stated, "The older brother should be respectful to the highest degree." This, he insisted, is the true meaning of the verse in the *Book of Odes*: "Brothers should be good to each other but should not imitate each other."³⁴

It would be misleading to suppose that self-sacrifice or a simple psychology of detachment is the message here. A fiduciary community means that the moral well-being of each member is the personal concern of all. In a specific dyadic relationship where an obvious asymmetry occurs, as in the case of the younger brother's lack of reverence, conscious effort is required of the righteous (the older brother) for his own self-cultivation to help the other (the younger brother) to resume his course of moral learning. The *locus classicus* for this is the Confucian *Analects*: "In order to establish oneself, one helps others to establish themselves; in order to enlarge oneself, one helps others to enlarge themselves."³⁵ Therefore, in the light of self-education, the reciprocal relationship is always a two-way communication. The ruler, the parent, the teacher, the senior friend, and the older brother are as much involved in making themselves obedient, faithful and dedicated to the shared values of the community as are the minister, the child, the student, the junior friend, and the younger brother.

It is conceivable that occasionally one may have to find a way to help one's parent and, by implication, one's teacher (not to mention one's ruler who often falls short of a minimum standard of rulership) to behave properly. The necessity and desirability of doing so is taken for granted, but the actual style to bring the necessary and desirable result requires careful deliberation and, of course, finesse. Commenting on the line from the *Book of Change*: "In dealing with troubles caused by one's mother, one should not be too firm," Ch'eng I (1033–1107) had this to say:

> In dealing with his mother, the son should help her with mildness and gentleness so she will be in accord with righteousness. If he

disobeys her and the matter fails, it will be his fault. Is there not a way to obey with ease? If one goes forward with his strength and abruptly resists or defies her, the kindness and love between mother and son will be hurt. That will be great harm indeed. How can he get into her heart and change her? The way lies in going backward, bending his will to obey, and following his mother so that her personal life will be correct and matters well managed. The way for strong ministers to serve weak rulers is similar to this.[36]

This concern for the irreparable damage to the amiable relationship between mother and son caused by the son's blunt confrontation in order to right the wrongs of the mother is a concern for the moral well-being of the mother as well as the harmony of the family. Voluntary change of attitude is preferred; an arbitrary imposition of an external standard, despite its possible heuristic value for self-discipline, can never bring about genuine self-transformation. Thus,

In teaching people, Confucius "would not enlighten those who are not eager to learn, nor arouse those who are not anxious to give an explanation themselves."[37] For if one arouses them without waiting for them to become eager to learn and anxious to give an explanation themselves, their knowledge will not be firm. But if one waits for them to be eager and anxious before arousing them, they will learn irresistibly like the rush of water. A student must think deeply. If he has thought deeply but cannot understand, it will then be all right to tell him.[38]

On the surface, the conjugal relationship seems to be a significant departure from the principle of reciprocity. The common impression that the wife and daughter-in-law in a male-oriented society has no "rights" of her own is, however, a misconception of how the normative system actually works in Neo-Confucianism. It is true that, in response to the loaded question: "In some cases the widows are all alone, poor, and with no one to depend on. May they remarry?" Ch'eng I, apparently troubled by the questioner's intention to establish the strong claim that remarriage is sometimes necessary if not desirable, stated in an unusually stern manner: "This theory has come about only because people of later generations are afraid of starving to death. But to starve to death is a very small matter. To lose one's integrity, however, is a very serious matter."[39] This uncompromising articulation of faith in the sacredness of marriage as a total commitment was probably in Ch'eng I's mind applied equally to husband and wife. Furthermore, it was meant to be a critique of a common practice which seemed to have taken too lightly the true meaning of matrimony by using a simple economic justification. The very fact that Ch'eng I cited approvingly his father's decision to remarry a widowed relative as a manifestation of kindness[40] indicates that, while he was in principle against remarriage, he did not make a dogma out of it.

Ideally, in the Neo-Confucian order of things, the conjugal relationship is the most fundamental of all human relations. The Neo-Confucians argue that it is from husband and wife that all other familial ties are engendered.[41] Failure to establish genuine reciprocity between husband and wife destroys domestic harmony and indeed social stability. Therefore, in underscoring its importance, their emphasis is on mutual responsibility rather than romantic love. Injunction against devoting too much attention to the affective aspect of the conjugal relationship is readily available in Neo-Confucian literature:

> Tranquillity and correctness are the ways to enable husband and wife to live together for a long time, whereas indecent liberties and improper intimacies result in disrespect and cause husband and wife to drift apart.[42]

Reciprocity in the conjugal relationship is often characterized by "respect" (ching). A common expression in describing a proper husband-wife relationship is that they treat each other respectfully as guests. For example, Ch'eng I summarized his mother's relationship to his father as follows: "she and father treated each other with full respect as guests are treated. Grateful for her help at home, father treated her with even greater reverence. But mother conducted herself with humility and obedience."[43]

Like all other forms of dyadic relationships, the idea of mutual respect between husband and wife conveys a profound ethicoreligious import. Although it is basically correct to interpret the Neo-Confucian perception of the conjugal relationship in terms of social values such as the creation, maintenance and perpetuation of the family, the mutuality of husband and wife should also be taken as an integral part of the self-education of both of them. One wonders if Ch'eng I did not somehow simplify the complexity of the actual situation in his praise of the virtue of his mother as wife:

> She was humane, altruistic, liberal, and earnest. She cared for and loved the children of my father's concubines just as she did her own. My father's cousin's son became an orphan when very young, and she regarded him her own.[44]

Nevertheless, despite the male-centeredness of the culture, the active participation of the wife in shaping the form of human-relatedness in the family is fully recognized and strongly encouraged. The division of labor between the inner (domestic) and the outer (public) realm of responsibility makes it functionally necessary for the wife to assume a major role at home. Thus, Ch'eng I's mother's preference in consulting her husband even in small matters was noted as an indication of extraordinary considerateness.[45] Needless to say, the ultimate self-transformation of the wife-mother, like that of the husband-father, provides a standard of inspiration for the family and for society at large.

The Neo-Confucian conception of the proper conduct of a wife differs from the accepted standards of behavior in pre-modern China. Although no convincing evidence has been found to establish a causal relationship between the rise of Neo-Confucian culture in the tenth century and the prevalence of such appalling social customs as footbinding, the charge that Neo-Confucian ideology significantly contributed to the decline in the status of women in China has not yet been cleared. Certainly, the Neo-Confucian advocacy of a hierarchical ordering of the human community according to prescribed social roles may have oriented society to adopt what seems to us an unwarranted policy of sex differentiation. However, it is the structural limitation of the human condition, to which we earlier referred, that actually provides the justification for perceiving society as a highly differentiated "organic solidarity" of which sex differentiation is only a part. People are also differentiated by age, profession, wealth, power, reputation, family connections, and so forth. One does not choose but is simply fated to be a particular person. Yet, the recognition that one is inescapably situated in one's primordial ties, far from being an acceptance of fatalism, is a realistic understanding of the context in which one begins the task of learning to be human. This task involves a dynamic process of

growth rather than mere submission to assigned social roles. In this
sense, the dialectic interplay between contextualization and
decontextualization for the wife-mother, like that for the husband-
father, can also function creatively at each stage of her self-
realization. Like her male counterpart, she realizes herself through
the "procedural freedom" that she cultivates despite (we may even
say paradoxically because of) her structural limitation.

This Neo-Confucian position on the role of woman is predicated
on a vision of society in which women, like men, actively shape its
moral character. One cannot exaggerate the importance of the
mother in nourishing and educating the young and the wife in harmonizing and managing the family in traditional China. The
transformation of a daughter into a responsible wife-mother, like
the transformation of a son into a responsible husband-father,
is a major concern in Confucian culture. Indeed, within the symbolic resources of the Neo-Confucian tradition, there is a well-
spring of insights on how to cultivate true mutality between
man and woman. The functional cosmology that the Neo-
Confucians subscribe to is not anthropomorphic; therefore it is not
wedded to a male-dominated symbolism. A natural consequence of
the lack of a fully institutionalized mediating structure (such as the
priesthood) between the mundane and the transcendent in the Confucian tradition is the absence of any theological justification for the
creation of an exclusively male spiritual leadership. While women
were long excluded from state examinations and from higher education, these practices are not prescribed by Confucian moral
metaphysics. Rather, a society of like-minded followers of the Way
is and ought to be open to all members of the human community.
The universalistic claim that every human being (in the sense of the
sexually neutral form *jen*) has the potential to form a unity with
Heaven, Earth, and the myriad things is thus not only an intellectual assertion but also a spiritual commitment of the Neo-Confucian
masters.

Nevertheless, we cannot ignore the historical fact that Confucian
China was unquestionably a male-dominated society. The education of the son received much more attention than the education of
the daughter, the husband was far more influential than the wife,
and the father's authority significantly surpassed that of the mother.
The idea that a woman passed through three stages of dependency:
dependency on the father in youth, on the husband when married,

and on the son in old age clearly indicates her inferior status in the so-called hierarchical ordering of the human community. Surely, to criticize Neo-Confucian ideology as male-oriented is to introduce a modern feminist perspective beyond the realm of imagination in most traditional discourses Eastern or Western. Yet, if we take Neo-Confucian religiosity seriously as a viable persuasion rather than merely as a historical phenomenon, we must criticize the outmoded Neo-Confucian ideology in order to retrieve the deep meaning of its universal humanistic teachings. Only then will we encounter no theological or scriptural difficulty in stressing the necessity and desirability of the participation of women in influencing, shaping, and leading the Confucian Way in the future. Chu Hsi or Wang Yang-ming may not have adopted a conscious policy of training women to become Confucian masters, but their legacy speaks loudly in favor of such a tendency. While they may not have been egalitarian in the modern sense, the suggestion that they subscribed to a kind of class consciousness that prevented women and the uneducated masses from becoming fully human is a misreading of their message. Indeed, their insistence that respect is the governing virtue between husband and wife is based not only on the idea of the division of labor but also on the value of mutual appreciation. This, by implication, requires the formation of a functionally differentiated and substantively unified relationship between woman and man.

I have suggested that, in the perspective of Neo-Confucian thought, human-relatedness is an essential dimension of religiosity. As an ultimate self-transformation, being religious entails being actively engaged in a communal act. Religious consciousness so understood is a quest for the identity and continuity of one's communality as well as one's selfhood. Paradoxically, for the self to be ultimately transformed, it must travel the concrete path defined in terms of its primordial ties such as parentage, ethnicity, locale, historical moment, and so forth. Strictly speaking, if the self fails to transform the primordial ties into "instruments" for moral cultivation, it can only be contextualized and structured to assume a predetermined social role. Yet, its creativity as a moral agent cannot be manifested merely by transcending the context and the structure that determines its center of relationships. The authentic approach is neither a passive submission to structural limitation nor a Faustian activation of procedural freedom but a conscientious effort to make the dynamic interaction between them a fruitful dialectic for self-realization. Learning for the sake of one's self is ethicoreligious because it takes as its root idea the inseparability of the ethic of human-relatedness and the religiosity of the quest for personal knowledge.

NOTES

1. The idea occurs in the *Analects* (14:25) and is accepted as an underlying assumption by virtually all schools of Neo-Confucian thought.

2. This phrase, *"han-yang hsü-yung ching ching-hsüeh tsai chih-chih,"* is characteristic of the Ch'eng-Chu approach to moral self-cultivation. See Wing-tsit Chan, *A Source Book in Chinese Philosophy* (Princeton: Princeton University Press, 1963), p. 562.

3. The idea of *"chü-ching ch'iung-li"* can be taken as Chu Hsi's interpretation of Ch'eng I's method of education. Wing-tsit Chan notes: "Like Ch'eng I, Chu Hsi struck the balance between seriousness and the investigation of things in moral education. He said that seriousness is the one important word transmitted in the Confucian school, that it is the foundation in Ch'eng I's teachings, and that it is Ch'eng's greatest contribution to later students." See *A Source Book*, p. 607. It should be mentioned that the word *"ching"* is rendered as "reverence" or "respectfulness" in this essay, whereas Chan has chosen "seriousnessness" to convey its many-sided meanings.

4. It is commonly known that Lu Hsiang-shan builds his moral philosophy on the Mencian idea, *"hsien li-hu ch'i ta-che,"* *Mencius*, 6A:15.

5. *"Chih liang-chih"* has been variously rendered as "extension of innate knowledge," "extension of conscientious consciousness," "extension of knowledge of the good," and "extension of intuitive knowledge." In this essay, *liang-chih* is rendered as "primordial awareness" and *chih* as "full realization." See *Mencius*, 7A:15.

6. Liu Tsung-chou's teaching of *shen-tu* is based on the *Great Learning* and the *Doctrine of the Mean*.

7. See Ch'eng Hao's essay, "On Understanding Humanity" ("Shih-jen"), in *Erh-Ch'eng i-shu*, 2A:3a-b.

8. This is based on the anthropocosmic vision in the *Doctrine of the Mean*, chap. 22. See Tu Wei-ming, *Centrality and Commonality: An Essay on Chung-Yung* (Honolulu: The University Press of Hawaii, 1976), chap. IV.

9. Thomé H. Fang, *Chinese Philosophy: Its Spirit and Its Development* (Taipei: Linking Publishing Co., 1981), pp. 446–469.

10. This is also based on the *Doctrine of the Mean*, chap. 33. However, the idea originally came from the *Book of Poetry*, no. 235.

11. *Mencius*, 5A:5. It should be noted that this "democratic" or "populist" idea is found in the *Book of History*; see James Legge, trans., *The Shoo King* in the *Chinese Classics*, vol. 3 (Oxford: Clarendon Press, 1865), p. 292.

12. Wilfred Cantwell Smith, *The Meaning and End of Religion* (New York: The Macmillan Company, 1964), pp. 19–74.

13. Tu Wei-ming, "Ultimate Self-Transformation as a Communal Act: Comments on Modes of Self-Cultivation in Traditional China," *Journal of Chinese Philosophy* 6 (1969), 237–246.

14. Tu Wei-ming, "The Neo-Confucian Concept of Man," in *Humanity and Self-Cultivation: Essays in Confucian Thought* (Berkeley: Asian Humanities Press, 1980), pp. 71–82.

15. An expression borrowed from the title of Herbert Fingarette's thought-provoking book, *The Self in Transformation: Psychoanalysis, Philosophy and the Life of the Spirit* (New York: Basic Books, 1963).

16. *The Great Learning*, chap. 1.

17. Ibid.

18. Robert N. Bellah, "Father and Son in Christianity and Confucianism," in his *Beyond Belief: Essays on Religion in a Post-Traditional World* (New York: Harper & Row, 1976), p. 81.

19. Ibid., p. 95.

20. Thomas Metzger, *Escape from Predicament: Neo-Confucianism and China's Evolving Political Culture* (New York: Columbia University Press, 1977), pp. 29–47.

21. Max Weber, *The Religion of China*, trans., from the German and ed., Hans H. Gerth (New York: Free Press, 1964), p. 235.

22. Weber, p. 236.

23. Weber, pp. 235–236.

24. Bellah, p. 95.

25. Ibid.

26. Wing-tsit Chan, *A Source Book in Chinese Philosophy* (Princeton: Princeton University, 1963), p. 497.

27. Ibid.

28. Ibid., p. 550. This phrase is often rendered as "principle is one and its manifestations are many." In this essay, I follow Wm. T. de Bary's translation. See his *The Liberal Tradition in China* (Hong Kong: The Chinese University Press and New York: Columbia University Press, 1983), p. 51.

29. The *locus classicus* for this is again *Mencius*: "According to the way of man, if they are well fed, warmly clothed, and comfortably lodged but without education, they will become almost like animals. The sage (emperor Shun) worried about it and he appointed Hsieh to be Minister of Education and teach people human relations, that between father and son, there should be affection; between ruler and minister, there should be righteousness; between husband and wife, there should be attention to their separate functions; between old and young, there should be a proper order; and between friends, there should be faithfulness." (3A:4) See Wing-tsit Chan, *A Source Book*, pp. 69–70.

30. The "three bonds" are those binding the minister with the ruler, the son with the father, and the wife with the husband. The Han philosopher, Tung Chung-shu (c. 179 - c. 104 B.C.) discusses these relations in terms of moral education. The idea

of one-dimensional dependency is a highly politicized interpretation of the whole matter. See Wing-tsit Chan, *A Source Book*, pp. 277–278.

31. Lien-sheng Yang, "The Concept of 'Pao' as a Basis for Social Relations in China," in *Chinese Thought and Institutions*, ed., John K. Fairbank (Chicago: The University of Chicago Press, 1957), pp. 291–309, 395–397.

32. Wing-tsit Chan, trans., *Reflections on Things at Hand: The Neo-Confucian Anthology Compiled by Chu Hsi and Lü Tsu-ch'ien* (New York: Columbia University Press, 1967), p. 260.

33. *Analects*, 4:15 reads: "The Way of our Master is none other than conscientiousness (*chung*) and altruism (*shu*)." See Wing-tsit Chan, *A Source Book*, p. 27.

34. Wing-tsit Chan, trans., *Reflections*, pp. 181–182.

35. *Analects*, 6:28.

36. Wing-tsit Chan, trans., *Reflections*, pp. 171–172.

37. *Analects*, 7:8.

38. Wing-tsit Chan, trans., *Reflections*, p. 226.

39. Ibid., p. 177.

40. Ibid., p. 179.

41. The underlying philosophy of this assertion is found in the *Book of Change* where it states: "The great characteristic of Heaven and Earth is to produce." See Wing-tsit Chan, *A Source Book*, p. 268.

42. Wing-tsit Chan, trans., *Reflections*, p. 173.

43. Ibid., p. 179.

44. Ibid.

45. Ibid.

IX. Neo-Confucian Ontology: A Preliminary Questioning

The mode of questioning in Neo-Confucian thought may give us the impression that metaphysical or ontological problems are either relegated to the background or subsumed under the category of ethics. One can easily point to the dialogues between masters and disciples in the "recorded sayings" (*yü-lu*) of the Neo-Confucian thinkers to confirm such an impression. Indeed, it seems that the central concern of the Neo-Confucians, motivated by a strong will to fully realize themselves (*chien-hsing*),[1] is simply an all-encompassing psychological process: *how* to become a sage. Questions of what and why, it seems, do not feature as prominently as the practical considerations of how.[2] Understandably it is commonly observed that Neo-Confucianism is predominantly a moral philosophy. Even though it may occasionally depart from the concrete issues of everyday existence, it seems always to return to the ethical realm.[3] And it is in moral philosophy, we are told, that the strength of Neo-Confucian thought really lies.

Viewed from this perspective, discussions of ultimate reality in Neo-Confucianism such as Chou Tun-i's (1017–1073) treatise on the "great ultimate" (*t'ai-chi*) and Chang Tsai's (1020–1077) reflection on the "great harmony" (*t'ai-ho*) are sometimes explained, or explained away, in terms of conscious responses to the metaphysical challenges of Buddhism and Taoism. The argument, in a simplified form, is that these Neo-Confucian masters were not primarily interested in these problems but that they were compelled to take up the task of investigating them because the Buddhists and the Taoists, having developed highly sophisticated metaphysical systems, had already set the shape of intellectual discourse in those terms. Unless Buddhist and Taoist methods of metaphysical speculation were confronted directly, the argument continues, the Confucian position could not be securely established. Therefore, the Neo-Confucian thinkers, for the sake of delivering their message, learned the art of metaphysicizing as a strategic necessity. According to this interpretation, Neo-Confucian metaphysics, if the term is permissible, is at best a preparation for social ethics, which is to them, as it were, the real thing.

Although such a genetic explanation is unsatisfactory in many respects, it has contributed much to the wide currency of the view that the Neo-Confucian tradition is an outstanding example of ethical thought in China. The textbook account of the Chinese mind as exemplifying an effortless eclecticism of Taoist or Buddhist sacredness on the one hand and Confucian secularity on the other further enforces the belief that Neo-Confucianism, far from being concerned with the problem of reality, focuses its attention on man's everyday existence. Neo-Confucian thought so conceived seems not unlike a Chinese counterpart of the later Stoa with its insistence on the practical and moral principles of human life.[4]

The intention of this essay is to present an analysis of the Neo-Confucian approach to ontology. It is based on the belief that Neo-Confucian ethics, in its effort to formulate a holistic way of being human, is indeed predicated on an ontological vision without which its moral philosophy would be incomplete and its social thought groundless. The purpose, however, is not so much to work out a systematic critique of the "common-sense" interpretation of Neo-Confucianism as to show that if we undertake a serious inquiry into the underlying structure of Neo-Confucian ethics it is not difficult to see that precisely because its moral and social ideas are anchored on a highly integrated metaphysical plane they take on meanings significantly different from those of other ethical systems.

I. *The Metaphysical Grounding of Sagehood.* A defining characteristic of the Neo-Confucian mode of questioning is, as already mentioned, its emphasis on the problem of attaining sagehood. It may not be far-fetched to suggest that sagehood, as the highest and the profoundest manifestation of humanity, is the philosophical locus wherein all the major realms of concern in Neo-Confucian thought converge. And it is probably in this sense that the Neo-Confucians characterize their "learning" (*hsüeh*) and "teaching" (*chiao*) as the Sagely Way.[5] Therefore, in a strict sense, the Neo-Confucians do not simply *follow* the way of the ancient sages; they try to embody it so that they can manifest it in their own ways of life.[6] Sagehood so conceived is not an inaccessible ideal but a realizable state of existence. The alleged founder of the Neo-Confucian tradition, Chou Tun-i, has made it explicit that sagehood is attainable through learning:

Can one become a sage through learning?

Yes.

Is there any essential way?

Yes.

Please explain it to me.

The essential way is to [concentrate on] one thing. By [concentrating on] one thing is meant having no desire. Having no desire, one is vacuous (*hsü*, being absolutely pure and peaceful) while tranquil, and straightforward while in action. Being vacuous while tranquil, one becomes intelligent and hence penetrating. Being straightforward while active, one becomes impartial and hence all-embracing. Being intelligent, penetrating, impartial, and all-embracing, one is almost a sage.[7]

Whether or not "desirelessness" (*wu-yü*) is an authentically Confucian way of self-realization should not concern us here. Suffice it to note that Chu Hsi (1130–1200) has raised serious doubts about the suitability of defining oneness, a concentrated state of mind, in terms of having no desire.[8] But the insistence on the centrality of sagehood and the presumption that it can be attained by self-effort indicates such a general belief in Neo-Confucianism that all schools of thought within the tradition, despite serious arguments concerning issues such as whether or not having no desire is the right method of spiritual cultivation, subscribe to this belief as self-evidently true.

However, sagehood in the Neo-Confucian sense is much more than a simple personality-ideal, and its implications cannot begin to unfold if the proposed inquiry remains only at the levels of psychology and ethics. It is true that Chou Tun-i states that "sagehood is nothing but sincerity (*ch'eng*)."[9] Taken at its face value, this may be interpreted to mean that honesty is all that is required to become a sage. But sincerity, far from being just a psychological or ethical idea, is actually an ontological concept. Thus Chou continues:

It [Sincerity] is the foundation of the Five Constant Virtues (humanity, righteousness, propriety, wisdom, and faithfulness) and the source of all activities. When tranquil, it is in the state of non-being, and when active, it is in the state of being. It is perfectly correct and clearly penetrating. Without sincerity, the Five Constant Virtues and all activities will be wrong. They will be depraved and obstructed.[10]

The term which is here translated as "sincerity" has also been rendered as "truth" or "reality."[11] After all the English word itself connotes the meaning of honest genuineness, signifying in a poetic sense a heartfelt feeling grounded not on semblances but on realities.

Indeed, Chou further states that "the sage is the one who is in the state of sincerity, spirit (*shen*), and subtle incipient activation (*chi*)."[12] This may be taken as a refinement of the earlier assertion that sagehood is nothing but sincerity. Quoting from the "Appended Remarks" of the *Book of Change*, Chou defines sincerity as "the state of absolute quiet and inactivity" and spirit as that which "when acted on, immediately penetrates all things."

> And the state of subtle incipient activation is the undifferentiated state between existence and non-existence when activity has started but has not manifested itself in physical form. Sincerity is infinitely pure and hence evident. The spirit is responsive and hence works wonders. And incipient activation is subtle and hence abstruse.[13]

This mode of presentation, as evident in Chou's other remarks in his highly acclaimed *Penetrating the Book of Change (T'ung-shu)*, is not only characteristic of Neo-Confucian thought but also reminiscent of the Mencian tradition of classical Confucianism. The following statement in Mencius is a case in point:

> The desirable is called "good." To have it in oneself is called "true." To possess it fully in oneself is called "beautiful," but to shine forth with this full possession is called "great." To be great and be transformed by this greatness is called "sage;" to be sage and to transcend the understanding is called "divine" ["spiritual"].[14]

One might easily infer from these explanatory sentences that just as the sage symbolizes a continuous perfection of the good, the true, the beautiful, and the great, the spiritual is a further refinement on the sage. But, as Chu Hsi maintains, the idea of the spiritual in this connection by no means signifies a "spiritual being" (*shen-jen*) which rises above the sage. Rather, it indicates that the transforming power of the sage is beyond ordinary human comprehension.[15] This line of thinking is in perfect accord with the "moral metaphysics" of the *Doctrine of the Mean (Chung-yung)*:

Only those who are absolutely *sincere* can fully develop their nature. If they can fully develop their nature, they can then fully develop the nature of others. If they can fully develop the nature of others, they can then fully develop the nature of things. If they can fully develop the nature of things, they can then assist in the transforming and nourishing process of Heaven and Earth. If they can assist in the transforming and nourishing process of Heaven and Earth, they can thus form a trinity with Heaven and Earth.[16]

It can therefore be argued that Chou Tun-i's deceptively simple statement, "Sagehood is nothing but sincerity," is actually buttressed by a fully developed metaphysical vision. To be sure, sagehood as a mode of experience rather than as an abstract principle is not devoid of psychological and ethical implications. Yet since it is as much an idea about ultimate reality as one about the deepest meaning of human existence, it should be understood and appreciated from a much broader perspective. Indeed, no matter how much weight one puts on the psychological and ethical dimensions of it, sagehood in Neo-Confucian thought is always grounded in a metaphysical structure. Only then do concepts such as "sincerity," "spirit," and "subtle incipient activation" seem compatible with it.

II. *Kantian Mode of Questioning Compared.* In the light of the above, although it is true that one can interpret the Neo-Confucian spiritual orientation as a form of philosophical anthropology, the metaphysical grounding of sagehood must be construed as the ultimate fruition of an ethicoreligious insight wherein the conventional distinction between ethics and religion becomes merely a heuristic device. The central questions underlying the attainment of sagehood are, then, Who am I? and What can I become? Or, in other words, What is it to be hunan? Even thought the Neo-Confucian masters do not appear to have posed their questions in precisely such terms, a brief survey of their main concerns should be sufficient to illustrate this point.

The question which is alleged to have been first raised by Confucius' best disciple, Yen Yüan, is most instructive in this connection: "What sort of man was Shun (the Sage-King)? And what sort of man am I? Anyone who can make something of himself will be like that."[17] Intent on expounding the philosophical implication of Yen Yüan's questioning, Ch'eng I (1033–1107) wrote the famous treatise entitled "What Master Yen Loved to Learn." Despite his seemingly simple answer that "it was to learn the way of becoming a sage," Ch'eng I elaborates on the reason why every person is in essence a sage and therefore in practice can well become one. The argument, as we shall see, is very much in the spirit of Chou Tun-i:

> From the essence of life accumulated in Heaven and Earth, man receives the Five Agents (Water, Fire, Wood, Metal, and Earth) in their highest excellence. His original nature is pure and tranquil. Before it is aroused, the five moral principles of his nature, called humanity, righteousness, propriety, wisdom, and faithfulness, are complete.[18]

Therefore, Ch'eng I continues, "the way to learn is none other than rectifying one's mind and nourishing one's nature. When one abides by the Mean and correctness and becomes sincere, he is a sage."[19]

We may, at this particular juncture, insert a comparative note. On the basis of what has been said so far, the Neo-Confucian problematic does not seem directly responsive to any of the three Kantian questions:

1. What can I know?
2. What ought I do?
3. What may I hope?

To be sure, the Neo-Confucian concerns, so far as they have been mentioned above, may be subsumed under question 2, since they seem to fall into the category of human activity involving the personality and freedom of moral choice. Accordingly, one can go so far as to conclude that Neo-Confucianism, instead of focusing its attention on cosmology or on theology, is exclusively preoccupied with psychology. Yet this kind of unexamined assertion does a serious injustice not only to Neo-Confucian metaphysics but also to the Kantian perception of morality.

Kant, in his *Foundations of the Metaphysics of Morals*, insists that the ground of obligation (pure morality) "must not be sought in the nature of man or in the circumstances in which he is placed, but sought *a priori* solely in the concepts of pure reason."[20] Problems of translation and equivalence of terms aside, this would seem to conflict with the Neo-Confucian teaching that morality is deeply rooted in human nature. While Kant stresses "the utmost necessity to construct a pure moral philosophy which is completely freed from everything which may be only empirical and thus belong to anthropology,"[21] the Neo-Confucians strongly believe that moral cultivation is inseparable from man's knowledge of himself as an integral and "natural" being. However, these apparent incompatibilities only scratch the surface of a much more fundamental difference.

Viewed from a Neo-Confucian perspective, it seems that Kant is particularly concerned about the secret incentives undiscoverable even by the most searching self-examination. For the "dear self," which is capable of eluding the strictest scrutiny, remains powerful behind our thoughts and aspirations, although they are often falsely believed to have been dicated solely by the idea of the good.[22] Therefore, the stern command of duty (which would often require self-denial) becomes the only basis for moral action.[23] And this is predicated on the conviction that "reason of itself and independently of all appearances commands what ought to be done."[24] Perhaps this is why Kant, for fear that the will might not of itself be in complete accord with reason, stipulates the categorical imperative, an objective principle which acts as a command of reason.[25] Since the categorical imperative, or the imperative of morality, "concerns not the material of the action and its intended result but the form and the principle from which it results," it can be taken as a practical *law* rather than merely a principle of the will.[26]

Time and again, Kant urges us not to think that the reality of this law can be derived from "the constitution of human nature."[27] Indeed, "we cannot too much or too often warn against the lax or even base manner of thought which seeks principles among empirical motives and laws, for human reason in its weariness is glad to rest on this pillow."[28] Therefore it is extremely important to stress that the categorical imperatives, either as conformity to law by actions or as the prerogative of rational beings as such, must "exclude from their legislative authority all admixture of any interest as an incentive."[29] This leads Kant to the observation that

> Man is subject only to his own, yet universal, legislation, and that he is only bound to act in accordance with his own will, which is, however, designed by nature to be a will giving universal laws.[30]

With this background in mind Kant introduces the principle of *autonomy of the will* and the concept of a *realm of ends.*

Whether or not Heidegger is justified in depicting Kant as "recoiling in fear, in the second edition [of his *Critique of Pure Reason*], from

the abyss of human subjectivity opened up by the schematizing imagination,"[31] his perception of Kant's problematic is worth noting:

> Through the laying of the foundation of metaphysics in general,
> Kant first acquired a clear insight into the character of the "univer-
> sality" of ontologico-metaphysical knowledge. . . . In the struggle
> against the superficial and palliative empiricism of the reigning
> moral philosophy, Kant attached increasing importance to the
> distinction which he established between the *a priori* and the em-
> pirical. And since the essence of the subjectivity of the subject is to
> be found in personality, which last is identical with moral reason,
> the rationality of pure knowledge and of [moral] action must be af-
> firmed. All pure synthesis, indeed, all synthesis in general, must as
> relevant to spontaneity depend on that faculty which in the strictest
> sense is free, the active reason.[32]

Heidegger is suggestive in maintaining that a fourth question,
What is man? must be added to the three previously cited Kantian
questions.[33] But in the light of the above discussion, one can at least
doubt whether, without stretching the truth, it is possible to contend
that metaphysics, in the Kantian sense, belongs to "human
nature."[34] Of course, this is not to deny that by underscoring the im-
possibility "for the subtlest philosophy as for the commonest reasoning to argue freedom away,"[35] Kant in a sense has grounded his *a
priori synthetical practical proposition* on the "inner man." However, it is
highly problematic whether Kant ever believed that human intelligence can really know the "inner man," or the "true self," if such
a being actually exists:

> The subjective impossibility of explaining the freedom of the will is
> the same as the impossibility of discovering and explaining an in-
> terest which man can take in moral laws. Nevertheless, he does ac-
> tually take an interest in them, and the foundation in us of this in-
> terest we call the moral feeling. This moral feeling has been er-
> roneously construed by some as the standard for our moral judg-
> ment, whereas it must rather be regarded as the subjective effect
> which the law has upon the will to which reason alone gives objec-
> tive grounds.[36]

III. *The Ontological Status of Human Nature.* Undeniably,
Heidegger's attempt to describe the real result of the Kantian laying

of the foundation in terms of the discovery of an "[essential] connection between the question of the essence of man and the establishment of metaphysics"[37] requires an unusually rigorous intellectual effort. And Heidegger himself admits that "the indefiniteness of this question [What is man?] indicates that even now we are not yet in possession of the decisive result of the Kantian laying of the foundation."[38] As we have seen, however, in Neo-Confucian thinking, the inseparability of human nature and ontological reality is a point of departure. This does not necessarily imply that the Neo-Confucian mode of questioning can be better understood and appreciated in the Heideggerian language. Actually, Professor Mou Tsung-san of New Asia Research Institute, in a powerfully argued monograph, asserts positively that the Heideggerian course of establishing a fundamental ontology on the basis of developing a metaphysics of *Dasein* is incompatible with the Neo-Confucian insistence on the "nontemporality" of human essence.[39] But the issue involved is not merely a mapping out of similarity and difference in a kind of typological analysis of philosophical systems. Rather, the task is to see how a real 'confrontation' of two fundamentally different modes of questioning can deepen our awareness of the limits as well as the strengths of our own chosen approach to ontology.

Chang Tsai, in one of the most celebrated essays in Chinese literature, sets forth the Neo-Confucian position in a highly condensed form:

> Heaven is my father and Earth is my mother, and even such a small being as I finds an intimate place in their midst. Therefore that which fills the universe I regard as my body and that which directs the universe I consider as my nature. All people are my brothers and sisters, and all things are my companions.[40]

This eloquent and condensed expression may appear simply to introduce an "organismic" vision, advocating that human beings are integral parts of a cosmological whole.[41] To be sure, that human beings are intrinsically related to Heaven, Earth, and the myriad things is essential to Chang's insight. And what he propounds can in a general way befit an organic structure. However, the *Western Inscription (Hsi-ming)*, as the essay is commonly known, is first of all a statement on man's ontological status.

A human being so conceived is not merely a creature who, by

definition, has no knowledge of his ontological ground of existence. Rather, as the son or daughter of Heaven and Earth (the receiver of the cosmic forces in their highest excellence),[42] humanity is the embodiment of that which is most refined in the creative process of the universe. This is in perfect accord with the assertion in the *Doctrine of the Mean* that human nature is what Heaven imparts to man.[43] And it is in this sense that Chang Tsai reminds us that no matter how small a being we find ourselves to be in the vastness of the cosmos, there is not only a locus but also an intimate place for each of us. For we are all potentially guardians and indeed co-creators of the universe. In this holistic vision of man, an ontological gap between Creator and creature would seem to be almost inconceivable. It appears that there is no post-lapsarian state to encounter and that alienation as a deep-rooted feeling of estrangement from one's primordial origin is nonexistent. Furthermore, the idea of man as a manipulator and conqueror of nature would also seem to be ruled out.[44]

This apparently childlike belief in the euphonious continuum of Heaven, Earth, man, and things is predicated on the cosmology of "great harmony." However, if we examine Chang's cosmos clearly, it is not so much the sweet sounds of an innocent garden as the powerful currents of the mighty ocean:

> [The Great Harmony as the Way] embraces the nature which underlies all counter processes of floating and sinking, rising and falling, and motion and rest. It is the origin of the process of fusion and intermingling, of overcoming and being overcome, and of expansion and contraction. At the commencement, these processes are incipient, subtle, obscure, easy, and simple, but at the end they are extensive; great, strong, and firm. It is *ch'ien* (Heaven) that begins with the knowledge of Change, and *k'un* (Earth) that models after simplicity.[45]

The influence of the *Book of Change* behind the whole conceptualization is readily noticeable. The metaphor, far from being static, seems to suggest a dynamic process of transformation. This is clearly shown even in his notion of the "Great Vacuity" (*t'ai-hsü*), the original substance of material force (*ch'i*). For "its integration and disintegration are but objectifications caused by Change."[46]

Yet it would be a mistake to suppose that since the cosmos is in a constant flux the idea of permanence is not applicable to Chang's cosmology. In fact, he unequivocally notes that "as an entity, material force simply reverts to its original substance when it disintegrates and becomes formless. When it integrates and assumes form, it does not lose the eternal principle (of Change)."[47] This is because "although material force in the universe integrates and disintegrates, and attracts and repulses in a hundred ways, nevertheless the principle (*li*) according to which it operates has an order and is unerring."[48] Underlying the discussion, then, is the famous thesis attributed to Chang that *principle is one but its manifestations are many (li-i fen-shu).*[49]

The phenomenal world, from this perspective, exhibits an infinite variety of dynamic interactions through which things come into existence. The act of creation as a conscious design by a supernatural being completely beyond the comprehension of human intelligence, which is undoubtedly a rather simplistic reading of Christian theological doctrine, is absolutely incompatible with this cosmological insight. Contrary to the idea of creation as a divine function which brings things into existence *ex nihilo*, the process of transformation in Chang Tsai's thought is an unceasing operation of creativity. Thus a thing comes into existence not because it has been molded by a mysterious agent. Rather, it is the result of a continuous procedure of differentiation. In this sense, a thing becomes a thing only after it has achieved, as it were, a state of differentiatedness:

> According to principle nothing exists alone. Unless there are similarity and difference, contraction and expansion, and beginning and end among things to make it stand out, it is not really a thing although it seems to be. To become complete (to attain individuality), a thing must have a beginning and an end. But completion cannot be achieved unless there is mutual influence between similarity and difference (change) and between being and non-being (becoming). If completion is not achieved, it is not really a thing although it seems to be. Therefore it is said [in the *Book of Change*], "Contraction and expansion act on each other and thus advantages are produced."[50]

However, to achieve its thingness, so to speak, a thing must endeavor to become itself; it is not enough simply to leave the whole matter to its natural course. This is predicated on the following premise:

> Sincerity implies reality. Therefore it has a beginning and an end.
> Insincerity implies absence of reality. How can it have a beginning
> or end? Therefore it is said [in the *Doctrine of the Mean*], "Without
> sincerity, there will be nothing."[51]

One may suspect that this is a case of transposing the realm of
nature into the context of morality. But it is misleading to interpret
this line of reasoning in terms of a moralization of natural
phenomena. What is exemplified here, to borrow from Heidegger,
signifies "the endeavor to make being manifest itself."[52] Whether or
not such an idea represents merely "the last cloudy streak of
evaporating reality,"[53] to Chang Tsai, reflecting on the "highest concepts" such as the Great Vacuity is the authentic way of understanding the true meaning of concrete things.

Therefore, it is vitally important to note that by positing the
oneness of ultimate reality and the multiplicity of its manifestations
Chang Tsai by no means advances a doctrine of dualism. On the
contrary, he envisions that "the integration and disintegration of
material force is to the Great Vacuity as the freezing and melting of
ice is to water."[54] And he further states that "if we realize that the
Great Vacuity is identical with material force, we know that there is
no such thing as non-being."[55] This mode of thought has clear implications for the concept of man: human nature as well as the
nature of things lies in the unity of the Great Vacuity and material
force.[56] With this basic assumption in mind, Chang contends that
"one's nature is the one source of all things and is not one's own
private possession."[57] Thus, in an exceedingly interesting passage,
Chang depicts the ontological status of man as follows:

> The Heavenly endowed nature in man is comparable to the nature
> of water in ice. It is the same whether the ice freezes of melts.
> Water's reflection of light may be much or little, dark or bright,
> but in receiving the light, it is the same in all cases.[58]

To be sure, as Professor Wing-tsit Chan has pointed out, Chang
Tsai's philosophy of "vacuity" has never been propagated by any
later Neo-Confucianist.[59] But, notwithstanding this idiosyncrasy,
Chang's postulate that since all human beings are endowed with the
same essence which underlies the creative transformation of Heaven
and Earth, each person has the inner ability to know and experience

ultimate reality in its all-embracing fullness, remains a defining characteristic of Neo-Confucian thought.[60]

IV. *Humanity as the Fundamental Question*. In an essay 'On Understanding Humanity' (*Shih-jen*), Ch'eng Hao (1032–1085) asserts emphatically that true humanity actually "forms one body with all things without any differentiation." For the sake of underscoring man's inner ability to know and experience ultimate reality, Ch'eng further suggests that "the purpose of (Chang Tsai's) 'Western Inscription' is to explain this substance (of complete unity) fully."[61] Humanity, or *jen*, so conceived is not only the innermost sensitivity but also an all-pervading care. Citing the description of paralysis as "absence of humanity (*pu-jen*)" in traditional Chinese medicine, he uses the following analogy to illustrate this point:

> The man of *jen* regards Heaven and Earth and all things as one body. To him there is nothing that is not himself. Since he has recognized all things as himself, can there be any limit to his humanity? If things are not parts of the self, naturally they have nothing to do with it. As in the case of paralysis of the four limbs, the vital force no longer penetrates them, and therefore they are no longer parts of the self.[62]

At first sight the statement seems to refer to "a subject which cancels out everything objective, transforming it into mere subjectivity."[63] However, far from advocating subjectivism or even anthropocentrism, what Ch'eng intends to convey here is simply that "since man and Heaven and Earth are one thing, why should man purposely belittle himself?"[64] In fact, he freely admits that "man is not the only perfectly intelligent creature in the universe. The human mind (in essence) is the same as that of plants and trees, birds and animals."[65] For once a thing is produced, it by necessity possesses the complete principle.[66] Therefore, the Mencian idea that "all things are already complete in oneself" is not only applicable to man but to things as well.[67] The difference merely lies in the fact that man can extend the principle in him to others whereas things in general cannot do so. Even then, Ch'eng notes that "although man can extend [the principle], when has he augmented it to any extent? And although things cannot extend it, when have they diminished it to any extent?"[68]

Indeed, Ch'eng Hao further observes that existentially "everyone's nature is obscured in some way and as a consequence he cannot follow the Way. In general the trouble lies in resorting to selfishness and the exercise of cunning. Being selfish, one cannot take purposive action to respond to things, and being cunning, one cannot be at home with enlightenment."[69] Although Ch'eng repeatedly urges the student (one who learns to be human) not to seek afar but to search within himself so that he can enlarge his humanity through self-cultivation,[70] he never denies the necessity of what Heidegger suggestively terms the "right time, i.e. the right moment, and the right perseverence."[71] In his own words, "Not the slightest effort is exerted!"[72] For Mencius has made it clear, "Always be doing something without expectation. Let the mind not forget its objective, but let there be no artificial effort to help it grow."[73]

Ch'eng Hao's way to preserve humanity so that the self and the other can be identified[74] does bear some resemblance to the Heideggerian notion of "waiting." To be sure, Heidegger's effort to confront the ontological challenge resulting from modern man's "forgetfulness of being" symbolizes a shape of thought significantly different from the Neo-Confucian insistence on the inseparability of being (principle) and being-human (humanity). But Ch'eng's caution that "to force things and to drag things along is naturally not to be in accord with the Way and principle" and that "as soon as [the Way and principle] is obscured by selfish ideas, it will be diminished and feeble"[75] reminds us of Heidegger's perceptive observation on how men have become alienated from being:

> They thrash about amid the essence, always supposing that what is most tangible is what they must grasp and thus each man grasps what is closest to him. The one holds to this, the other to that, each man's opinion [Sinn] hinges on his own [eigen]; it is opinionatedness [Eigen-sinn]. This opinionatedness, this obstinacy, prevents them from reaching out to what is gathered together in itself, makes it impossible for them to be followers [Horige] and to hear [horen] accordingly.[76]

Similarly Ch'eng observes that "simply because of selfishness, man thinks in terms of his own person, and therefore, from the point of view of principle, belittles [things]. If he lets go this person of his and views all things in the same way, how much joy would there be!"[77]

For "what is gathered together in itself" is the principle which enables "all things [to] form one body."[78]

Nevertheless, what Ch'eng Hao advocates and, for that matter, what his teacher Chou Tun-i and his uncle Chang Tsai also advocate is that, despite man's finitude in his everyday existence, ontologically his ability to apprehend in the sense of "embodying" ultimate reality is unlimited: "the reason why the man of humanity can serve Heaven and be sincere with himself is simply that he is unceasing in his humanity."[79] This vision of humanity differs in a fundamental way from Parmenides' image of man as "historical being (as the historical custodian of being)," which Heidegger hails as a crucial definition of being human for the West.[80] The governing perspective in Neo-Confucian thought is neither historicity nor temporality but the (non-temporal) unfolding of humanity as the self-disclosure of ultimate reality. This, perhaps, is what Mou Tsung-san means when he identifies as a basic assumption of the Chinese mode of thinking: all human beings are endowed with the ability of "intellectual intuition" (*chih te chih-chüeh*).

Indeed, Neo-Confucian thought, with its single-minded concern for the realization of sagehood, is an outstanding example of "intellectual intuition" at work. The following statement from Chang Tsai is a case in point:

> By enlarging one's mind, one can enter into all the things in the world [to examine and understand their principle]. As long as anything is not yet entered into, there is still something outside the mind. The mind of ordinary people is limited to the narrowness of what is seen and what is heard. The sage, however, fully develops his nature and does not allow what is seen or heard to fetter his mind. He regards everything in the world to be his own self. This is why Mencius said that if one exerts his mind to the utmost, he can know nature and Heaven. Heaven is so vast that there is nothing outside of it. Therefore the mind that leaves something outside is not capable of uniting itself with the mind of Heaven. Knowledge coming from seeing and hearing is knowledge obtained through contact with things. It is not knowledge obtained through one's moral nature. Knowledge obtained through one's moral nature does not originate from seeing or hearing.[81]

This possibility, that one can enter into all the things in the world

and that one can obtain knowledge through one's moral nature
without the sensory perceptions of seeing and hearing, is never allowed
in Kant's philosophy. In fact, the kind of intellectual intuition that is
necessary for apprehending things as they are is, from the Kantian
point of view, humanly impossible.

Kant's considered opinion that it is impossible that human beings
are capable of apprehending things-in-themselves through intellectual intuition seems to signify not only his own idiosyncratic approach to philosophy but a basic assumption in Western thought. To
be sure, following Heidegger's interpretation, the reason why Kant
is barred, in principle, from actually bringing the "fundamental ontology" to fruition is in a way connected with this:

> In the broadest terms, the reason lies in Kant's inability or perhaps
> his ultimate reluctance to shake loose from the metaphysics of ob-
> jectivity, from the assumption that the meaning of being is ade-
> quately determined in function of the relation of being-an-object-
> for-subjectivity.[82]

However, as Ernst Cassirer observes, Kant's alleged "turning from
the metaphysical realism of the external world to a concern about
man, the basis of his finitude, and the relationship between his
finitude and the question of being which he is ontologically structured and impelled to raise"[83] is basically a Heideggerian imposition
on the philosophical intention of Kant.[84]

It should be mentioned in this connection that Husserl, not unlike
Fichte on this particular point, also sharply criticized Kant's failure
or refusal to acknowledge an intuitive knowledge of the acting ego.[85]
In the words of James Collins, Husserl's argument is as follows:

> The Kantian method of regressive reconstruction of the conditions
> of possibility for judgments in the mode of scientific objectivity is
> lacking precisely in that *intellectual intuition* which could save it from
> becoming lost in objectivity, and could complete the turn toward
> the life of subjectivity. Hence there is no Kantian experience of the
> transcendental life of the ego, the I-actuality which is not just the
> ego-pole correlated with the objective world.[86]

Whether or not Husserl's "transcendental phenomenology" can fur-
nish both the method of understanding and the reflective experience
itself of the pure ego, the central problem of Kant and by extension a
most important issue in Western philosophy is now identified.

The claim that the "simple and easy" method of the Neo-Confucians consists fundamentally in taking intellectual intuition for granted as an inner ability of man is not likely to satisfy the critical mind of a Husserl or a Heidegger, but as Mou Tsung-san suggests, if taken seriously this mode of thinking, by whatever name one calls it, has the potential of bringing forth a philosophical vision more congenial to Kant's original insight than either the Husserlian phenomenology or the Heideggerian ontology.[87]

As already mentioned, the fourth Kantian question, What is man? must be added to the three major problem areas in philosophy. It can be further argued, as Heidegger has already done in his reflection on Kant, that the question of human nature, in terms of the magnitude of philosophical importance, actually precedes problems of knowing (epistemology), doing (psychology), and hoping (theology). Of course, this by no means suggests that the science of man (anthropology) alone is the fundamental discipline of philosophy. In Neo-Confucianism as well as in Heidegger's thought, there is the necessity of developing an intrinsic relationship between the problem of man and a laying of the foundation of metaphysics.[88] However, while Heidegger focuses his attention on the finitude in man and thus on the importance of *Dasein* as temporality, the governing perspective in Neo-Confucian thought is the realization of humanity in the absolute unity of man and Heaven. The central question for the Neo-Confucians is, then, How can I really know my true self? or, put in the context of the above discussion, How can I cultivate my capacity for intellectual intuition as a way of manifesting my true self and participating in the fundamental unity of the cosmos? To borrow from Mou Tsung-san, the question can be simply restated as the ontological possibility of intellectual intuition for human beings.[89]

NOTES

1. Although the expression first occurs in the *Book of Mencius*, "Our body and complexion are given to us by Heaven. Only a sage can give his body complete fulfillment (*chien-hsing*)," the concept is widely used in Neo-Confucian literature. Literally meaning to bring one's bodily design to fulfillment, *chien-hsing* makes it clear that self-cultivation in the Confucian sense, far from being a form of asceticism, is aimed at a complete realization of the person, body as well as mind. See D. C. Lau, trans., *Mencius* (Middlesex, England: Penguin Classics, 1970), VIIA:38, p. 191.

2. For a brief discussion of this issue, see Tu Wei-ming, "Toward an Integrated Study on Confucianism," *Akten des XIV. Internationalen Kongresses für Philosophie* (Wien, 1968), VI, 532–537.

3. For instance, the late Sinologist Étienne Balazs characterized all Chinese philosophy as preeminently social philosophy; "even when it attempts to detach itself from the temporal world and arrive at some form of pure, transcendental metaphysics there can be no hope of understanding it without recognizing its point of departure to which sooner or later it returns." See his "Political Philosophy and Social Crisis in the End of Han," in Étienne Balazs, *Chinese Civilization and Bureaucracy: Variations on a Theme*, trans. by H. W. Wright, ed. by Arthur F. Wright (New Haven: Yale University Press, 1964), p. 195.

4. For a discussion on the Later Stoa, see Frederick Copleston, S. J., *A History of Philosophy: Greece & Rome*, Vol. I, Pt. II (New York: Doubleday, 1962), pp. 172–181. It is interesting to note that Marcus Aurelius' *Meditations*, so far as its aphoristic statements are concerned, is compatible with some of the collected sayings of the Neo-Confucian masters.

5. The Sagely Way (*sheng-jen chih tao*) is also known as the "learning of the body and mind" (*shen-hsin chih hsüeh*) or the "teaching of mind and human nature" (*hsin-hsing chih chiao*). The emphasis in all three cases is on the problem of how to become a sage through moral self-cultivation.

6. It is interesting to compare this observation with the following statement in the *Book of Mencius*: "[The Sage-King Shun] followed the path of morality. He did not just put morality into practice," D. C. Lau, trans., *Mencius*, IVB:19, p. 131. Of course, the idea of "following" in this connection signifies that, instead of putting morality into practice as an object, Shun, who had embodied morality in his life, was able to walk in its path without exerting any artificial effort.

7. See *Chou Tzu t'ung-shu*, SPPY edition (Taipei: Cheng-chung Book Co., 1966; reprint), XX, 4b. For this translation, see W. T. Chan, *A Source Book in Chinese Philosophy* (Princeton: Princeton University Press, 1969), p. 473.

8. For Chu Hsi's comment, see the *Cheng-i-t'ang ch'üan-shu* (1896) edition of *T'ung-shu* or the *Wan-yu wen-k'u* edition of *Chou Tzu ch'üan-shu*, p. 165. Also see Wing-tsit Chan, *A Source Book*, pp. 473–474.

9. *Chou Tzu t'ung-shu*, II, 1a.

10. *Ibid.* See Wing-tsit Chan, *A Source Book*, p. 466.

11. I have made a general analysis of the concept of *ch'eng* in a monographic study of the *Doctrine of the Mean* in *Centrality and Commonality: An Essay on Chung-yung* (Honolulu: The University of Hawaii Press, 1976), pp. 106–141.

12. *Chou Tzu t'ung-shu*, IV, 1b. See Wing-tsit Chan, *A Source Book*, p. 467.

13. *Chou Tzu t'ung-su*, IV, 1b; Wing-tsit Chan, p. 467.

14. D. C. Lau, trans., *Mencius*, VIIB:25, p. 199. It should be noted that the Chinese character *shen* is more commonly rendered as "spiritual."

15. See Chu Hsi's comment on this statement in his *Ssu-shu chi-chu*, quoted in Shih Tz'u-yün, annotated *Meng Tzu chin-chu chin-i* (Taipei: Commercial Press, 1973), p. 403, note 7. It should be noted that in making this remark, Chu Hsi cites a statement from Ch'eng Tzu (either Ch'eng Hao or Ch'eng I) to support his point.

16. *Chung-yung*, XXII: Wing-tsit Chan. *A Source Book*, p. 107–108. The concept of "moral metaphysics" (*tao-te hsing-shang-hsüeh*) is developed by Mou Tsung-san in the light of Kant's *Foundations of the Metaphysics of Morals*; see his *Hsin-t'i yü hsing-t'i* [Mind and Nature] in 3 vols. (Taipei: Cheng-chung Book Co., 1968), I, 115–189.

17. D. C. Lau, trans., *Mencius*, IIIA:1, p. 96.

18. For a reference to Yen Yüan (Yen Hui or Yen Tzu), see *Analects*, 6:2. The complete essay is found in *I-ch'üan wen-chi*, 4:1a–2a. According to Chu Hsi, the essay was composed by Ch'eng I when he was only eighteen years old; see *Chu Tzu yü-lei* (1880 edition), 93:9a Yao Ming-ta contends that it can be dated even earlier; see his *Ch'eng I-ch'uan nien-p'u*, p. 16. The above information is taken from W. T. Chan, *A Source Book*, p. 547, note 19. For the translated statement, see W. T. Chan, p. 547.

19. See W. T. Chan, p. 548.

20. Immanuel Kant, *Foundations of the Metaphysics of Morals*, trans. Lewis White Beck (New York: The Bobbs-Merrill Co., 1959), p. 5.

21. Ibid.

22. Ibid., p. 23.

23. Ibid., pp. 23–24.

24. Ibid., p. 24.

25. Ibid., pp. 29–30.

26. Ibid., p. 33. For a brief discussion on the idea of a practical *law*, see *ibid.*, p. 37.

27. Ibid., p. 43.

28. Ibid., p. 44.

29. Ibid., p. 50.

30. Ibid., p. 51.

31. In the words of James Collins, see his *Interpreting Modern Philosophy* (Princeton: Princeton University Press, 1972), p. 310. Also see Heidegger, *Kant and the Problem of Metaphysics*, trans. by James S. Churchill (Bloomington: Indiana University Press, 1962), p. 222.

32. Heidegger, *Kant*, pp. 173–174.

33. Ibid., pp. 214–215.

34. It is interesting to note that while Kant makes it explicit that the categorical imperative cannot be derived from the constitution of human nature (*Metaphysics of Morals*, p. 43), Heidegger asserts that "metaphysics, with the laying of the foundation of which we are concerned, belongs to 'human nature.'" (*Kant*, p. 176).

35. Kant, *Metaphysics of Morals*, p. 75.

36. Ibid., pp. 79–80.

37. Heidegger, *Kant*, p. 220.

38. Ibid., p. 221.

39. For Mou Tsung-san's interpretive position, see his *Chih te chih-chüeh yü Chung-kuo che-hsüeh* [Intellectual intuition and Chinese philosophy] (Taipei: Commercial, 1971), pp. 346–367. It should be noted that although in his *Hsin-t'i yü hsing-t'i* (1968) Professor Mou hardly mentions Heidegger, his recent study on "intellectual intuition and Chinese philosophy" takes Heidegger's reflection on Kant as its point of departure; see *Chih-te chih-chüeh yü Chung-kuo che-hsüeh*, pp. 24–59.

40. These are the opening lines of the *Hsi-ming* ("Western Inscription"). Originally entitled *Ting-wan* ("Rectifying Obstinacy"), the essay was inscribed on the western wall of Chang Tsai's study. Thus Ch'eng I later gave it the new title "Western Inscription." See Wing-tsit Chan, *A Source Book*, p. 497; also cf. note 2 on the same page. It should be noted that the same lines are rendered somewhat differently by Siu-chi Huang: "Heaven (*ch'ien*) is my father, and earth (*k'un*) is my mother; I, as a small, finite being, occupy a central position between them. Therefore, what fills heaven and earth is my body (*t'i*), and what commands heaven and earth is my Nature (*hsing*). All men are my brothers, and all things are my companions." See her "The Moral Point of View of Chang Tsai," *Philosophy East and West* XXI (1971), 141.

41. Joseph Needham has made some very insightful observations on this point. For his characterization of the Neo-Confucian view of the universe as "organic," see his "History of Scientific Thought" in *Science and Civilization in China* (Cambridge: Cambridge University Press, 1969), II, 412, 502. Although Needham here only refers to the "organic naturalism" of the Ch'eng-Chu (or Hsing-li) school, it can well be argued that the Lu-Wang (or Hsin) school also subscribes to this cosmological view.

42. Actually Chou Tun-i states, "It is man alone who receives (the Five Agents) in their highest excellence, and therefore he is most intelligent." See his *T'ai-chi-t'u shuo*, which is translated in full by Wing-tsit Chan, *A Source Book*, p. 463.

43. *Chung-yung*, I.

44. See Tu Wei-ming, *Centrality and Commonality*, pp. 1–2, 19–22.

45. *Cheng-meng*, I:1. See Wing-tsis Chan, *A Source Book*, p. 500.

46. *Cheng-meng*, I:2, See Wing-tsit Chan, p. 501.

47. Ibid., I:3; see Wing-tsit Chan, p. 501.

48. Ibid.

49. The idea of the oneness of reality and the multiplicity of its manifestations has exercised tremendous influence on Neo-Confucian thought. However, the implication of this seminal idea has to be understood in the context of Chang Tsai's philosophy. For some helpful suggestions in this regard, see T'ang Chün-i, "Chang Tsai's Theory of Mind and Its Metaphysical Basis," *Philosophy East and West* VI (1956), 113–136; T'ang Chün-i, "Spirit and Development of Neo-Confucianism," in Arne Naess and Alastair Hannay, eds., *Invitation to Chinese Philosophy* (Oslo: Universaitets-forlaget, 1972), pp. 56–83; Siu-chi Huang, "Chang Tsai's Concept of Ch'i," *Philosophy East and West* SVIII (1968), 245–259; Siu-chi Huang, "The Moral Point of View of Chang Tsai," *Philosophy East and West* XXI (1971), 141–156; Wing-tsit Chan, "Neo-Confucian Solution to the Problem of Evil," *Studies Presented to Hu Shih on His Sixty-fifth Birthday* (Tapei: Academia Sinica, 1957), pp. 780–783; Wing-tsit Chan, *A Source Book*, p. 495; and Joseph Needham, *Science and Civilization in China*, II, 472–485.

50. *Cheng-meng*, V, SPPY edition, 2:16b. See Wing-tsit Chan, *A Source Book*, p. 515. In Chan's translation, *I Ching* is rendered as *Book of Changes*.

51. Wing-tsit Chan, p. 508. For the quotation from the *Doctrine of Mean*, see *Chung-yung* XXV.

52. Martin Heidegger, *An Introduction to Metaphysics*, trans. by Ralph Manheim (New York: Doubleday, 1961), p. 34.

53. Quoted by Heidegger from *The Twilight of Idols*, in Nietzsche's *Complete Works* (Edinburgh and London: Heinemann, 1911)). XVI, 19. See Heidegger, *Metaphysics*, p. 29.

54. Wing-tsit Chan, *A Source Book*, p. 503.

55. Ibid.

56. Ibid., p. 504.

57. Ibid., p. 508.

58. Ibid., p. 59.

59. Ibid., pp. 504–505.

60. To be sure, it is still problematical whether by identifying the principle solely with human nature and by characterizing the mind as a refined stuff of material force, Chu Hsi has emphasized man's ability to attain sagehood through self-effort as strongly as the Neo-Confucian thinkers in the Lu-Wang tradition. But it is undeniable that, although Chu Hsi time and again stresses the importance of learning, he strongly believes that "each person has the inner ability to know and experience ultimate reality in its all-embracing fullness." For a thought-provoking interpretation of Chu Hsi's position on this issue, see Mou Tsung-san, *Hsin-t'i yü hsing-t'i*, III, 464–485.

61. "Shin-jen" in *Erh-Ch'eng i-shu*, 2A:3a–b. See Wing-tsit Chan, *A Source Book*, p. 524.

62. Ibid., p. 530.

63. Heidegger, *Metaphysics*, p. 117.

64. Wing-tsit Chan, *A Source Book*, p. 539.

65. Ibid., p. 527.

66. Ibid., p. 533.

67. The whole statement reads as follows: "All the ten thousand things are there in me. There is no greater joy for me than to find, on self-examination, that I am true to myself. Try your best to treat others as you would wish to be treated yourself, and you will find that this is the shortest way to benevolence [humanity]." See D. C. Lau, trans., *Mencius*, VIIA:4, p. 182, Also see Wing-tsit Chan, *A Source Book*, p. 534.

68. Wing-tsit Chan, *A Source Book* p. 534.

69. Ibid., p. 526.

70. Ibid., p. 532.

71. Heidegger, *Metaphysics*, p. 172.

72. Wing-tsit Chan, *A Source Book*, p. 524.

73. D. C. Lau, trans. *Mencius*, IIA:2, p. 78.

74. Wing-tsit Chan, *A Source Book*, p. 524.

75. Ibid., p. 532.

76. Heidegger, *Metaphysics*, p. 110.

77. Wing-tsit Chan, *A Source Book*, p. 533.

78. Ibid.

79. Ibid., p. 508. It should be noted that some deletions have been made. The original statement reads: "The reason why the man of humanity and the filial son can serve Heaven and be sincere with himself is simply that they are unceasing in their humanity and filial piety."

80. Heidegger, *Metaphysics*, p. 119.

81. Wing-tsit Chan, *A Source Book*, p. 515.

82. James Collins, *Interpreting Modern Philosophy*, p. 301.

83. Ibid. For a brief discussion of the Cassirer-Heidegger Seminar of 1929 in Davos, Switzerland, see ibid., pp. 201–203.

84. For a summary of Cassirer's critique of Heidegger's interpretation of Kant as well as other Heideggerian themes, see Carl H. Hamburg, "A Cassirer-Heidegger Seminar," *Philosophy and Phenomenological Research* XXV (1964–65), 208–222.

85. James Collins, *Interpreting Modern Philosophy*, p. 295.

86. Ibid., Italics added.

87. See Mou Tsung-san, *Chih-te chih-chüeh yü Chung-kuo che-hsüeh*, pp. 184–202. Although Professor Mou does not seem to have discussed Husserl's phenomenology in his published studies, it is clear that in his forthcoming monograph on "phenomenon and thing-in-itself," his single-minded attention to Kant's problematics is by implication a critique not only of Heidegger but also of Husserl.

88. Heidegger, *Kant*, p. 225.

89. Mou Tsung-san, p. 157.

Glossary

ai-jen 愛人

Bito Masahide 尾藤正英

Cao Xuequin (see Ts'ao Hsüeh-ch'in)

Chan Wing-tsit 陳榮捷

Ch'an 禪

Chang Liwen 張立文

Chang Tai-nien 張岱年

Chang Tsai 張載

Ch'en Wen Tzu 陳文子

Cheng 鄭

Cheng-chung 正中

cheng-hsin 正心

Cheng-i-t'ang ch'üan-shu 正誼堂全書

ch'eng (sincerity) 誠

ch'eng (complete) 成

ch'eng-chi 成己

Ch'eng-Chu 程朱

Ch'eng Hao 程顥

Ch'eng I 程頤

ch'eng-i 誠意

Ch'eng I-ch'üan nien-p'u 程伊川年譜

ch'eng-jen 成人

Ch'eng Tzu 程子

chi 幾

Chi-lu 季路

ch'i 氣

chia (family) 家

chia (false) 假

chiao 教

chien 健

chien-hsing 踐形

ch'ien 乾

Ch'ien-Chia 乾嘉

chih (intelligence) 知

chih (extension) 致

chih-chih 致知

chih liang-chih 致良知

chih te chih-chüeh 智的直覺

Chih te chih-chüeh yü Chung-kuo che-hsüeh 智的直覺與中國哲學

ch'in 親

ching 敬

Chin-hsiu hsien-sheng wen-chi 静修先生文集

Ch'ing 清

Ch'iu 丘

Chou I (see *Chou-i*)

Chou-i 周易

Chou Li (see *Chou-li*)

Chou-li 周禮

Chou-li chu-shu 周禮注疏

Chou Tun-i 周敦頤

Chou Tzu ch'üan-shu 周子全書

Chou Tzu t'ung-shu 周子通書

chu 助

Chu Hsi 朱熹

Chu Tzu yü-lei 朱子語類

chü-ching ch'iung-li 居敬窮理

chün-tzu

Chuang Tzu 莊子

Chuang Tzu ying-te 莊子引得

chung 忠

Chung-hua 中華

Chung-kuo che-hsüeh fa-wei 中國哲學發微

Chung-kuo che-hsüeh shih yen-chiu 中國哲學史研究

"Chung-kuo hsiao-tao ssu-hsiang te 中國孝道思想的形成演變

    hsing-ch'eng yen-pien chi-ch'i 及其在歷史中的諸問題

    tsai li-shih chung te chu-wen-t'i"

Chung-kuo i-shu ching-shen 中國藝術精神

Chung-kuo ssu-hsiang shih 中國思想史

Chung-kuo ssu-hsiang shih lun-chi 中國思想史論集

Chung-kuo wen-hua hsin-lun 中國文化新論

Chung-yung 中庸

Dai Kan-Wa ji-ten 大漢和字典

Daishū Kan 大修館

erh-te 耳德

Fang Keli 方克立

Fang Ying-hsien 方穎嫺

Feng Qi 馮契

Fu Hsi-hua 傅惜華

fu-jen chih jen 婦人之仁

Fung Yu-lan 馮友蘭

Han 漢

hang-yang hsü yung ching 涵養須用敬

　　ching-hsüeh tsai chih-chih 進學在致知

Hou Wai-lu 侯外廬

Hsi-ming 西銘

Hsi-yu chi 西遊記

"Hsiang-tang" 鄉黨

hsiao-t'i 小體

Hsieh 契

hsien li-hu ch'i ta-che 先立乎其大者

hsin (heart-and-mind) 心

hsin (true, faithfulness) 信

hsin-hsing chih chiao 心性之教

Hsin-t'i yü hsing-t'i 心體與性體

hsing (nature) 性

hsing (form) 形

Hsing-li 性理

hsing-sheng 形生

hsü 虛

"Hsü-hsüeh" 叙學

Hsü Fu-kuan 徐復觀

Hsü Shen 許慎

hsüeh 學

hsüeh tso-jen 學作人

Hsün Tzu 荀子

Hu Shih 胡適

Hu Shih wen-ts'un 胡適文存

Hua 華

hua-sheng 化生

Huang-Lao 黃老

Huang Siu-chi 黃秀璣

Huang Ti 黃帝

Hung-lou meng 紅樓夢

Hui 回

i (art) 藝

i (righteousness) 義

i (meaning, intention) 意

I Ching (see *I-ching*)

I-ching 易經

I-ch'üan wen-chi 伊川文集

I Yin 伊尹

Jan Ch'iu 冉求

jen 仁

jen-cheng 仁政

Jen-min 人民

jen-yü 人欲

ju 儒

kan-ying 感應

Kao Yu-kung 高友工

ke-chi fu-li 克己復禮

k'un 坤

kung-fu 工夫

Kung Kung 共工

Kung-sun Ch'ou 公孫丑

K'ung Tzu chia-yü 孔子家語

kuo 國

ko-i 格義

ko-wu 格物

Lao Tzu 老子

Lee Kwang Kyu 李光奎

Lee Sang-eun 李相殷

Li (the *Book of Rites*) 禮

li (ritual) 禮

li (principle) 理

Li-chi chin-chu chin-i 禮記今註今譯

li-chih 立志

li-i fen-shu 理一分殊

liang-chih 良知

Lien-ching 聯經

Lien-hsi 濂溪

Lin Fang 林放

Liu-hsia Hiu 柳下惠

liu-i 六藝

Liu Tsung-chou 劉宗周

Liu Yin 劉因

Lu Hsiang-shan 陸象山

Lu-Wang 陸王

Lü Tsu-ch'ien 呂祖謙

Ma-wang-tui 馬王堆

Maruyama Masao 丸山真男

mei 美

Meng Tzu chin-chu chin-i 孟子今註今譯

Ming 明

ming 命

Morioka Kiyomi 山根常男

Morohashi Tetsuji 諸橋轍次

Mou Tsung-san 牟宗三

nei 內

Pai-she-chuan chi 白蛇傳集

Pai-she ku-shih yen-chiu 白蛇故事研究

P'an Chiang-tung 潘江東

Pang Pu 龐樸

pao 報

Pao-yü 寶玉

Park Song-bae 朴性焙

pen 本

pen-t'i 本體

Po I 伯夷

pu-jen 不仁

pu-jen chih hsin 不忍之心

pu-neng 不能

pu-wei 不爲

san-kang 三綱

shan 善

shan--ch'uan ching-ying 山川精英

"*Shan-ch'uan ching-ying*— 山川精英

   yü te i-shu" 玉的藝術

Shang 商

Shao 韶

shen (spirit) 神

shen (body) 身

shen-chiao 身教

shen-hsin chih hsüeh 身心之學

shen-hui 神會

shen-jen 神人

shen-tu 慎獨

sheng 聖

sheng-jen chih tao 聖人之道

Shih 詩

"Shih-jen" 識仁

Shih-san-ching chu-shu 十三經注疏

"Shih-t'an Chung-kuo che-hsüeh 試談中國哲學中的三個基調
   chung te san-ko chi-tiao"

shih-tao 師道

Shih Tz'u-yün 史次耘

Shu 蜀

shu 恕

Shun 舜

"Shuo ju" 說儒

Shuo-wen 說文

Sofue Takao 祖父江孝男

Song-bae Park (see Park Song-bae)

ssu (think) 思

ssu ("self") 私

Ssu-shu chi-chu 四書集註

ssu-yü 私欲

suan-shu 算術

Suenari Michio 末成道穗

Sun K'ang-i 孫康宜

Sung-Ming 宋明

ta (great) 大

ta (convey, reach) 達

ta-hua 大化

Ta-lu tsa-chih 大陸雜誌

ta-pen 大本

"Ta-ssu-t'u" 大司徒

ta-t'i 大體

ta-t'ung 大同

t'ai-chi 太極

T'ai-chi-t'u shuo 太極圖說

t'ai-ho 太和

t'ai-hsü 太虛

T'ai-yüan 太原

Takao Sofue (see Sofue Takao)

Tang Ijie

T'ang Chün-i 唐君毅

Tao 道

Tao Chi 道濟

tao-te hsing-shang-hsüeh 道德形上學

te 德

Teng Shu-p'in 鄧淑蘋

"Ti-kuan" 地官

t'i 體

T'ien 天

t'ien-hsia 天下

t'ien-hsing 天行

t'ien-lai 天籟

t'ien-li 天理

Ting-wan 訂頑

t'ing-te 聽德

ts'ai 宰

tsao-wu chu 造物主

Ts'ao Hsüeh-ch'in 曹雪芹

Tseng Tzu 曾子

ts'un-hsin 存心

Tu Wei-ming 杜維明

t'ui 推

Tung Chung-shu 董仲舒

T'ung-shu 通書

Tunghai 東海

Tzu-hsia 子夏

tzu-jan 自然

Tzu-lu 子路

Tzu-wen

Wan-yu wen-k'u 萬有文庫

wang 忘

Wang Fu-chih 王夫之

Wang Hsin-chai hsien-sheng ch'üan-chi 王心齋先生全集

Wang Ken 王艮

Wang Liang 王良

Wang Ling 王鈴

Wang Meng-ou 王夢鷗

Wang Su 王肅

Wang Yang-ming 王陽明

wei-chi 爲己

wei-jen 爲人

wu 物

Wu Ch'eng-en 吳承恩

wu-hsing 五行

wu-lun 五倫

wu-yü 無欲

yang 陽

Yang Lien-sheng 楊聯陞

Yao 堯

Yao Ming-ta 姚名達

Yao Tien (see *Yao-tien*)

Yao-tien 堯典

yen 言

yen-chiao 言教

Yen Hui 顏回

Yen Yüan 顏淵

Yen Tzu 顏子

Yi Ching (see *I-ching*)

yin 陰

yu 憂

yu-tao 友道

yü 愚

Yü Kuo-fan 余國藩

yü-lu 語録

"Yü Nan-tu chu-yu" 與南都諸友

Yüan 元

"Yüan-jen lun—tzu Shih Shu chih 原仁論一自詩書至
　　K'ung Tzu shih-tai kuan-nien 孔子時代觀念之演變
　　chih yen-pien"

Yüan-tung 遠東

Yüeh 岳

"Yüeh-chi" 樂記

yung 勇

Zen (see Ch'an)

Bibliography of Tu Wei-ming

1968

"The Creative Tension between *Jen* and *Li*," *Philosophy East and West*, XVIII: 1–2 (January–April 1968), 29–39.

The Quest for Self-Realization — A Study of Wang Yang-ming's Formative Years (1472–1509), thesis presented to the Committee on the Degree of Doctor of Philosophy in History and Far Eastern Languages (Harvard University, 1968), 271 pp.

"Towards an Integrated Study on Confucianism," paper presented to the 14th International Congress of Philosophy (Wien: Akten des XIV Kongresses für Philosophie, 2–9 September, 1968), V:532–537.

1970

Traditional China, coedited with James T. C. Liu (Prentice-Hall, 1970), 179 pp.

San-nien ti hsü-ai 三年的畜艾 (Three years of cultivating the moxa; Taipei: Chih-wen 志文 Book Co., 1970), 191 pp.

"The Unity of Knowing and Acting — From a Neo-Confucian Perspective," in *Philosophy: Theory and Practice*, ed., T.M.P. Mahadevan (Madras: Proceedings of the International Seminar on World Philosophy, December 7–17, 1970), pp. 190–205.

1971

"The Neo-Confucian Concept of Man," *Philosophy East and West*, XXI:1 (January 1971), 79–87.

189

"Mind and Human Nature," review article, *The Journal of Asian Studies*, XXX:3 (May 1971), 642–647.

1972

"Li as Process of Humanization," *Philosophy East and West*, XXII:2 (April 1972), 187–201.

1973

"Jih-pen T'ien-li ta-hsüeh ts'ang 'Wang Yang-ming chiang-hsüeh ta-wen ping ch'ih-tu' chüan ch'u-t'an" 日本天理大學藏 王陽明講學答問並尺牘卷初探、   (A preliminary examination of Wang Yang-ming's unpublished letters from the T'ien-li University collection in Japan), *Ta-lu tsa-chih* 大陸雜誌, XLVI:3 (March 1973).

"Subjectivity and Ontological Reality - An Interpretation of Wang Yang-ming's Mode of Thinking," *Philosophy East and West*, XXIII: 1-2 (January–April 1973), 187–205.

"Wang Yang-ming ta Chou Tao-t'ung shu wu-feng"   王陽明答周道通書五封   (Wang Yang-ming's five unpublished letters to Chou Tao-t'ung), *Ta-lu tsa-chih*, XLVII:2 (August 1973).

"On the Spiritual Development of Confucius' Personality," paper read at the XXVII International Congress of Orientalists in Ann Arbor, Michigan (August 7, 1967), *SSu-yü yen* 思與言 (Thought and Word), XI:3 (September 1973), 29–37.

1974

"An Introductory Note on Time and Temporality," *Philosophy East and West*, XXIV:2 (April 1974), 119–122.

"Reconstituting the Confucian Tradition," review article, *The Journal of Asian Studies*, XXXIII:3 (May 1974), 441–454.

"An Inquiry into Wang Yang-ming's Four-Sentence Teaching," *The Eastern Buddhist*, new series, VII:2 (October 1974), 32–48.

1975

"Yen Yüan: From Inner Experience to Lived Concreteness," in *The Unfolding of Neo-Confucianism*, ed., Wm. T. de Bary (New York: Columbia University Press, 1975), pp. 511–541.

1976

"Ou-yang Te," in *Dictionary of Ming Biography*, eds., L. Carrington Goodrich and Chaoying Fang (New York: Columbia University Press, 1976), pp. 1102–1104.

"The Confucian Perception of Adulthood," *Daedalus*, 105:2 (April 1976), 109–123.

Centrality and Commonality: An Essay on Chung-yung, monograph no. 3 of the Society for Asian and Comparative Philosophy (Honolulu: The University Press of Hawaii, 1976), 181 pp.

"Hsiung Shih-li's Quest for Authentic Existence," in *The Limits of Change*, ed., Charlotte Furth (Cambridge: Harvard University Press, 1976), pp. 424–275; 396–400.

"Transformational Thinking as Philosophy," review article, *Philosophy Est and West*, XXVI (January–April 1976), 75–80.

"Confucianism: Symbol and Substance in Recent Times," *Asian Thought and Society: an International Review*, I:1 (April 1976), 42–66.

Jen-wen hsin-ling te chen-tang 人文心靈的震盪 (The resonance of the humanist mind; Taipei: China Times Publication Co., 1976), 197 pp.

Neo-Confucian Thought in Action: Wang Yang-ming's Youth (1472–1509) (Berkeley: University of California Press, 1976), 218 pp.

"Wang Yang-ming's Youth: A Personal Reflection on the Method of My Research," *Ming Studies*, no. 3 (1976), 11–17.

1977

"Inner Experience: The Basis of Creativity in Neo-Confucian Thinking," in *Artists and Tradition, Uses of the Past in Chinese Culture*, ed., Christian Murck (Princeton: The Art Museum, Princeton University, 1977), pp. 9–15.

"Chinese Perceptions of America," in *Dragon and Eagle: United States-China Relations, Past and Future*, eds., Michel Oksenberg and Robert B. Oxnam (New York: Basic Books, 1977), pp. 87–106.

1978

"On the Mencian Perception of Moral Self-Development," *The Monist*, 61.1 (January 1978), 72–81.

"The *Problematik* of Kant and the Issue of Transcendence: A Reflection on 'Sinological Torgue'," *Philosophy East and West*, XXVIII:2 (April 1978), 215–221.

"The 'Moral Universal' from the Perspective of East Asian Thought," in *Morality as a Biological Phenomenon*, ed., Gunther S. Stent (Berlin: Dahlem Konferenzen, 1978), pp. 187–207.

"Yi Hwang's Perception of the Mind," *T'oegye Hakpo*, No. 19 (October 1978), 76–88. [Also available in Korean translation].

"T'oegye hsin-hsing lun shu-hou" 退溪心性論書後 (Further thoughts on Yi Hwang's perception of the mind), *T'oegye Hakpo*, No. 20 (December 1978), 18–21. [Available in Korean translation only].

1979

Humanity and Self-Cultivation: Essays in Confucian Thought (Berkeley: Asian Humanities Press, 1979), 364 pp.

"Shifting Perspectives on Text and History: A Reflection on Shelly

Errington's Paper," *Journal of Asian Studies*, XXXVIII:2 (February 1979), 245–251.

"The Value of the Human in Classical Confucian Thought," *Humanitas*, XV:2 (May 1979), 161–176.

"Ultimate Self-Transformation as a Communal Act: Comments on Modes of Self-Cultivation in Traditional China," *Journal of Chinese Philosophy*, 6 (1969), 237–246.

"*Hsi-yu Chi* as an Allegorical Pilgrimage in Self-Cultivation," review, *History of Religions*, 19.2 (November, 1979), 177–184.

"The 'Thought of Huang-Lao': A Reflection on the Lao Tzu and Huang Ti Texts in the Silk Manuscripts of Ma-wang-tui," *The Journal of Asian Studies*, XXXIX:1 (November 1979), 95–110.

"A Note on Wittfogel's Science of Society," *Bulletin of Concerned Asian Scholars*, 11.4 (October–December 1979), 38–39.

1980

"Neo-Confucian Ontology: A Preliminary Questioning," *Journal of Chinese Philosophy* 7 (1980), 93–114.

"A Religiophilosophical Perspective on Pain," in *Pain and Society*, eds. H. W. Kosterlitz and L. Y. Terenius (Berlin: Dahlem Konferenzen, 1980), pp. 63–78.

1981

"Jen as a Living Metaphor in the Confucian *Analects*," *Philosophy East and West*, 31.1 (January 1981), 45–54.

"Ts'ung i tao yen" 從意到言 (From intention to word), *Chung-hua wen-shih lun-ts'ung* 中華文史論叢 (Shang-hai: January, 1981), 225–261.

"Shih-t'an Chung-kuo che-hsüeh chung ti san-ko chi-tiao" 試談 中國哲學中的三個基調 (A preliminary discussion on the three basic motifs in Chinese philosophy), *Chung-kuo che-hsüeh shih yen-chiu* 中國哲學史研究 (Beijing, March 1981), 19–25.

"Kung Tzu jen-hsüeh chung ti tao hsüeh cheng" 孔子仁學中的
道學政 (The Way, learning and politics in Confucius' learning of
humanity), *Chung-kuo che-hsüeh* 中國哲學 (Beijing, 1981), 17–
32.

1982

"T'oegye's Creative Interpretation of Chu Hsi's Philosophy of Principle," *Korean Journal*, XXII:2 (February 1982), 4–15.

"Towards an Understanding of Liu Yin's Confucian Eremitism," in
Hok-lam Chan and Wm. T. de Bary, eds., *Yüan Thought: Chinese
Thought and Religion under the Mongols* (New York: Columbia Univer-
sity Press, 1982), pp. 233–277.

1983

"Perceptions of Learning (*hsüeh*) in Early Ch'ing Thought," in *Symposium in Commemoration of Professor T'ang Chün-i* (Taipei: Student
Book Co., 1983), pp. 27–61.

"Die neokonfuzianische Ontologie," in Wolfgang Schluchter ed.,
Max Webers Studie über Konfuzianismus und Taoismus (Frankfurt:
Suhrkam, 1983), pp. 271–297. A German translation of "Neo-
Confucian Ontology: A Preliminary Questioning" published in
1980.

1984

"The Idea of the Human in Mencian Thought: An Approach to
Chinese Aesthetics," in Susan Bush and Christian Murck, eds.,
Theories of the Arts in China (Princeton: Princeton University Press,
1984), pp. 57–73.

"A Confucian Perspective on Learning to be Human," in *The World's Religious Traditions*, ed., Frank Whaling (Edinburgh: T. & T. Clark, 1984), pp. 55–71.

"On Neo-Confucianism and Human-Relatedness," in *Religion and Family in East Asia*, eds., George De Vos and T. Sofue (Osaka: The National Museum of Ethnology, 1984), pp. 111–125.

"The Continuity of Being: Chinese Visions of Nature," in *On Nature*, Vol. 6 of *Boston University Studies in Philosophy and Religion*, ed., Leroy S. Rouner (Notre Dame, Ind.: University of Notre Dame Press, 1984), pp. 113–129.

"Wei-Chin hsüan-hsüeh chung ti t'i-yen ssu-hsiang—shih-lun Wang Pi 'sheng-jen t'i-wu' kuan-nien ti che-hsüeh i-i" 魏晉玄學中的體驗思想—— 試論王弼 " 聖人體無 " 觀念的哲學意義 (Personal experiential thought in the Wei-Chin period—a preliminary discussion on the philosophical meaning of Wang Pi's concept, "the sage embodies nothingness"), *Yen-yüan lun-hsüeh chi* 燕園論學集　 (Essays in memory of T'ang Yung-t'ung's ninetieth birthday; Beijing: Peking University Press, 1984), pp. 197–213.

"Ts'ung shen-hsin-ling-shen ssu ch'en-ts'i k'an Ju-chia ti jen-hsüeh" 從身心靈神四層次看儒家的人學　 (Confucian humanist learning in the four related perspectives of body, mind, soul and spirit; Hong Kong: *Ming-pao yüeh-k'an* 明報月刊　). December 1984), 41–44.

Confucian Ethics Today: The Singapore Challenge (Singapore: Federal Publications, 1984), 247 p.

Forthcoming

"Subjectivity in Liu Tsung-chou's Philosophical Anthropology," in *Individualism and Holism: The Confucian and Taoist Perspectives*, eds., Donald J. Munro and Chad Hansen (Ann Arbor: University of Michigan Press).

"Yi T'oegye's Perception of Human Nature: A Preliminary Inquiry into the Four-Seven Debate in Korean Neo-Confucianism," in *The*

Rise of Neo-Confucianism in Korea, eds., Wm. T. de Bary and Jahyun Haboush (New York: Columbia University Press).

"Yi T'oegye's Intellectual Self-Definition: An Exploration," *Korean Studies International* (Cambridge, Mass.: Harvard University and Seoul: Seoul National University).

"Profound Learning, Personal Knowledge and Poetic Vision," in *The Vitality of the Lyric Voice: Shih Poetry from the Han to T'ang*, eds., Shuen-fu Lin and Stephen Owen (Princeton: Princeton University Press).

Index